William's
almanac

Everything You Ever Wanted to Know About

Video Games

Canadian Cataloguing in Publication Data

William, Jean-François

William's Almanac: everything you ever wanted to know about video games

(IQGuides)
Includes bibliographical references and index.

ISBN 2-922417-29-8

1. Video games. 2. Computer games. I. Title. II. Series.

GV1469.3.W5413 2002   794.8   C2002-940613-7

Legal Deposit:
National Library of Canada
Bibliothèque nationale du Québec

Distributed in North America by:
General Distribution Services
325 Humber College Boulevard
Toronto (Ontario)
Canada
M9W 7C3
http://www.genpub.com

Distributed in Europe by:
Gazelle Books Services
Queen Square
Lancaster LA1 1RN
United Kingdom
http://gazellebooks.co.uk

Producers: Jean-François William and Serge Ethier for Productions Fauve Inc.
Translation: Bernard Dubreuil and Maryse Tardif
Revision: Gary Rosenberg
Research: Simon Desjardins (Chapter 6), Jean-Maurice Duplessis (Chapter 2)
Illustrations: Stuart Harrison <stuart.harrison@virgin.net> and Mike Krahulit <www.penny-arcade.com>
    (compliments of www.gamespy.com)
Cover and page layout: Olivier Lasser and Jean-Philippe Gaudet
Cover illustration: Studio Brunelle

© Isabelle Quentin éditeur, 2002
http://iqe.qc.ca
ISBN: 2-922417-29-8

PRINTED IN CANADA

1 2 3 03 02

J.F. William

William's
almanac

Everything You Ever Wanted to Know About

 Guides

IQ Guides focus on change.

Designed to be practical and in accordance with scientific concepts and studies, these texts help readers develop informed strategies for change based on their unique situations.

We look forward to your comments and questions. Please feel free to contact us.

Isabelle Quentin
iquentin@sim.qc.ca
http://iqe.qc.ca

To my wife Catherine Hugo, without whom none of this would have been possible,
and to my son Frederic, from whom I still have much to learn...

Table of contents

In the beginning was
the pixel...

Introduction:
the video game industry is
in complete overhaul!

We are witnessing the birth of a new art form, and a very popular one at that! It took cinema, the 7[h] art form, almost 40 years to come up with a chef d'œuvre like *Citizen Kane.* Amazingly enough, 30 years ago, the video game industry didn't even exist. Hail to the 10th art form!

I was giving a lecture about the influence of 3-D and interactivity on what seemed to be understood by the public and the organizers as the 9th art form: the comic strip. As a connoisseur and collector, I totally agreed with that premise. At the end of my talk, I declared that if the comic strip was ranked as art form number nine, it was evident that video games were to be art form number ten. I used that momentum in my column about video games and declared: "Long live the 10th art form"

I later found out that two writers from France, Alain and Frédéric Le Diberder, authors of *L'Univers des Jeux Vidéo* had already welcomed the idea.

But then something else occurred to me: If cinema was the seventh art, which one was the eighth? A shiver went down my spine… Not TV, please! I did some research, I asked some of my learned friends and realized that none of them knew for sure. Worse still when asked to name them all, they had to think real hard to identify how artistic expression had settled into different art forms. I eventually did come up with a list. Here it is, in a tentative chronological order. The debate is still open.

(1) Music; (2) Sculpture; (3) Painting; (4) Dance; (5) Theatre; (6) Literature; (7) Cinema; (8) ?; (9) Comic Strips; (10) Video Games. So what was the elusive eighth art form? I suggested photography, architecture and sex on a rainy day, but no one I asked seemed to know for sure. Can you help? Send me your answers to:

<jfwilliam@hotmail.com>

Books, music and films have had to reposition themselves to become part of the digital revolution. Not so with video games! Quite the contrary, in fact. The first generation of game players is coming of age and its rallying cry is: Power to the gamer!

Interactivity is completely redefining the world of entertainment. The battle to attract your attention is just starting! In today's world, the video game industry is the black sheep of world culture, just the way rock 'n'roll was in the 50's, just the way psychedelia was in the 60's pumk in the 70's and rap in the 80's. Video games are the Rock'n'roll of the mind! The new creative frontier. Get used to it. Some even say that video violence has replaced sex as the latest taboo. The recent ban of *Grand Theft Auto* in Australia certainly seems to bear that out.

Nintendo's GameCube (the Panasonic version) as exposed at 2001's E3 expo.

The video game industry is in a perpetual state of flux. With Vivendi-Universal, Infogrames, Ubi Soft and Titus, the French recently bought into more than 30% of the American market. Sony and Microsoft will be at each other's throats for the next 10 years. Japanese game developers are spending fortunes on astounding titles! PS2, Gamecube and Xbox have given the industry a complete facelift. We, the lucky players, are witnessing the birth of a new age of creation, where creativity is based on technology, which, only a few years back, was pure science fiction! We are embarking on a world of totally new tools. Fasten your seat belt, interactive entertainment is coming of age!

Analysts are already talking about game sales worth over 10 billion dollars (US) by 2003. By then, 70% of all North American households will have a game console of some sort. Video-cassette players and game consoles are now both in the Major Leagues! This is quite a change from the days when video games were dubbed as a niche market for teenagers!

We live in an age when the United Arab Emirates can send press releases stating boldly that *Pokemon* is forbidden on their territory... and, at the very same moment, off-shore casinos demonstrate that national frontiers are a meaningless concept on the Internet. In societies all over the world, video games are big news. The age of entertainment is at hand!

The more they change, the less they remain the same!

According to IDSA (Interactive Digital Software Association), 60% of all regular game players play with friends and 33% play with siblings. *EverQuest* and the upcoming *Sims online* encouraged people to explore and discover new avenues in human communication. These games are based on a kind of interaction between human beings which has never taken place before. Adults and kids are exploring roles they have never had a chance to play in real life. In the virtual

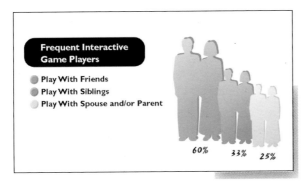

Frequent Interactive Game Players

- Play With Friends
- Play With Siblings
- Play With Spouse and/or Parent

60%   33%   25%

world, they are responsible for their each and every move. This is a far cry from the sort of passive attitude TV has been peddling on us.

The days when the lonely geek sat glued to a console or computer screen are over. Gamers now come from all walks of life and they can meet for collaborative or competitive games over the Internet. On almost every video game console, 2 to 4 players can now interact. Video games have become a social occasion, almost a family event. This is quite a change indeed!

<www.idsa.com>

Video games lead the entertainment industry

The world of entertainment is undergoing radical changes. In one of its reports, IDSA indicates that 35.5% of the population use video games as a way to relax and have fun. Television accounts for 18.2% and the Internet 15.3%. 13% of the population relax reading a book, and 11.1% going to the movies. Video game rentals account for 6.5% of the total while 0.5%

tune in to pay-per-view TV. The proportion of female players is steadily growing. Right now, it stands at 43%. At GDC 2000 (Game Developers Convention) Kornelia Tabacs, one of the Quake3 champions, ended the 3 day competition with a score of 1179 to 27 frags in her favor. With hordes of male players trying to dislodge her. There is hope for humankind!

Game developers have never had so many platforms, computer systems and computer languages at their disposal. Watch out, here comes a geek attack: Xbox, PlayStation 2, GameCube, Game Boy Advance, Palm, WindowsCE, WAP, BREW, Java, Synovial, FOMA, WildTangent, Real Arcade, Macromedia Shockwave, Adobe Atmosphere, Windows, Mac OS9, Linux and many others. Mind boggling, isn't it!

Production costs for consoles are skyrocketing. A triple A title, with a good promotional campaign, can cost anywhere from 10 to 15 million dollars. Some titles have already gone way beyond that limit. It is a frightening fact of life that 5% of all titles account for 95% of all revenues. Independent developers, in that context, are an endangered species. Those who are lucky enough to achieve success are quickly bought off by the major companies.

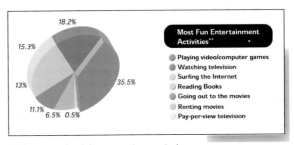

Most Fun Entertainment Activities

- Playing video/computer games
- Watching television
- Surfing the Internet
- Reading Books
- Going out to the movies
- Renting movies
- Pay-per-view television

18.2%   15.3%   13%   11.1%   6.5%   0.5%   35.5%

Video games lead the entertainment industry

Quality in quantity!

More than 3000 video games are published every year. So it's not surprising that no one can follow every twist and turn of the game saga. The amazing thing is that more and more good games appear on the market. Strategy games and RPG's ask you to work hard for your pleasure. Platform games are pure entertainment. They offer lots of interactive escape and very little mental effort, they are honey pots for the nimble thumbs! I get a kick out of games like *Sonic, Crash Bandicoot* and *Rayman*. I simply adore games like *Deus Ex, Half-Life* and the likes of *Tribes2* and *Counter Strike*. I could not survive without an adventure game like *Monkey Island*. And what about *Diablo, Metal Gear Solid 2, Twisted Metal Black* and *Warcraft 3*, coming out soon...

To be quite frank, there is a whole load of excellent games. The only thing missing is time to play them all. When is life going to become all play and no work?

Has the anti-trust action against Microsoft had an effect on the new economy? Can President Bush give Bill Gates a pat on the shoulder and get the new economy back on its wheels again? 2001 and 2002 are going to be most important years in the video game industry. PS2 is going to show us what it's got. Xbox is going to do double flips and somersaults! Sega is going to reinvent itself and continue to explore console-based massive multiplayer games over the Internet. Nintendo will remain the undisputed master of its own domain, and Microsoft will be the unrelenting contender. You can expect quite a show!

The video game industry

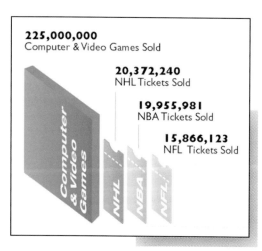

An art form more popular than professional sports

Comparing sales today and sales five years ago is simple: they have doubled. It is difficult to quote figures with pinpoint precision, but according to my estimates, in North America, we are talking about a $25 billion industry, that is counting software sales ($6.02 billion), hardware sales ($2 billion) peripherals ($1 billion), license rights and distribution ($1.75 billion), plus indirect on-job creations ($7.2 billion in wages for 219,600 workers) plus an indirect economic impact of $5.65 billion, including taxes ($1.7 billion) publicity spending, transport, magazines, etc. 70% of the total goes to consoles and related games. The present number of video game players in North America is 145 million. This is

60% of the total population. For a broader understanding of the market, check IDSA's *Economic Impact study* at: <www.idsa.com/pressroom.html>

IDSA data is clear enough

Although Playstation, N64 and Game Boy have been a real bonanza for stores, the coming four years are going to be even better in terms of revenue. The Yankee group has anticipated that by 2003, 85% of households already equipped with a console will have graduated to a 128-bit system (GameCube, Playstation2, or Xbox). 23% of households are expected to own 2 systems and 20% will own three. Global sales for 2003 are expected to reach 45 million units.

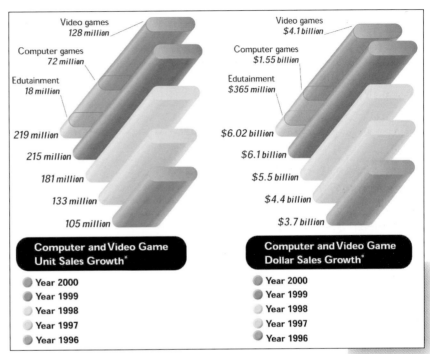

IDSA data is clear enough

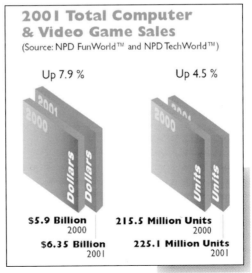

Sales still on the rise

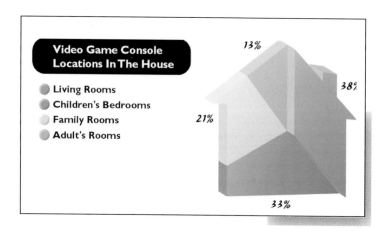

Recession? What recession?

The world of finance does not sound too optimistic at the moment, yet it looks like the video game industry is heading for a record year. The first 9 months of 2001 have generated $4.3 billion, while the first 9 months of year 2000 generated only $3.2 billion. North Americans spend more and more leisure time at home. The video game, slowly but surely, is becoming North America's number one pastime, much more popular than family chats around the fireplace!

The demise of the dotcoms is still sending aftershocks down the bank corridors. Quite a few cyber speculators are still paying for their NASDAQ folly. Yet comparing the first three quarters of 2000 and 2001, NPD Funworld has shown that console, game and accessory sales have gone up 33%.

Grand Turismo 3, Diablo 2: Lord of Destruction and *The Sims* are all outselling themselves. GameBoy Advance is being sold at a rate of 20 units per minute. Nintendo's GameCube and Microsoft's Xbox were introduced in November 2001. Consider 150 million North Ame-rican citizens watching Microsoft spend a good 500 million dollars on its promotional campaign... Talk about a top of mind product!

Now there is one bad piece of news: the economic slowdown in the telecommunication industry, which is going to affect the deployment of the high speed infrastructure. High speed for all will come, for sure, but not as soon as expected. Unfortunately, PS2 and Xbox had both based their strategic plan on the availability of broadband communication lines.

At the same time, a number of disappointed dot-com investors are now moving into the video game arena. Some shares have gone up a full 100%. Acclaim, which was nearly wiped out in 2000, has seen its shares go up from $0.35 to $4. THQ has seen a 143% increase. EA has gone up 33%. The arrival of Microsoft in the video game industry has been an eye-opener for Wall Street experts. Video game producers are going to be closely scrutinized by experienced stock brokers!

Games are everywhere!

According to a recent study by IDSA, a typical American family uses its console or PC for 10 to 11 hours per week. This is one hour more than last year. Games played over the Internet attract 24% of players, while 32% use portable consoles. As for age, 70% of all hardcore gamers are 18 years old and more. 40% are over 35 years of age. Console players are younger: 43% are 18 years old or less.

37% of all play sets are to be found in the living room, 33% in the kids' room, 21% in the family room and 13% in the parents' bedroom. Guess why the birth rate is going down?

2001 has been a transition year for the video game industry. Sony's PS1 and Nintendo's N64 have been on the decline. Dreamcast has not met with as much success as expected, and PS2, for quite a while, has been hard to find in stores. On the whole, however, 2001 has been a very good year! Most surprisingly, portable console games have gone up a whole 28%. The *Pokemon* phenomenon is still riding high: throughout the year, it has occupied the first four positions on the charts; and it has placed seven titles in the top 20.

Part 1

The Industry

Digital based entertainment invades society

Despite their humble start in coin-op machines, video games today are a well-established cultural phenomenon. Over the past 25 years, the video game industry has gone through incredible ups (with GameBoy and PS1) and pretty rough downs. Call it a roller-coaster history!

In a previous life, I was a rock singer moving from one club to the next. I saw with my own eyes how an interactive game called *Pong* started to invade the space reserved for pin-ball machines. I remember that one of my first attempts was to slice the ball and give it some spin. All in vain. It took a good twenty years for this real time physics effect to become available on PS2 and on Xbox.

The evolution of the industry was shaped by visionaries and nerds, but also by the young people who became involved in this techno art form. They never gave up. Rather, they piggybacked on the technological improvements that offered them more and more ways to express their talent.

The first video game was created by Willy Higinbotham, a research scientist. In 1958, he concocted an interactive tennis game on his oscilloscope. The first computer game, *Spacewar*, was created in 1961-62 by Steve Russel and his MIT pals. Steve designed it on a PDP-1, a $120,000 machine the

An oscilloscope: the first console?

size of four filing cabinets! The game was about two rockets firing at each other as they were pulled by the gravitational field of a dangerous sun.

The father of the first video console is Ralph Baer. He has more than 70 patents to his name, he was celebrated as inventor-of-the-year in the State of New York. In 1972, he developed what was to become the console called Odyssey, made by Magnavox. At the time, he was working for Sanders Associates, a subcontractor for the US Army.

From nerds to the general public

The first console would probably have gone down the drain had not *Pong,* the arcade game, been so incredibly successful. *Pong* was manufactured and distributed by Nolan Bushnell, the founder of Atari, the first dynasty in the video game industry.

Pong has it was first presented to the public

1981 was the golden age of arcade games. In the US, there were approximately 24,000 major arcade parlors and 400,000 smaller, "round the corner" joints. All in all, they housed over 1.5 million coin-ops. In an article in *Time* magazine, the American population was said to spend 20 billion dollars and 75,000 person/years on this new hobby. The article also stressed that video game revenues were twice as big as casino revenues in Nevada. And three times bigger than revenues from all baseball, basketball and football major leagues combined. A cultural phenomenon was born.

The video game industry timeline

1889

Fusajiro Yamauchi creates the Manufuku company, specializing in card games. In 1951, the company's name was changed to the Nintendo Playing Card Company. In Japanese, the word "Nintendo" means, "Leave Luck to Heaven", or "Work hard, but in the end, it is in Heaven's hands".

H. Hollerith develops an electro-mechanical counting machine based on the perforated card system.

1947

Akio Morita and Masaru Ibuka launch the Tokyo Telecommunications Engineering Company. In 1952, Morita and Ibuka painstakingly put together $25,000 and buy the right to use Bell Lab's patent on the transistor. They create the first portable transistor radio set operating on batteries. The name of their company is too complex for the American market. They change it to Sony (from the Latin word "sonus" meaning "sound").

1951

Ralph Baer, an engineer from Loral, is asked to develop "the best TV set in the world." To give it extra competitive advantage, he offers to create a new form of content: an interactive game. Management turns down the idea.

Ralph Baer is the founding father of the industry

1954

A Korean war veteran, David Rosen, notices how popular coin-op machines are in military barracks. He creates Services Games and exports pin-ball machines to American bases in Japan. In 1960 he decides to create machines under his own brand name: Sega (SErvices GAmes) is born!

1958

Jack Kilby, from Texas Instruments, Dallas, Texas, invents the integrated circuit.

Scientist Willy Higginbotham comes up with the first interactive tennis game ever. It operates on his lab's oscilloscope.

1961

MIT student Steve Russell creates *Spacewar*, the first video game. He uses a DEC PDP-1, a minicomputer the size of 4 filing cabinets.

<http//lcs.www.media.mit.edu/groups/el/ projects/spacewar/>

1966

Richard Greenblatt's chess program wins several tournaments at beginner's level.

Ralph Baer develops a hockey game. Four years later, it will be on the Odyssey console.

Sega launches its first arcade game in Japan. It is a submarine simulator called *Periscope*.

1967

Texas Instruments puts the first solid-state hand-held calculator on the market.

Games based on the Star Trek storyline appear on a number of mainframe computers.

1968

RAM memory is first introduced in the data processing industry.

1969

The US Defense Department launches its Advanced Research Projects Agency Network (ARPANET). Later it will become the Internet.

Life, a game created by John Conway, is played on quite a few university mainframes.

1971

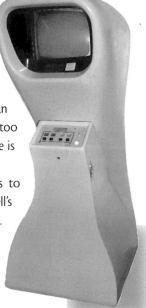

Game manufacturer Nutting delivers the first 1,500 copies of their arcade machine. The design is quite futuristic. The public finds Nolan Bushnell's *Computer Space* too difficult to play. The game is a flop.

Bally/Midway refuses to put *Pong*, Nolan Bushnell's game, on the market. Bushnell decides to create Atari Inc. Intel creates its first 4-bit microprocessor, the 4004.

Computer Space makes a cameo appearance in the SF classic Solient Green

1972

Pong undergoes its first real-life test in a bar room close to where the inventor lives. It is an enormous success!

Paul Allen and Bill Gates buy an Intel 8008 chip for $360. They build a computer to control road traffic. They create their first company, Traf-O-Data.

Nolan Bushnell and it's beloved PONG

Bally/Midway finally publishes the game called *Winner Pong*. The first wave of video game madness begins.

Magnavox starts industrial production of the Odyssey console.

First trade add for a game console

1974

Gary Gygax and Dave Arneson publish *Dungeons and Dragons*.

Sears asks Atari to manufacture 100,000 copies of *Pong*, with the Sears Logo on them.

Coleco launches its famous arcade game *Telstar.*

The Sears financed version of Pong for the home

1975

Steve Jobs plays a dirty trick on his good friend (and Apple co-founder) Steven Wozniack: he says he will split the $700 he got from Atari for the game called *Breakout* that he and Steven designed together. Instead of the $700 he said he got, Steve had received $5000!

Exidy Corporation releases *Death Race 2000* for the arcade game circuit. For the first time in arcade history, a game is banned for moral reasons. The public considers that the goal of the game — running over innocent passersby — is really revolting.

Bill Gates and Paul Allen create their first BASIC compiler for the Altair computer. They start a new company: Microsoft Inc.

1976

Nolan Bushnell sells Atari corporation to Warner Bros. for 28 million dollars.

Steve Jobs persuades Steven Wozniack to start selling the Apple 1, a motherboard with no case, no keyboard and no screen.

1977

The Apple II is launched. This is the first computer with color graphics capability.

Its clock delivers 1,000000 ticks per second, a fantastic speed (1 MHz)!

Mattel is the first to manufacture a console with a mini-LED screen. The game's name is *Football.*

Atari launches its video computer system (VCS). Better known under the code name of "the 2600", it will keep selling until 1990, becoming the most popular console of all times.

The 2600 was still being sold as late as 1990

1978

Atari's *Asteroïds* becomes so popular that the company is forced to stop production of *Lunar Lander*, the first game ever to use vector graphics.

Atari's four best game designers jump ship and create Activision.

1979

Atari's *Battlezone* is the first 3-D arcade game using vector graphics.

Taito launches *Space Invaders*. Residents from Mesquite, Texas, go to court to prevent the game from being played in their

town. Their case goes all the way to the Supreme Court, and is lost.

Nintendo of America is founded. It launches *Donkey Kong* in its arcade format.

Namco introduces the first color game, *Galaxian.*

1980

Pacman is launched in Japan. First called Puckman, it was later changed to Pacman to prevent vandals from turning P's into F's... The game will become the best selling game of all times.

Mattel Electronics introduces its Intellivision console, Atari's first competitor.

1981

IBM's first PC is released. The desktop computer and the mouse become a regular fixture.

Trip Hawkins leaves Apple and starts a new venture, which will give birth to Electronics Arts.

Ken and Roberta Williams establish Sierra On-Line; Bill Stealey and Sid Meier create Microprose Software.

A man has a heart attack playing *Berzerk*. He is and remains the only documented video game casualty.

1982

Coleco launches its Colecovision console with games from a company that is soaring in the charts... Nintendo. Nintendo

offers Coleco the license to *Donkey Kong* and *Donkey Kong Junior*.

Infocom's *Zork* is the best-selling PC game.

Atari pays Spielberg 21 million dollars for the rights to E.T. and comes out with a game, which is really rotten. Legend has it that thousands and thousands of copies are buried in the sands of Alamogordo, New Mexico.

On December 7, Atari announces sales won't meet the mark. In one day, Warner Communications lose 32% on the Stock Exchange.

1983

A revolution is underway in Japan

The video game crisis hits small developers.

Electronic Arts launches its first line of products, including *M.U.L.E.*

In Japan, Nintendo introduces its Family Computer (the FamCom). On the North American market, it becomes the NES (Nintendo Entertainment System).

Don Bluth's *Dragons Lair* is the first arcade game on laser disc.

Commodore 64 is introduced on the market, with specs that leave all other consoles way behind.

Time Magazine elects its Person of the Year and the winner is… the computer.

1984

Apple puts a bombshell on the market: the Macintosh.

Mattel sells Intellivision, Warner sells Atari.

Commodore introduces the Amiga.

Brett Sperry and Louis Castle create Westwood Studios.

1985

The video game industry seems to bottom out. Nintendo tests its new console in New York. Buyers are given a satisfaction-or-money-back guarantee.

Intel introduces its 386 chip, centupling the number of transistors found in the 4004 original series. Grand total for the 386: 275,000 transistors!

Habitat, by Lucas films, appears on Quantum Link network, AOL's forerunner.

1986

Nintendo launches NES, with *Super Mario Brothers* and 15 other cartridges. *Super Mario* is an immediate success, outselling the competition 10 to 1.

An unknown plumber begins his carrer in America

Modem to modem games make their first appearance, with two splendid scenarios: *Strategic Conquest Plus* for the Mac and Sierra's *Helicopter Simulator* for the PC.

Capcom's *Streetfighter* beats all arcade game records.

Acclaim becomes Nintendo's first American developer.

In the wake of Nintendo's NES' success, the Sega Master system is launched in North America.

Atari introduces a new console, the 7800.

1987

Nintendo's already steep ascent turns vertical when *Zelda* and *Metroïds* hit the stores.

Activision is the first American developer to create games for two platforms at the same time, Nintendo and Sega.

Maxis launches *Sim City*.

Tonka starts distributing Sega games and increases its market share, eating chunks of Nintendo's market.

1988

Millions of law-abiding citizens suddenly get hooked on *Tetris*, the new buzz in town.

Sega launches the Genesis console.

Atari's, portable console is the first to offer color games. Coleco is wiped out of business.

Nintendo GAME BOY™

The original version of a 120 million units legacy

1989

Nintendo launches *Game Boy* and Sega follows up with the 16-bit version of Genesis.

Activision is the first to market a game on CD-Rom: *Manhole*.

NEC introduces the Turbografx card.

RPG game inventors, the Steve Jackson Games company, are raided by police and their equipment is impounded! They were working on a Cyberpunk game and the federal government decided they were dangerous hackers. The obvious conclusion is: for certain people, it is difficult to draw the line between fiction… and reality.

Intel introduces its 486 chip. For the first time, the chip carries an integrated math co-processor, speeding up computing considerably. PC computers are now ready for the point-and-click interface.

1990

Nintendo launches *Super Mario 3*, the most popular cartridge in the history of video games. Nintendo also delivers the 16-bit *Super Nintendo* console to the Japanese market.

Nintendo takes Blockbuster to court, arguing that game rentals hurt game sales. Nintendo looses the court game.

Nintendo keeps delivering the hits

Sega is still absolute king in the arcade game market.

1991

Origin's *Wing Commander* is the year's big hit.

Nintendo releases the Super Nintendo console.

Id Software is founded by John Carmack, John Romero, Tom Hall and Adrian Carmack.

Sid Meier launches *Civilization*.

Super Nintendo is launched on the North American market.

Sega introduces *Sonic*.

Sony and Nintendo announce a CD-rom player for the Super NES.

Despite Nintendo's effort to stop the move, the Game Genie is launched. It allows players to use cheat codes.

1992

With *Wolfenstein*, Id Software introduces the first person shooter category (FPS).

Nintendo breaks its contract with Sony and signs with Phillips. Sony gets really upset and decides to start manufacturing its own 32 bit console: the PlayStation is born.

Launch poster for the 3D0

1993

Trip Hawkins launches the 3DO console and Atari retaliates with the Jaguar: two flops on the market.

Doom takes all gamers to the next level.

Mortal Combat by Acclaim causes a big scandal among American parents. Senator Joseph Lieberman starts his anti-violence crusade.

Sony starts its own entertainment software division.

Intel introduces the first Pentium processor.

Sega and Nintendo announce their next generation of consoles.

The most popular PC game of all time

1994

Broderbund launches *Myst*, which becomes a phenomenon of its own.

Electronic Arts starts a series of mergers, buying off Bullfrog.

The X-Com is a big success with experienced gamers.

The Entertainment Software Rating Board (ESRB) is established.

Donkey Kong Country is launched, taking everybody by surprise with its 3-D look.

Two new consoles for Japan: Sega launches the Saturn and Sony the PlayStation.

1995

PlayStation arrives on the North American market, $100 below the announced price tag.

Squaresoft announces that their *Final Fantasy* series will appear on Playstation, not N64 as first announced. Nintendo's fiery president is still fuming!

Windows 95 sets a new environment for developers. One year later, DOS is dead.

Nintendo's N64 is launched in Japan with *Mario 64*: success is immediate.

The N64, it's silicon graphic chip and revolutionary gamepad

1996

Quake rides solo and reigns supreme on the web.

3-D Video acceleration cards are mushrooming everywhere. Voodoo introduces 3dfx.

Voodoo3: 3dfx's last horray !

An EA subsidiary, Origin, launches *Ultima Online*: this is the beginning of a new era for online gaming.

Warcraft II becomes the new standard for real time strategy games.

Eidos launches *Tomb Raider*. Lara Croft becomes the industry's pin-up girl.

Nintendo announces the sale of its billionth cartridge. It sells 1.6 million N64s in the first three months.

Over the Christmas period, Sony averages sales of 12 million dollars a day.

1997

Thanks to *Diablo*, RPGs come back into fashion.

Bungie's *Myth* is the first strategy game to be published in 3-D.

About 50 strategy games are launched, all hoping to dislodge *Warcraft II* from top place.

The Tamagotchi and Pokemon phenomena takes everybody by surprise

20 million PlayStations are sold around the world.
The Tamagotchi craze sweeps over Japan.

In 5 days, more than 300,000 copies of *Star Fox 64* are sold on the American market. In Japan, *Final Fantasy VII* sells two million copies in three days.

Gumpei Yokoi, who fathered the Game Boy, dies in an automobile accident.

GameBoy Color takes over the legacy

1998

The 3-D TNT2 NVIDIA acceleration card is released. The 3dfx sees its market share dwindle severely.

With *Rainbow Six*, Red Storm creates a game sub-category: tactical combat simulation.

Sega's Dreamcast is launched in Japan.

Half-Life meets with incredible success. An FPS with a strong storyline can really hold its own! Blizzard launches *Starcraft*: a new standard is born.

Nintendo announces *Pokemon*'s release in America and launches the Game Boy Color.

The Interactive Digital Software Association (IDSA) announces that industry sales are up a record 30%. Arcade games, on the contrary, are on a steep decline.

Over the Christmas period *Zelda: Ocarina of Time* generates more money than any other Hollywood film.

Sega's console endeavour hangs by a thread

1999

With *Unreal*, Epic Entertainment takes the multi-player crown from Id Software.

On the Internet, *EverQuest* is so popular that it is nicknamed Evercrack.

Half-Life's official extension, *Team Fortress Classic*, is one of the year's best games; it comes free of charge.

Sega launches Dreamcast. 98 million dollars in sales the first day.

Sony unveils the specs of its PS2 console. Everybody falls on their knees and thank the Creator!

There's a war going on in our living rooms

The war of the consoles

According to the US Census Bureau there were 115.9 million housing units and a total population of 281,420,000 in the US in 2000.

In a study published in 2001 by the IDC, the future of console sales looked bright. For PC-based games sales revenues were expected to grow from $2.73 billion in 2001 to $2.73 billion in 2003. For console games the projected increase was much more significant: from $4.17 billion to $10.43 billion.

The *Gaming in America Survey*, another 2001 study sponsored by Ziff Davis Media, compiled responses from 2700 gamers. It described the statistical profile of PC and console gamers: their buying habits, their lifestyle, etc.

The survey established that there were 37.7 million households equipped with video gaming hardware. Almost half the 37.7 million owned both kinds of equipment, while 34 million owned only a computer and 21 million owned only a console. With a minimum of 1 to 2 players per household, that's a lot of people.

According to the IDSA, sixty percent of all Americans age six and over, or about 145 million people, play computer and video games. In 2000, over 219 million PC and video games were sold, almost two games for every household.

Xbox and GameCube both sold 1.5 million units over the 2001 holiday season. PS2 sold 5 million. Basically that says that video games are part of the American way of life.

The average gamer does not correspond to the "nerd" stereotype. In fact, 48% practice extreme sports. Their average household revenue is $64,000. 77% are single. 88% are males. 60% own cell phones. 78% spend less time in front their TVs because of their video gaming hobby.

Your average gamer has evolved

The average PC gamer is 28 years old. The average console gamer is 17. They are active consumers. They own an average 29 games and intend to rent or buy 4.5 games within the 60 days following the survey, spending an average $66. 60% rent 2 games a day for 4 days. 78% have a game in mind before they make a purchase.

Hardcore gamers are a very important minority. Of a total population of 44 million console gamers, there are only 11.2 million hardcore gamers (i.e. 25.45%), but they account for 55% of all sales: 41% of them buy games every week!

The *Electronic Gaming Segmentation Study* has a different spin on things. It established that 43% of all gamers can be considered "hardcore", a 17% increase over the proportion observed in 1997. They play on PCs or consoles an average of 4 times a week and 50% of them play online. They all spent over $100 in games over the past 6 months. Next are high tech gamers, representing 25%. They are professionals in their late twenties, with a higher income. Moderate players come next, accounting for 20%. They mostly use consoles. Younger players represent 12%. They too are console players.

The most important piece of data is the number of online players — 80 million — who have become the number one group. We will be talking more about them a little later on.

<www.idc.com>
<www.ziffdavis.com>

In the 80's Nintendo jumped started a dying Industry.

Dreamcast vs Playstation 2

What happened?

The war between consoles has begun and it is going to change the face of the electronic entertainment world forever.

Here's a summary of what's happened so far: Nintendo and Sega fought each other off, while lots of US consoles went down the drain. Then Sony, retaliating against Nintendo's breach of contract, launched the PlayStation and gained huge chunks of the market pie. Xbox is the Americans' last chance to get out of the PC basement.

Sega was not supposed to be a major player any more and yet, against all odds, its Dreamcast broke *Star Wars'* $23 million record for a first day showing with sales of $98 million (372,000 units). That compared to Dreamcast 350,000 units over the first 6 days. One week after launch N64 had sold 410,000 units, and the 500,000 mark was reached soon after that. Sega's new console came with a superior line of games: *Sonic 3-D, NKL2K*, the best football game ever and *Soul Calibur*, a fantastic sword fighting game.

Sega and Sonic have a few tricks up their sleeves

In its second year on the market Dreamcast gave the competition a run for its money. With *NFL2K1*, it was the first console to hook up to the Internet, gaining universal praise. *Quake III, Ferrari 355, NBA2K1* and *Phantasy Star* soon followed. But the shadow of a new launch from Sony stopped Sega's momentum and Dreamcast never reached the base of 5 million units it needed to become viable.

Indeed when Playstation 2 appeared things changed for Sega. With its 128-bit retro-compatible "emotion engine" delivering 75 million polygons per second, Playstation 2 could display characters showing an unprecedented level of movement, reactions and feelings. And you could play your DVDs on it too! Today there are more than 300 titles available and just as many developers.

According to Sony's 2001 business report, the average number of software items per PS2 user was 3.7 at the end of September 2001, but the number had moved up to five per PS2 user by end of December 2001. Since sales of PS2 began almost 2 years ago the total number of units shipped has reached the 25 million mark. This is three times the number for PS1 game console sales over the same period. 18 million units were shipped during fiscal year 2001 alone.

In January 2002, NPD Funworld reported that Playstation 2 games dominated the video game sales

charts. It placed 12 titles in the top 20, including Take-Two's Blockbuster, and *Grand Theft Auto 3*. Sony is clearly the reigning champion.

PS2: an installed based of 25 million units

Console prices play a significant role. Announced at $229, Dreamcast dropped to $99 after it decided to stop production, then to $49 for the 2001 Christmas period. Prices like that can't be beat!

Playstation 2 prices tell a different story. The console cost $449. You need at least one game. So add $79. Then a second joystick to be able to play with a friend, i.e. $49 more. Add taxes and the sum climbs to $650! 25 million units later, it looks like a rather good pricing idea! You can now get a game pack that includes: a PS2 console, an additional controller and a memory card for $369.

Yet because Xbox comes loaded with a modem and a hard disk in its standard version, Sony is thinking about putting its PS3 on the market for Christmas 2004, sooner than expected.

Alea jacta est!

3 contenders are now fighting it out in the arena: PS2 (October 2000), Xbox (November 15, 2001),

Xbox vs GameCube

GameCube (November 18, 2001). As anyone could expect, we had a hot video game winter!

Bill Gates looked at the PS2 and demanded double the specs for his Xbox. It is indeed the most powerful machine on the market now. The CPU runs at 733 MHz and the graphic processor is a 250 MHz engine developed conjointly by Microsoft and NVIDIA. It delivers 150 million polygons per second. It has 64 3-D sound channels. It can play DVDs and is Ethernet and is 56K modem ready.

Developers are all breaking down Bill Gates'gate, eager to exploit the console's new capabilities!

Nintendo's GameCube has a different approach. The idea is not to flex technological muscle, but to bank on a long line of hit characters. Nintendo has been around for so long that everybody knows their star games. GameBoy is now 10 years old and has sold over 100,000,000 units. Nintendo's image has become equated with kids. The more mature gamers have moved to other consoles and games. So Nintendo is now trying to lure the older gamers back with games like *Perfect Dark* and *Conquer*. In addition to *Mario*, *Donkey Kong* and

Star Fox, we can expect all Nintendo star games to appear on GameCube. On launch date, Shigeru Miyamoto was ready with the first game based on Mario's brother: *Luigi's Mansion*. There was also an extension to the irresistible game called *Smash Brothers Melee*, featuring all of Nintendo's star characters.

Although Xbox is definitely the most powerful console for the moment, a few questions remain: Is it going to be confused with a PC? Are Microsoft's Xbox games and PC games going to cross-fertilise? Cross-fertilisation is probably what most gamers are hoping for. But we don't know yet.

The Trojan horse theory

What looks like a console battle is in fact much more than that. Sony and Microsoft are using their console hardware as a Trojan horse: they both want to invade North America's digital home entertainment market. The fascinating thing for us players is that the path to success, for both of them, is to offer top quality games.

Sony wants PS2 to pave the way for its digital entertainment portal. But that's not all. Sony also wants PS2 to become a shopping center connected to our credit card. Go to their site and check out their business plan. Every artist, every movie, every game has its own web site. Every piece of intellectual property they own has a site! There is only one thing missing for the moment: a button to quickly download our favorite product to our hard disk.

Photos: Charles Meyer

A launchday promo for the Xbox

With Xbox he wants to establish a firm base of digital entertainment hardware, thereby gaining direct access to your credit card... Just like Sony!

<www.sony.com>

PC vs consoles

Netting 30% of the industry's revenues at best, the PC video game market seems to have reached a plateau. The arrival of the Xbox, which is a PC in disguise, could hurt PC games. Consoles have been penetrating the home market very fast. Developing a game for a console is, in fact, easier than for a PC: developers do not have to take the vast number of existing configurations into consideration! Throughout the lifetime of a console, which is about 5 years (and getting shorter every second) the specs remain the same. Consoles are also a lot easier to play with. Their intuitive, life-like interface is one of the main reasons for their success.

Microsoft announced it was going to spend $2 billion during its first two years on the market. It is easy to understand why small companies can't compete! Microsoft plans to lose about $120 with every Xbox sale. Every manufacturer uses its console as a loss leader and makes up for lost dollars with game sales. Financial circles predict yearly returns of $500 to $1 billion per year, a mere 5% of the company's profits. In other words... peanuts! But Bill has a hidden agenda.

Prices for PC games and for consoles are steadily going down. At the same time, costs for the production of quality games are skyrocketing. Game manufacturers and game publishers are obviously entering a danger zone. The mergers and acquisitions that have taken place over the last few years are a sure sign that the market is in pretty turbulent waters.

Specialists will say that the success of a video game is a multi-variable phenomenon. Even with huge marketing budgets and top-notch technology, the real competitive advantage is the experience the game provides. Players know when the feel is good.

Today, competitive games are 3 to 15 million dollar projects. Production takes 2 to 5 million dollars, marketing gobbles two or three million more, not to mention the licensing costs.

Solo endeavours are pretty much extinct. Production teams can range anywhere between 20 to 100 people. *Pong*-like stories belong to the past! But small developers could make a come back with episodic games delivered directly to a console. (An episodic game is brought to you in small chunks of a level or two. The idea is to hook you and then lure you into paying for more. This business model was pioneered by id Software with *Doom*, and caused a small revolution in the way games were marketed to the public).

The upward spending trend is not going to stop. Think how demanding graphics are in terms of processing power. Think how much more time and money must be spent on software so that programs can integrate artificial intelligence, special effects and real time physics.

The Big Two (Sony and Microsoft) are getting their digital supermarkets ready. This is where they expect their revenues to come from. To increase their market shares, they have concocted the same plan. I say: Viva la competition! The end winner is going to be the consumer. He will enjoy the best titles in history. And the best home entertainment equipment, for very little money.

Sony entered the 21st century with the best console the world had ever seen. Capitalizing on its success, it is clearly aiming at the digital, high speed, entertainment market. But the absence of add-ons such as a modem and hard disk could reduce the PS2's life span.

In 2000, Merrill Lynch put together a list of the 10 reasons why Sony will sell 100 million units of the PS2 and 960 million games between 2001 and 2005.

1. The video game market is in full bloom.
2. The PS2 will be much more than a game console.
3. As a console, it offers DVD capabilities.
4. The console is backward compatible.
5. Playstation fans are a very loyal bunch.
6. The console is the tech champion (not true any more, with the arrival of Xbox).
7. The PlayStation franchise is a world success.
8. Developers are all aboard!
9. Competition is weak. (Not true any more, with Xbox and GameCube).
10. Production costs are going to go down.

Whatever happens on the high-speed digital entertainment scene, Sony will play a major role. Nintendo will keep catering to the family market. High-end players as well as the general public will keep an eye open for guru Miyamoto's new products. For a while, Dreamcast will remain the best console for arcade game adaptations and for outlandish Japanese games. Xbox is still an enigma. Bill Gates' decision to invade the video game market is certainly one of the biggest gambles of his life.

Year 2000 and 2001 News

Since this is the first version of *William's Almanac, Everything You Ever Wanted to Know about Video Games* (the *William's Almanac* for short), we will go further back in history than just a year or two. We'll see how important video games have become in our lives. Starting this year, *William's Almanac* will provide an overview of the achievements and trials of this fascinating new industry. As you know, video games have already become a source of creativity and riches equal to none... and this is only the beginning!

August 2000

- In Japan, in 5 months, Sony sells 3 million units of the PS2. The PS1 had reached that mark after 19 months.
- Sega cuts Dreamcast prices down to $149.
- Sony buys RTIME, acquiring its network expertise.
- Ubi Soft confirms it has acquired Red Storm.
- INVIDIA graphic cards sell like mad. They take 3dfx to court.
- Nintendo unveils Game Boy Advance (an upgraded version of Game Boy) and announces their new generation console, the GameCube.
- Thanks to *Diablo II* sales, Havas ranks first among PC video games publishers.
- EA wins the bid race to the *Harry Potter* rights.
- Intel announces the Pentium 4, with a brand new architecture and a 400MHz system bus, roughly three times faster than the system bus on the Pentium III.
- Presidential candidate Al Gore chooses Joseph Lieberman to run with him as vice-president. Lieberman is an arch opponent of violence in the entertainment industry.

- Sony confirms that the release date for the PS2 in Europe has been postponed. European prices will be set $150 above US prices.

September

- Mattel grudgingly accepts to sell The Learning Company (TLC), which they bought only the year before.
- Sony announces there will be no more than 500,000 PS2s up for sale on launch day, October 26.
- Microsoft unveils the Xbox logo.

Nintendo unveils its new line of products

- Sony launches the PS One, the upgraded version of PlayStation 1.
- Two of Infograme's investors take the company to court over the fact that the company has squandered some of GT Interactive's assets.
- The Federal Trade Commission publishes its study on "Marketing Violent Entertainment to Children". Film, music and video game industries are heavily criticized for the way they market their products to children. The Commission points a finger at violence in their promotional campaigns.
- Pre-sales for *Pokemon Gold* reach 600,000 copies. Another record sale for Nintendo.
- THQ buys Volition. 3dfx announces losses of up to $100 million.
- vEA founder Trip Hawkins invests 20 million dollars in 3DO, his other venture.

Microsoft show's off
its colors

October

- Due to repeated losses, Sega is forced to do some restructuring.
- *EverQuest* goes beyond the 300,000 registered player mark.
- Oddworld spreads the word that the PS2 is hell to program, then signs an exclusive agreement with Microsoft for the Xbox.
- It turns out that Eidos, finally, will not be sold to Infogrames.
- The PS2 is launched amidst a lot of confusion.
- Hasbro cuts 550 jobs.
- A ruling by the city of Indianapolis, barring minors from arcade parlors, is confirmed by a federal judge. Chicago and Saint-Louis are discussing a similar ruling.
- vSan Francisco's mayor lashes out at a graffiti competition based on Sega's *Jet Grind Radio*.
- In its first month in operation, Sega Net attracts 100,000 users.
- Sony vigorously denies that the limited supply of PS2s is a marketing ploy intended to boost popular demand.

November

- Direct X 8.0 is released. Direct X is Microsoft's standard set of routines for multimedia application development on the Windows platform.
- SEGA announces that Dreamcast is going to change a lot over the next two years. It unveils an ambitious strategic plan, based on its ability to deliver the best games on the planet.

Abe and Oddworld abandon Sony's ship to jump abord the Xbox bandwagon

- Sony presses Great Britain's customs officials to re-categorize PS2 as a computer.
- While profits reached 38 million dollars in 1999, Acclaim announces losses of 131.7 million for year 2000.
- Eidos announces losses of 116.4 million dollars for the first six months of 2000.
- Over the same period, Nintendo announces profits of 400 million dollars.
- In a public statement, Infogrames announces revenues of 75 million dollars, half of which come from sales on the US market.
- Only three days into the market, Sony nets 165 million dollars in PS2 sales.

The new console juggernaut marches on

- Basing its case on a United Nations regulation, Nintendo forces a Tennessee citizen to abandon his ownership of the name "Pokemon Center".
- Brian Hook leaves Verant on friendly terms and has harsh words about Sony's corporatism.
- Seagate Technology wins the 8 Gig hard-disk contract for the Xbox.

December

- Rumor has it that Nintendo is going to buy Sega. The *New York Times* writes about it. The rumor is denounced by all as pure sham.
- Infogrames buys Hasbro Interactive and Games.com for 100 million dollars.
- Electronic Arts announces that 10 of its titles will be available on the Xbox as soon as it comes out.
- J.F. Cecillion, chairman of the board for Sega Europe, resigns in the wake of the Dreamcast's poor results.
- NVIDIA acquires 3dfx pour 70 million dollars.
- Paul Steed joins the Wild Tangent team as game producer.
- Microsoft buys Digital Anvil.
- Nintendo restructures its distribution circuits in Europe.
- The Irish Police Corps accuses the IRA's terrorist branch of financing its activities with the sale of illegal copies of PS2 games. It claims the terrorist branch generates 30,000 dollars in sales per week.
- The Canadian Federal Police investigates illegal sales of the PS2 over the Internet.
- Angelina Jolie's first photographs as Lara Croft are published in the press.

Crash Bandicoot is one of the rare American icons to have been adopted in Japan

January 2001

- Sony buys Naughty Dog, developers of the mega success *Crash Bandicoot*.
- SEGA confirms that all of its titles will be released in PS2, GameCube, Game Boy Advance and Xbox format.
- Sony's sale projections for PS2 are revised downwards: 9 million units rather than 10 million.
- SEGA stops the production of Dreamcast. Selling price drops to $99.95.
- EA decides to use its license for *The Sims* on the Internet. *Sims Live* and *Sims Online* are launched.
- Microsoft retracts a previous statement announcing that graphics for Xbox would be generated by a 300 Mhz chip. Current speed will be 250 MHz. The poly count falls from 300 million to 125 million per second.
- In Europe, a number of complaints about PS2 raise questions about the console's overall quality.
- The Surgeon General's Office blames the media for the level of violence among young people.

The new 3D king is in town

February

- NVIDIA launches its revolutionary graphics card, GForce3.
- Sony announces that for budget year 2001 (starting in April), 20 million PS2 units will be put on the market.
- 3DO cuts down 30% of its workforce.
- Majesco sells Sega's Game Gear for $29.99 a piece.
- Ubi Soft announces sale results are up by 49%.
- Shiny confirms the rumor: yes, there will be a video game based on the license to the *Matrix*.
- Flipside, Vivendi's online game portal announces it is buying arch competitor Uproar for 140 million dollars.
- Ubi Soft buys German company Blue Byte.
- Nintendo confirms the launch date of Game Boy Advance on the American market. The system will be available as of March 31st in Japan, and June 11th in the US.
- NVIDIA's revenues for budget year 2000 are up 96%, with sales totaling 735.3 million dollars.
- THQ announces record breaking revenues of 347 million dollars.

- Sega cuts down 300 jobs; workers all go into early retirement.

March

- Sega announces that since it first came out in December 2000, *Phantasy Star online* has registered 200,000 players.
- Saudi Arabia bans *Pokemon* from the country.
- Nintendo announces that Game Boy Advance will be available on the US market for $99. Games will cost anywhere from $29.95 to $39.95. In Japan, on its first day, Game Boy Advance sells 650,000 copies.
- Microsoft decides to upgrade Xbox's hard disk capacity from 8 Gigs to 10 Gigs.
- EA buys Internet game portal POGO.com, getting access to its 17 million registered players.
- Ubi Soft buys the Learning Company, the best educational software publisher.
- Microsoft estimates it will take 5 years and 2 billion dollars to reach the break-even point for Xbox.
- Sony asks IBM and Toshiba to create a 10 micron superchip for the PS3. This is a 400 million dollar project!
- Sega's Chairman of the board dies from a heart attack.

The first RPG designed for on line consoles id is a success

All the marketing power in the world could not help GameBoys' opponents

April

- Bill Gates opens the Tokyo Game Show by introducing the Xbox, along with an ex-development manager from Sony who moved over to Microsoft.
- IDSA's annual report is published. The number of games sold has gone up. But the number of consoles hasn't. Overall US sales have gone down from $6.1 billion in 1999 to $6 billion in 2000. The report mentions the fact that prices for 64 bit console games have gone down, due to the fact that the 64 bit consoles are now at the end of their life cycle.
- Sega admits it is ogling Electronic Art's market.
- In the aftermath of the tragedy at Columbine high school in Columbus Ohio, Nintendo, Sega, Sony, id Software and Infogrames, along with 25 other video game companies, are named in a lawsuit filed by the family of the assassinated teacher.
- Daily Radar, one of the most influential web sites on video games, is closed rather abruptly by its publisher Imagine Media.

- Nintendo announces it has set aside 75 million dollars for the Game Boy Advance marketing plan.

May

- A new study by IDSA estimates that jobs in the video game industry are standing at 29,500. This is a 15% increase over the 2000 figure. The US economy has had a 6% job overall increase.
- Vivendi-Universal Publishing buy the exclusive right to create video games based on J.R.R. Tolkien's *The Hobbit* and *Lord of the Rings.*
- Microsoft buys Ensemble, which has sold 8.5 million copies of *Age of Empire.*
- Nintendo announces that its GameCube will hit the stores on November 5 and will sell at $200, $100 below Xbox. Xbox is scheduled for launch on November 8.
- 65,000 visitors go to E3. 450 companies, from 100 countries, are represented.
- Interplay announces it is up for sale.
- Sony announces an agreement with AOL, whereby PS2 owners will be able to use AOL's Internet services

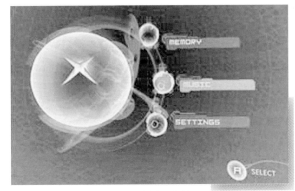

The interface to access a console's hard drive: a first !

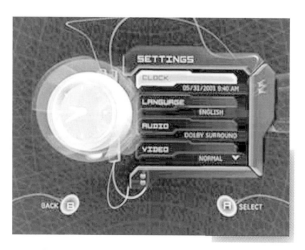

- Wall Mart decides to stop making its sales results available to companies like NPD.

June

- The Xbox command interface is unveiled.
- PS2 prices are lowered in Japan and England.
- Will Atari be resurrected? Infogrames bought Atari's remains when it acquired Hasbro. Infogrames official Bruno Bonnel says the company is toying with the idea of changing Atari's name on the US market and maybe on all world markets.
- Midway axes its arcade division.
- Negotiations with THQ are not getting anywhere: French firm Titus Interactive announces that its Interplay Entertainment shares (46.5%) are not for sale any more.
- Game Boy Advance is launched and, as usual, meets with instant success.

Nintendo seduces Merrill Lynch

- With *Myst III: Exile*, the *Myst* franchise hits another record mark.
- PS2 will be able to process Java scripts, making programming a whole lot easier.
- Namco, Square and Enix announce a joint effort and a common Internet game offer strategy.
- Tomb Raider, the movie, is number one on the box-office.
- Philips is chosen by Microsoft as manufacturer for Xbox's DVD player.
- Ubi Soft will distribute Capcom titles in Europe. Infogrames will do the same with Sega titles.
- The appeal court gives Microsoft a second chance.

July

- While the dotcoms hit rock bottom lows, the video game industry enjoys a 28% sales increase over the first 6 months.
  - Game Boy Advance sells 20 units per second, for a total of one million copies over the first 6 weeks.
  - Christmas price for Dreamcast is set at $49.
  - *Diablo II: Lord of Destruction*, the extension, sells 1 million copies within a month.
  - Sony finally delivers *Gran Turismo 3 A-Spec* and meets with immediate success.
- Nintendo America's CEO goes into retirement after Christmas. Peter MacDougall, CEO of Nintendo Canada will take his place.
- Merrill Lynch, the consulting firm, calculates that Nintendo is losing only $20 per GameCube sold, which is a lot less than competitors Sony and Microsoft lose on their console.

- Thanks to a 12.9 million dollar investment by American company Global Emerging Market, French company Kalisto escapes bankruptcy.
- John Romero and Tom Hall leave Ion Storm. Eidos closes Ion Storm offices in Dallas.
- Sega.com transfers its registered clients to Earthlink.
- Microsoft anticipates sales of 4.5 to 6 million units of the Xbox during its first year on the market.
- In Japan, *Final Fantasy X* gets really close to the 2 million copy sales mark.
- British publication Edge, considered to be the best monthly magazine on the video game industry, celebrates issue number 100.

August

- Former executives from Disney and Digital Domain found Rebel Arts. They want to offer a powerful new platform for massive multiplayer gaming.
- Infogrames reports a 29 percent increase in full-year sales.
- Take Two closes its subsidiary Godgames New York offices. Godgames titles will not be affected by the change. Founder Mike Wilson leaves the company to start Substance TV, a subscription-based interactive DVD magazine.
- id Software confirms that it has asked Raven Software to develop *Quake 4*. An Xbox version of *Doom 3* is also on the way.
- Sega of America lowers the Dreamcast price to $79.95, down from $99.95.
- Nintendo announces that, early into 2002, it will release a 56k-compatible V.90 modem and a broadband adapter for faster connections.
- *Pokemon Crystal* for Game Boy Color sells almost 600,000 units in its first two weeks on the market.

- Microsoft strongly denies reports that problems with the motherboard could delay the delivery of the Xbox. Xbox game price is set at $49.99.
- Titus Interactive takes majority control over Interplay Entertainment.
- Nintendo delays the release of GameCube to Nov. 18, two weeks after the promised date of November 5.
- Microsoft delays the Japanese and European launch of Xbox until early 2002.
- An SCEA study reports that 93% of PS2 owners have used the console to watch a DVD movie.

September

- Toys R Us and Amazon.com sell their first batch of $499 Xbox bundles in just 30 minutes.
- Sega reveals its aim to grab a 15 percent share of the consumer game software market in Japan and in the US over the 2003/04 business year.
- The horrible tragedy on September 11th places the video game industry in a state of shock. Immediately after the attacks, many games are delayed because scenario changes must be made. Video game manufacturers see their stocks plunge. The same happens with industry in general.
- Nintendo's next generation GameCube console hits stores in Japan, selling around 80 percent of the 500,000 units available. The event is generally regarded as "low-key" compared to the dizzy scenes of GBA and PS2 launches.
- Ranking 255th, EA is the only interactive entertainment publisher to make it on the annual Information Week 500 list.
- The November 8 launch of Xbox is delayed by one week to allow Microsoft to meet the demand for the console.

- For the fourth consecutive year, THQ is named on the Los Angeles Technology Fast 50 list. While BioWare is awarded the Ernst & Young Entrepreneur of the Year Award in the Software and Information Services category, it files a lawsuit against Interplay over a breach of two contracts for sublicensing distribution of BioWare games to third parties without BioWare's consent.

October

- The PlayStation 2 is making a profit for Sony and the company expects its games division to get out of the red.
- The 2002 Spring Tokyo Game Show is cancelled due to waning attendance from both exhibitors and visitors.

PS2 standing tall with 25 million units sold

- Sony buys 19% of Japanese developer Square for 124 million dollars. Square was hit hard by the poor performance of its movie *Final Fantasy*.
- The well respected Japanese company SNK (NeoGeo) closes shop.
- Activision is named by Fortune Magazine as one of the top 100 fastest-growing publicly held companies in the U.S.
- Worldwide shipments of PlayStation 2 have hit the 20 million mark. (Japan: 6.86 million units, North America: 8.55 million units, Europe/PAL: 4.63 million units).
- EA is appointed as the distributor of three forthcoming Disney Interactive PC titles.

- Sega announces an alliance with Microsoft for the Xbox. *Shenmue II* and *PSO* may only be the tip of the iceberg.
- Sega is also working to jointly develop an arcade board using Xbox hardware.

November

- Tecmo launches a lawsuit against a Japanese software company that has re-released *Dead or Alive 2* with nude characters.

DEAD OR ALIVE 3
Bouncing breasts are OK, but nudity is not!

- Sony's President Kunitake Ando says Xbox will change the traditional five-year console lifecycle and could force Sony to release PlayStation 3 sooner than it would have liked.
- Contrary to what was announced before, the hybrid DVD player for the GameCube will not be released in the United States.
- Peter Moore, president and CEO of Sega of America, publicly apologizes for the cancellation of *Shenmue II* on Dreamcast in the U.S. *Shenmue II* will now be released on the Xbox. He also revealed that Sega did have talks with Microsoft regarding a possible merger.
- Following the combined effects of strong sales and lower costs of producing the Game Boy Advance, Nintendo anticipates profits over 375 million dollars.
- AOL Time Warner and Sony create a new open broadband home networking environment.
- Microsoft closes its store in the Sony owned San Francisco Metreon center. The fact that the store closes shortly before the launch of Xbox is sheer coincidence.

December

- Imagine Media's consumer videogame publication, *Next-Generation*, closes down. *Next-Generation* magazine started in January 1995.
- PS One shipments targeted for Europe are halted by Netherlands authorities after its cables are tested with excessive levels of cadmium.
- The Federal Trade Commission report states that the motion-picture and electronic-game industries have "made commendable progress in limiting their advertising to children of R-rated movies and M-rated games, and in providing rating information in advertising".
- VM Labs Inc., the maker of Nuon technology is forced into involuntary bankruptcy.
- The latest *EverQuest* expansion, *The Shadows of Luclin*, sells more than 120,000 units during its first 24 hours on store shelves. According to Sony, its release is "one of the largest PC game debuts in history."
- A study entitled *Fair Play? Violence, Gender and Race in Video Games*, reveals that "the top-selling videogames offer very little racial and gender diversity".
- Microsoft confirms that the Xbox console will start selling in Japan on February 22.
- Microsoft's Xbox receives the Consumer Electronics Association 2002 Innovation Award for best product in Electronic Gaming and for Best designed and engineered product.
- According to NPD Funworld the amount of sales brought in by videogame hardware, software and accessories was approximately $6.4 billion from January to November. During the same time period last year, overall sales figure was $4.7 billion.

All your base are belong to us

Doesn't make any sense, right? Well, that's precisely the point. No one in his right mind could understand what the sentence means! It first appeared in a game called Zero Wing, published for Sega's Genesis by Toaplan in Japan. It was such a blatant translation error that people started quoting it right and left, making fun of it. CEO's used it as joke in corporate meetings all over America. In 2001, the story became an explosively popular phenomenon. Follow the joke's history at:

<www.memecentral.com>
<www.planettribes.com/allyourbase/index.shtml>
<www.allyourbase.net>

With Sega's decision to focus on game creation, Electronic Arts and all other smaller developers are now faced with a powerful competitor. Sega's titles are going to be available on all existing pieces of hard-

Dreamcast is dead but Sega, like a phoenix, rises from its ashes

ware: Sony, Nintendo, Microsoft, Palm, PCs, WAP phones and DVD players. Sega will also produce some of the most popular licensed games in history. The Dreamcast chip is available for all TV set-top manufacturers. Sega may have had clay feet, but it is still a giant.

As mentioned earlier, Sega was founded in 1952 by Marty Bromley. Sega (SErvice GAmes) was providing American bases with all sorts of coin-op machines: pin-ball machines, juke-boxes, etc. In those days, the pin-ball machine was illegal in New York city and in many states across the US. Eventually, Sega and Sonic the mascot did so well that it beat Nintendo at its own game. But then the bad days rolled in. Sega's Dreamcast had to compete with Sony, Nintendo and Microsoft's brand new machines.

Future according to Sega

Was it last-ditch energy? Was it sheer genius as a reaction to danger? The fact is that Sega did come up with design solutions, which may well have a lasting effect.

When Dreamcast came out, it was selling 10 units per minute. During its first year, it was doing better than PS1, with 2 million consoles and 6 million games sold. Game figures included 1.5 million units by third parties. Experts found *Dead or Alive* was better on Dreamcast than on PS2! How did Sega react?

The first console with web capability

Sega followed the flow of digital business. It decided its console would be free of charge... provided you chose SegaNet as your internet provider for the next 2 years, at $21.95 a month.

For $526.80, Sega offered Dreamcast, a keyboard and unlimited access to the Internet. Gifts included, that was half the price it would have cost to sign up with AOL or MSN for 2 years. SegaNet was designed and optimized for games. Real-time multiplayer games were made available to 56K modem owners one year before competitors even thought about it! At the time, Sony and Microsoft were talking a lot about high speed. It was "high speed or nothing". But that was talk only. Sega showed them!

At the Millia 2000 convention in France, Sega President Scoichiron Irimajari had identified latency as gaming enemy number 1. For an RPG game, one second latency is OK. But in a simulation game or, worse, in a race game, fractions of a second make a huge difference. Sega announced its remedy: a Game Center linked to a fiber optics network, to be launched in Japan in 2001.

In the US the answer was GTE Internetworking.

On both networks, latency is supposed to drop to 200 milliseconds or less. Titles such as *NBA2K1, NFL2K1, Ready 2, Rumble 2* and *Quake 3* were made available and John Cormack, id Software's guru, said they were great!

The Sega Team also published *Phantasy Star Online* at the end of year 2000. This was the first multicultural online game ever. In *Phantasy Star Online*, real-time communication between players is achieved through a set of standard symbols. Teams of four, coming from all possible countries, get together and embark on a mission in a virtual world which changes all the time.

Sega's new CEO, Brad Huang, led the charge against Sony, stating publicly that high speed was still 5 years away.

Figures seem to prove him right:
- According to Jupiter, 22 million young people under 18 identify online games as their number one activity on the Internet. 68 million gamers will be online by 2003.
- In 2002, according to Forrester, 24% of the video game industry's revenues will come from online games.
- 20% of Dreamcast owners are registered SegaNet gamers.

Sega's views on the digital economy have had their effect. Sony, in 2002, will offer a modem and a hard disk for PS2. Xbox had learned the lesson and was fully equipped from the start. Yasushi Nagumo, marketing manager for the Dreamcast Japanese market said:

'Of the 2 million consoles we sold in Japan, 550,000 went to SegaNet online users. We are getting ready to offer banking, stock, medical, video-telephone and karaoke services. We are going to connect all our arcade parlors to our fiber optics network so that all gamers in the country can play together.'

Here is a list of a few of the gadgets available in Japan at the moment. Watch out for the technical vocabulary…
- MP3 on VMU platforms, wristwatches with an internet connection and Swatch's universal 1000 beat system, force feedback for online gear, ISDN high speed adaptors, LAN adaptors and Palm/cell phone adaptors for the Internet, online karaoke.
- As of May 16, 2001, it has become possible, with Dream Passport, to download any of 50 Genesis and Turbo-grafx-16 oldies. 15 new "oldies" are added to the library each month.
- Videoconferencing and videoch@t with the Dreameye camera on SegaNet. Just imagine what American teenagers could do if they could lay their hands on that joystick with integrated microphone! I am sure American kids can't wait to use the kind of high-speed network that goes with such cool video gear! I shiver at the idea of what American kids could do with these gadgets and a network ready to Webcast their every whim.

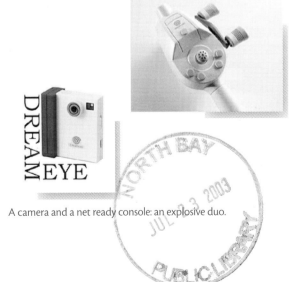

A camera and a net ready console: an explosive duo.

• For only $200, you can add the Samba de Amigo interactive maracas to your bag of tricks and, bingo, you're off on a new musical planet!

The most bizarre peripherials on the market

Beyond Dreamcast

Sega's developers are among the best in the industry

Sega was the first to reach the online Promised Land. Thanks to SegaNet, gamers have found massive milk and multiplayer honey on the other shore! Sega set the stage for tomorrow's action… then vanished!

But Nintendo is learning from Sega's pioneering advances. Check out what Nintendo is planning to do on the GameCube with Sega's award winning *Phantasy Star Online*: five different languages, a person-finding system allowing gamers to seek out who they want to play with, zillions of character options to choose from… Sega's generic seeds are now growing in Nintendo's garden!

2.

Creating a video game is like mixing an applied science with a variety of interactive arts. But above all, it is putting a product on the market. This is where business culture and the bottom line take over. Idealists have to adapt their vision of the ideal game and think in terms of what makes business sense.

Developing video games is not an easy task! There are lots of wannabes, but very few games actually make it to the finish line. What happens with games is pretty much the same as what happens in the film or the music industry: lots of producers and lots of artists line up and want to make it big. They all want to sign that fat production contract which will turn their pet project into reality. Likewise, in the video game industry, there is a horde of small developers who want to climb to the top.

Let see what it takes for a small developer to attract the attention of a publisher. Then let's take a look at the kind of contract that binds publishers to game developers.

The right person to talk to

If you know the right person to talk to, in this or that publishing firm, you may feel you have made big advances already... Well, not quite. That's only step one. Well established publishers do have people responsible for game project analysis. These analysts or development officers are inundated with projects. They can receive as many as 1,000 new projects a year. Conclusion number one, then, is quite simple: your project better be striking. If analysts cannot detect what is essential and what is innovative about your game, they won't even call you to say thank you. Now, if you catch their eye, be prepared for a rush meeting where they'll quickly get down to the nitty-gritty.

These people may sound distant and indifferent, but remember, they cannot pat each and every small developer on the back! Their job is to identify viable projects quickly.

Chose the right target!

There are quite a few publishers around. Only a few may be the right ones for you. What sort of games do they publish? What sort of platform or console do they publish on? What level of quality are they well-known for? A, AA, AAA? Do they need a new product? How many independent developers did they work with over the past few years?

Ask yourself these questions and then make a choice. Choose publishers who are the most likely to be interested in your kind of game. Gather as much information as you can about their company. Speak to developers who are presently working with them. Speak to insiders who work for departments other than production. Information is the key to a well-prepared presentation.

The top 20 publishers

1	Nintendo of America	12	Acclaim Entertainment
2	Electronic Arts		
3	Sony	13	Konami of America
4	Activision	14	Namco
5	Vivendi-Universal	15	Midway
6	Infogrames	16	Eidos Interactive
7	THQ	17	The 3DO Company
8	Sega of America	18	Square EA
9	Ubi Soft	19	Capcom USA
10	Take 2 Interactive	20	Interplay Productions
11	Microsoft		

What are the risks?

For a publisher, the project with the least amount of risk is a completely operational game. You'd be sur-prised to see how many well-polished projects publishers receive. A beta version does not carry the same clout as an alpha version. A playable level is more impressive than a technical demo.

Of course a team with experience and with a couple of hit games under its belt is less risky than a team which is made of star game designers who have never worked together before. It is fine and dandy for them to have produced major hits, but for any publisher, question number one always is: are they going to be able to work together and stick to schedule for the next 24 months?

The technology used to produce a game is also part of the risk evaluation process. If you are using a game engine that is well known on the market, your project is safer than if the engine is brand new and built specifically for your game.

A value-added product

Whatever the game category or the platform you are aiming at, your game must be better than any game on the market. It must be up to par with games scheduled to appear in the future. If your game is as good as the latest version of *Quake*, forget about it, it is already *passé*.

There are three basic criteria for game evaluation: look and feel, gameplay and technology.

Once you have compared your game to the market leaders, establish its assets and its weaknesses. Ask one of your colleagues or a friend to conduct the same evaluation you just did. Then compare results. When it comes to measuring up to competition, somebody else's point of view is always valuable.

With well over 4,000 games published every year, your game must have a well-defined, distinct competitive edge. It can't be the sort of game that no one has ever seen before. It can't resemble a game that is already famous except for a couple of new, cool functions. Your game must have something totally unique, what is called a unique selling point in marketing parlance. If it is the only one that does this or does that, then it's really got added value, and you are on the right track.

There is one thing you have to be wary of: if a publisher is looking for a game which "looks like mega hit x", then he will probably want to produce it with his own team or with someone he has already worked with before.

Will it sell?

If the publisher thinks that, despite your jazzy graphics and your great gameplay, the game won't sell, there is nothing you can do about it.

This is where the final verdict is given

Your game must have something gamers have been longing for. Something that acts like a magnet. It can be breathtaking graphics or a game based on a movie everybody knows, or on a book everybody has read, or on a famous table game. Or simply the extension to a very popular game.

New games also sell well when they "look familiar" or look "easy to understand". A potential consumer must be able to tell what the game is all about, simply by looking at the game box. The main character, the license or the title must be "tell all" right away.

A game that grabs you!

If you want to develop an interactive game you have to be part of the video game culture. Many film studios have made attempts to create video game versions of their own films. They thought they had the right resources in terms of graphic artists, software engineers or marketing whiz kids... Yet after a while, they all came to understand that interactive entertainment is indeed very different from traditional entertainment. They simply backed out. A video game must be exciting and a lot of fun to play... or it simply does not exist. It must be addictive to the point of generating hordes of addicts!

If you want to know how addictive your game is, ask people who do not belong to the development team. If they play with it with several times in a row, then your game may have what it takes!

The ideal project

The ideal game project is a game that is:
· almost completely operational ; not a concept, not a limited run-time demo
· produced by a team of old pros
· a technical marvel and a wonder to look at
· addictive, with great gameplay.

Let suppose you have everything in hand now. You really think you can get a publisher interested. You still have to find the right company. It may look easy, but it isn't. Even if you are very well prepared, it is hard work and quite time consuming. As you know, there are a whole lot of games competing against you. Statistics show us that 95% of all games are rejected.

Publishers have all gone through nightmares, what with projects going over budget and being long overdue or below standard in terms of quality. They know that the vast majority of games they publish won't be profitable. At the same time, they know that they can take risks: one successful title will pay for all the rest.

The standard contract

Despite the fact that production budgets may vary a lot from one console to another, most contracts are based on the same advance versus royalties system.

There is another kind of agreement called the "Affiliate label deal" which used to be popular but not any more. In the Affiliate label deal the publisher distributes the product, is given advertising space on the box and keeps a certain percentage of the sales. The developer pays for marketing, public relations and reproduction costs. This kind of deal has proved to be a nightmare for quite a few developers. More often than not, the publisher didn't push the product well enough and the developer found he had no control whatsoever over the inventory, although he was paying for all reproduction costs.

In the advance versus royalties kind of deal, the developer gets a 15% royalty on all net sales. The 15% royalty is paid to the developer when sales revenues match the amount of money handed down as an advance. In theory, the advance covers all production costs plus an estimated 30% envelope for day to day expenses. The developer will use his 30% to keep him afloat till the next project comes around. Unfortunately, what happens most of the time is that development ends up taking more time than expected. And so, the developer is forced to finance part of the production with his 30%.

Developer-valve tooks its time but delivered the classic *Half-Life:* a franchise was born

This, of course, puts developers under a lot of strain. On top of that, to minimize their risks, publishers tend to hold on to their advance payments as long as they can, usually until the end of the production cycle. This is a good way to force a developer to be on time and on budget, but when the project is cancelled and there is no special cancellation clause in the contract, it can leave him or her out in the cold!

Normally, an advance must be big enough to cover production costs, and there is an unwritten common sense rule, which says: the smaller the advance, the bigger the royalties.

The developer may ask for his royalties to increase with sale revenues. For example a fee could be 15% for the first 200,000 copies, then 25% until 400,000 copies are sold.

For the publisher, costs include sales taxes, distribution, reimbursements, royalties to console manufacturers and more often than not, marketing costs. Net revenues are defined as gross revenues minus allocation for unsold copies, minus sales costs.

Let's see what the breakdown for costs and revenues looks like for a publisher with distribution lines to Europe and North-America.

Wholesale price

The wholesale price varies from one territory to another. In Europe a PlayStation title costs $40. The return for the publisher is $20, as compared to $32 in the US. To simplify things, let's assume that the US wholesale price is $30 and the public price is $40.

Allocation for unsold copies

The publisher reserves a certain amount of money to cover the cost of copies that will be returned to him unsold. If inventory management, particularly for console titles, is not conducted properly, profits may well turn into losses. There is very little room for mistakes. For PC titles, there is more leeway because games cost a lot less than consoles.

Marketing and license fees

Marketing budgets usually represent 15% of net projected sales. License fees can range anywhere from 5% to 15% of net projected sales. Net sales are calculated as gross sales minus reserve allocations for unsold products. For example a FIFA license can cost as much as $250,000 per title and up to 20 million dollars for a long-term deal covering several platforms.

Promotion at the store level

A lot of promotion goes on at the store level, particularly with PC titles. It can take the form of publicity in the store's magazine or in the various leaflets the store puts out regularly. Depending on the title, a publisher will set aside from 0 to 15% (15% is when sales expectations are really high).

Console royalties

Up until very recently, for titles selling at around $40, publishers had to pay Sony $7 per copy. Today, however, 65% of all sales are generated by titles costing $20 or less. So Sony is currently reviewing its policy. Nintendo royalties have always been much higher than Sony's.

Duplication costs

Duplication costs include the manual, the CD, the cover, the case and the packaging. For a PlayStation 1 with one CD, the cost can be as low as $2. But for a title on 4 CDs or a PC title, the cost can be $4.

Distribution

Distribution costs represent about one or two percent of the total revenues. They cover transportation costs. For a publisher without his own distribution channels, costs can be from 12 to 15% higher. Now let's take a good look at the cost breakdown, item by item.

	CONSOLE	PC
Public price	$50	$40
Wholesale price	$30	$26
Projected sales (number of copies)	1	1
Gross revenue	$30.00	$26.00
Console royalties	$7.00	$0.00
Duplication	$2.00	$4.00
Marketing (15% projected sales)	$4.50	$3.90
Promotion (5%)	$1.50	$1.30
Allocation for unsold copies (8%)	$2.40	$2.08
Publishing costs	$17.40	$11.28
Net revenue	$12.60	$14.72
Developer's advance money (15%)	$4.50	$4.50
Net revenue for the developer	$8.10	$10.22
Developer's royalties	$1.22	$1.53
Publisher's profit	$6.89	$8.69

It looks more profitable to publish PC titles, but because sales volumes differ greatly, the opposite is true! The next table will highlight this. The developer of a console title has received a $4.50 advance per copy, with a 400,000 copy sale guarantee. For a PC title the advance is the same, but this time the guarantee is for 100,000 copies.

	CONSOLE	PC
Public price	$50	$40
Wholesale price	$30	$26
Projected sales	400,000	100,000
Gross revenue	$12,000,000.00	$2,600,000.00
Console royalties ($7)	$2,800,000.00	$0.00
Duplication	$800,000.00	$400,000.00
Marketing (15% projected sales)	$1,800,000.00	$390,000.00
Promotion (5%)	$600,000.00	$130,000.00
Allocation for unsold copies (8%)	$960,000.00	$208,000.00
Publishing costs	$6,960,000.00	$1,128,000.00
Net revenue	$5,040,000.00	$1,472,000.00
Developer's advance (15%)	$1,800,000.00	$450,000.00
Net revenue for royalties	$3,240,000.00	$1,022,000.00
Developer's royalties	$486,000.00	$153,300.00
Publisher's profit	$2,754,000.00	$868,700.00
Developer's total	$2,286,000.00	$603,300.00

The lion's share goes to the publisher, which is OK because he is taking all the risks. Now let's have a look at a different hypothesis. The developer pays for production costs and receives a 50% royalty.

	CONSOLE
Public price	$50
Wholesale price	$30
Projected sales	400,000
Gross revenue	$12,000,000.00
Console royalty ($7)	$2,800,000.00
Duplication	$800,000.00
Marketing (15% projected sales)	$1,800,000.00
Promotion (5%)	$600,000.00
Allocation for unsold copies (8%)	$960,000.00
Publishing costs	$6,960,000.00
Net revenue	$5,040,000.00
Developer's advance money (15%)	$0.00
Net revenue for royalties	$5,040,000.00
Developer's royalties	$2,520,000.00
Publisher's profit	$2,520,000.00
Developer's total	$2,520,000.00

If you compare the last two tables, you see that the difference is not very big. The ideal contract is a mix of the two agreements, where the developer accepts to pay for some of the production costs, so he can ask for higher royalties in return.

The reality may seem a bit grim. But one should always remember that whatever the sector, there is no such thing as a free ride. The entertainment industry is tough, but it is very gratifying. The production of your first video game is not the end of your dream, it is the beginning of a fantastic adventure.

To conclude on a positive note, let's take a look at an example where the developer has negotiated a 15% advance, with royalties growing up to 30%. The title has sold 1 million copies.

	CONSOLE
Public price	$50
Wholesale price	$30
Projected sales	1,000,000
Gross revenue	$30,000,000.00
Console royalties ($7)	$7,000,000.00
Duplication	$2,000,000.00
Marketing (15% projected sales)	$1,800,000.00
Promotion (5% projected sales)	$600,000.00
Allocation for unsold copies (8%)	$2,400,000.00
Publishing costs	$13,800,000.00
Net revenue	$16,200,000.00
Developer's advance money (15%)	$1,800,000.00
Net revenues for royalties	$14,400,000.00
Developer's royalties (30%)°	$4,320,000.00
Publisher's profit	$10,080,000.00
Developer's total	$6,120,000.00

*Depending on the agreement between the developer and the publisher, royalties for the developer increase gradually from 15% to 30% after the guaranteed minimum is reached.

Bigger than Hollywood

These days, if you have written a movie script based on a famous video game, you stand a better chance of seeing Hollywood back your project.

Regardless of how it was greeted by the critics and the public, *Tomb Raider*, the film, opened right at the top of the box office list. With *Final Fantasy, Resident Evil* and half a dozen other projects in the works, game-based scenarios have started a craze in Hollywood. The International Licensing Industry Merchandiser Association held its 2001 annual convention in New York. The 3,700 intellectual properties submitted to the 18,000 participants generated 97 billion dollars in transactions. Game related properties amounted to 11% of the total, which is enormous!

Well over 100 companies bought the rights to manufacture products under the *Tomb Raider* license. The first week it was shown, the film sold 47 million tickets and 850 licensed products were auctioned off on Ebay.

Street Fighter (1994) and *Mortal Kombat* (1995) were quite successful. But *Super Mario Brothers* (1993) and *Wing Commander* (1999) were total flops. Now that video games can generate as much money as films, now that President Bush admits he is a regular player, Hollywood studios have started to ask video game companies for new scenarios. It is so much easier to market a movie when the public already knows the main characters! The big studios simply can't resist. Game companies are well aware of it and they now

develop their intellectual properties with future partnerships in mind. The same thing happens the other way round. Both industries agree on the same bulletproof conclusion: game sales mean ticket sales and *vice versa*.

How about a game about Elvis' movie carrer?

The same thing happened with comic strips. It all started with Superman and Batman. The X-men and Spiderman now have the floor. There seems to be no end to this sort of exchange. Will movies become interactive one day? In any case, movies and games will be drawing their inspiration from the same source for a long time to come.

It is believed that since the dawn of time only 16 different stories have been told over and over again in different shapes and formats. Interactivity may well be an occasion to expand that common core and place the art of telling stories back into the limelight again.

3.

Science and technology

Video game companies invest an average 10 to 20% of their budgets in research and development. Hardware and middleware manufacturers are always fighting the clock to attract developers and please consumers. Gamer demands push R&D people to the outer limits of the computer galaxy. If you compare gamer demands and businessmen's needs, it is only fair to say that business needs have already been pretty well met, while gamers are still craving for more.

The military used to spend a lot of money on training simulations. But after the end of the cold war budget cuts were dramatic.

It is still a little early to predict what effect September 11th will have on the market. Military budgets have already been increased considerably. But what proportion will be spent on computer-based simulation is unknown. The return to home-based entertainment, the game version of cocooning, seems to favor the industry as a whole, however.

The video game industry is now the biggest and most hungry broadband consumer. Gamers need hyper effective networks for their death match games. 3-D, real time physics, music and voice also call for speed and reliability. Gamers are turning into sophisticated, exacting crowds! Gamers' needs are shaping the future of real-time interactivity. They are the clients the so-called new economy must really listen to. When the Pentium 3 was introduced in 1999, it came with 70 new instructions specifically designed to enhance graphics, 3-D, streaming audio, streaming video and speech recognition.

Nvidia's Geforce3

A revolutionary 3D card that swept the market

In 2001, for the second time in a row, NVIDIA corporation stole the show in *Business Week*'s report on the semiconductor industry. Not only was it number one in its own category, but in the high technology sector it was ranked number four. This was a first for a company almost entirely devoted to 3-D graphics for the game market. The company was also honored by the Fabless Semiconductor Association (FSA) for accomplishments during the year. The FSA voted it as the Most Respected Public Fabless company and the Best Financially Managed company. In addition, the FSA honored NVIDIA for its achievement as the fastest US-based semiconductor company to reach revenues of $1 billion. Sales have gone up 96%, reaching $735 million and, at $100 million, profits have increased 162%. To put mildly, competition for 3dfx has been wiped out in no time. NVIDIA is now offering its revolutionary GeForce3 to developers and consumers, for their enjoyment and pleasure.

Their graphics processor is the jewel of Xbox and their PC card sells like hot buns. For the moment, the card is still one step ahead of what gamers can do. It will take another few months before new games will use the full power of Xbox's processor or all the potential of GeForce3.

To enhance 3-D realism, GeForce3 integrates the nfiniteFX engine and Lightspeed Memory Architecture. For the first time the architecture is open. Using *Vertex* and *Pixel Shaders*, programmers and artists will be able to give their work a personal touch, creating their own special effects, their own graphic atmosphere. Games will have a different look.

With *Jet Grind Radio*, Sega provided an example of what could be done with an open architecture. At the time a toon shader had been used to enhance the 2-D/3-D renderings.

The GeForce3 is equipped with the fastest processor in the world. With its 57 million transistors, it can handle 800 billion operations per second. It offers 32 bit color images with a resolution of 2048 x 1536 pixels. Specs like that are going to keep professionals busy and consumers dizzy for quite a while!

Real-time physics

Reality now has a competitor! Two companies, Havok and Math Engine, are offering developers a way to incorporate real time physics in their games. Blizzard, Valve and Ubi Soft are some of Havok's clients. Their technology will be integrated in Macromedia's Shockwave 3-D. The computing power available today on PCs or on consoles has made it possible for games to exploit advances made in applied science.

Realtime interactive physics enhances the immersion level

Using Newton's laws, it is possible to predict the motions of inanimate objects in space. But why stop at objects? For R&D software engineers, the interactions between game characters and their environment is the next target. Solid body moves, articulated body moves and collisions have always preoccupied developers. How does a piece of material float on water? How do waves propagate on the surface of a pond? How do explosions unfold? Solving problems like these in real time is the new frontier. Gamers have found a way to exploit the potential of real-time physics with the rocket launcher in *Quake*. Because acceleration is equal to force divided by mass (Newton's second law), they found they could fire a rocket placed under a character's feet and produce incredibly high jumps!

Real-time physics is also used in games using artificial intelligence, the way *Black and White* is doing. The door is now open: surprise and wonder are on the other side!

The Game Theater XP

The Game Theater XP is one of the cheapest, most effective ways to expand your PC. Sound effects and music account for at least 50% of the impact of any audio-visual experience. Yet the two are treated like underlings in the multimedia family. All they have to chew on, most of the time, are the

The sound barrier is broken

cheap loudspeakers which come bundled with the computer. We all tend to forget that good audio is crucial to the game experience.

The Game Theater XP comes in two parts: an audio card and a sleek looking case, which is an external module. There is an incredible number of options to chose from. You may plug in your USB joysticks or your driving-wheels, plus your headset and microphone and enjoy total immersion when you engage in multiplayer games over the Internet. The power DVD option allows you to enjoy Dolby surround sound. The digital signal processor (DSP) outputs 3-D sounds to either two or four loudspeakers: the sound will literally blow your head off! The package comes with a number of sound applications: an MP3 encoder, a sequencer and a digital karaoke. All in all, this is really a must. It is complete, it is inexpensive, it is a sound processing center of unprecedented quality.

<http://fr.hercules.com/products/gt_xp/features_gt_xp.php>

The Game Commander 2

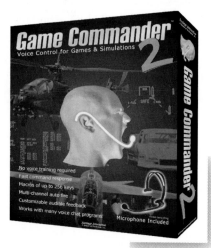

Now you can scorn your opponent in realtime while he bites the dust

The Game Commander 2 is more than a gadget: it will transform your online interactive experience. It offers real-time vocal communication. You suddenly feel yourself totally immersed in vocal exchanges, insulting your opponent or making fun of him. Tension becomes palpable as words escape your mouth in the middle of the wildest battle. You can trigger up to 256 keystrokes per voice command! The application has won several prizes, and gets us very close to the feel of Star Trek's holodeck.

<www.gamecommander.com>

Get yourself your own avatar

3Q Inc. is a pioneer in a very specialized sector, capturing the image of a human face and inserting it into a game. They have invented a kind of photo booth, similar to the booths at the supermarket. But instead of producing 2-D paper copies of people's faces for a buck or two, they burn a special CD you can use in your favorite online games: your own 3-D digital face

A 3D clone generator

can be displayed over the head of the character of your choice. This is the ultimate personalization! It works fine with the online versions of *Unreal Tournament, Quake III Arena, Half-Life* and *Counter Strike*. The technique was going to be extended to the console gaming world when publishers suddenly chickened out. They were afraid that the face of a politician or of a school principal could show up on characters that are consenting victims or all-round losers!

Another company, Cyberextruder Inc. has chosen a different approach: all you need is a photograph of yourself and they can produce a 3-D rendition you then paste over the face of a character.

<www.3qme.com>
<www.cyberextruder.com>

What impressed me most this year, was to see that what I had been dreaming about five years ago now exists for real. I was talking to my students about Moore's law and about miniaturization. In my vision, there was this handheld computer you could take along on the bus and do your homework on. It had 3-D color graphics and a Softimage environment that only Silicon Graphics high-end workstations could handle at the time. Most students thought I was going a little too far!

Create your own video game on the bus

But lo and behold, at the 2001 GDC, I spotted a Pocket PC, which was running Blender, a powerful 3-D package. It was possible to create a virtual world and the model of a ship, then to move the ship in that 3-D environment in real time... It was even better than what I had been talking about five years before. It is always spooky when you find out that your wildest dreams can't compete with reality!

Evolution comes to the Arcade world

Once inside Trio-Tech's Cyberpod, words can't describe the quality of immersion! The door closes on you and there you are, sitting on 600 watts of sound, facing an incredibly wide screen, your hands resting on the joysticks. Even *Unreal* never got so intense. Even a jaded mercenary would stand up to the occasion!

Total immersion: a gamers ultimate trip

In January 2001, the Cyberpod was on the cover page of *PlayMeter*, the industry's most important magazine. Elaine Shirley, who worked for Atari for 25 years, now works full-time for Trio-Tech. She has been showing off the Cyberpod to American distributors. Cyperpods can be networked for group sessions. There is a microphone you can use for expletives and sneers you want to share with your victims! Cruise ships have started to welcome Cyberpods aboard.

Ballistics, Trio-Tech's latest baby, was a big hit at IAAPA 2001 (The International Intellectual Property Alliance). This time you're in lay-down racing position and you pilot a jet-engine supersonic speeder. You really must try that one!

<www.trio-tech.com>
<www.iaapa.org>

4.

Associations

Academy of Interactive Arts and Sciences

First established in 1996, the Academy of Interactive Arts and Sciences is dedicated to the advancement and the promotion of a new art form: the interactive game. It organizes the awards ceremony, which is held every year in Las Vegas during the Academy's annual D.I.C.E. summit. Numerous prizes are handed out. The AIAS certainly brings the developer community together, whipping up pride in the art of video game design.

<http://64.49.205.17>
<www.interactive.org>

European Software Publishers Association

ELSPA is IDSA's European counterpart. It was founded in 1989. Today it represents over 100 organizations and companies. With its Video standards Council, it developed high production standards and also a code of ethics for the interactive entertainment industry. ELPSA promotes ECTS, a yearly convention taking place in London.

Entertainment Software Rating Board

The ESRB was formed in 1994 by IDSA, as described, below, and it is the rating board, which has related over 8,500 video games and console titles to date. The ERSB addresses online privacy issues and advertising practices in the interactive entertainment industry.

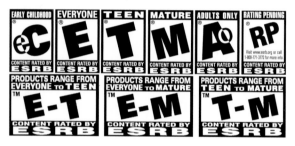

"Please be advised that the ESRB rating icons, "EC", "K-A", "E", "T", "M", "AO" and "RP" are copyrighted works and certification marks owned by the Interactive Digital Software Association and the Entertainment Software Rating Board and may only be used with their permission and authority. Under no circumstances may the rating icons be self-applied or used in connection with any product that has not been rated by the ESRB. For information regarding whether a product has been rated by the ESRB, please call the ESRB at 1-800-771-3772. For information regarding licensing issues, please call the IDSA at (212) 223-8936."

<www.esrb.org>

IDSA

id sa Interactive Digital Software Association

IDSA is an American born association. It is dedicated to the business and public affairs needs of the video game industry, across the PC, console and online platforms. In 2001, its members, representing 85% of the industry, generated 6.35 billion dollars in sales in the US. The IDSA is a strong opponent of software piracy. It owns the Electronic Entertainment Expo (E3). It acts as the industry's lobbyist in Washington DC and it conducts studies which are regularly published on the web site.

<www.idsa.com>

Interactive Entertainment Merchants Association

IEMA was created in 1997 and represents the interests of PC and console game retailers. After the May 2001 Columbine high school tragedy, it was made responsible for the sale of inappropriate hardware to young members of their clientele. The IEMA now publishes standards addressing this issue. 19 out the 20 major retailers are members of the Association. Altogether they sell 80% of all games and consoles across the US.

International Game Developers Association

IGDA is a non-profit organization. Its mandate is to help interactive game developers reach their collective goals. Local chapters offer members of the community all sorts of legal, financial and strategic advice. The IGDA also has foreign chapters that conduct regular meetings and seminars.

<www.igda.org>

Local chapter activities can be found at:

<www.igda.org/Chapters/chapters.htm>

The International Intellectual Property Alliance

There are over 1,350 companies worldwide managing intellectual property rights. In 1984, IIPA was created to represent their needs and interests. The Alliance covers intellectual property rights for movies, videos, music, books, newspapers, business software and entertainment software. In 1999, the last year a complete study was conducted, their industry was worth $457.2 billion.

5 .

Conventions

D.I.C.E.

Backed by the Academy of Interactive Arts & Sciences, the first annual D.I.C.E. summit (Design, Innovate, Create, and Entertain) will explore approaches to the creative process and to artistic expression as they apply to the development of interactive entertainment. The 2002 D.I.C.E. summit was at the Hard Rock Hotel in Las Vegas (February 28 - March 1st), in conjunction with the 5th Annual Interactive Achievement Awards. D.I.C.E. turned the Hard Rock Hotel into a think tank for the interactive entertainment industry. It addressed the most basic question of all: what is the interactive art form?

<www.dicesummit.org>

The Electronic Entertainment Expo

Every month of May, eyeballs turn towards Los Angeles where E3 is held. This is the major event in the industry. Just imagine 5 football fields covered with booths, with video game companies all vying for your attention. Gamers are asking for more in every corner! Four days of exciting activities, with 62,000 participants from 100 foreign countries. This yearly business fair brings together 450 companies: there are developers, publishers, manufacturers, distributors, retailers and also representatives from the media! Everybody is putting on their best interactive show! Business professionals will also attend seminars conducted by industry pundits: they will want to get the latest news on the state of the art; they will also want to hear about the world culture mushrooming right under their feet.

<www.e3expo.com>

Milia

2000 companies attended MILIA 2002 on the Riviera in Cannes, France. More than 50 countries were represented. Professionals made this huge European event a big success. The ThinkTank Summit, partnered by Forrester Research, drew hordes of delegates. High profile sessions, over two consecutive days, focused on strategic development and new trends in the business.

Now in its third year, The Game Developers' Village, backed by AMD, Biovirtuals, Discreet and MathEngine and media partners Joystick, Edge, PC Games and Alliance NumériQc, received an unprecedented number of entries for the 2002 competition. An astounding 83 projects from 21 countries competed this year, an increase of 26% compared to last year.

<www.milia.com>

ETCS

The North American and European video game markets are now roughly equivalent, with Europe standing at $6.3 billion. The ETCS started in 1989 in London, Great Britain. Over the years, it has grown bigger and bigger and is now the size of France's MILIA. While MILIA attracts spring crowds, ECTS takes place during the fall. In 2001, for the first time, it opened two days before GDC and attracted 23,000 visitors from 60 different countries. 2,500 members of the press were present and they gave the event top coverage.

<www.ects.co.uk>

The Game Developer Conference

GDC is the annual convention for all those who make a living out of game developing. They are a passionate bunch who play games, talk about games, dream about games, spend two years on a game and keep asking for more. They attend seminars and workshops led by their favorite industry luminaries. The creator of *The Sims*, for example, is a superstar for these guys and gals. All the best designers are there: with everything changing so fast and the industry forever redesigning itself, they cannot sit back and rest on their laurels. They cannot live in their ivory tower and risk alienating themselves from the needs, whims and wishes of their growing target audience, the occasional player.

IEMA Executive Summit

On the list of conventions and business fairs related to video games, the IEMA Executive Summit is really unique. It was designed to offer a quiet business setting for retail members of the association and for invited vendor company representatives. A lot of business done in a very comfortable environment! Three days of workshops and networking take place at the beautiful Ritz-Carlton Laguna Niguel in Southern California. Lecturers and workshop leaders are offered a choice of three different golf courses! VIPs will tell you it is one of their favorite stops on the circuit!

<www.executivesummit.com>

Nordic Interactive Media Expo: NIME 02

The Nordic Interactive Media Expo was launched in Scandinavia last year. Scheduled for October 30-November 1st this year, it will once again draw everybody's attention to Sweden. More than 50 different countries will flock to the Swedish Exhibition and Congress Center in Gothenburg. Seminars, workshops and prizes for developers demonstrate Sweden's ambition to promote the Northern European market. As project manager Per-Anders Gustafsson said, "Our goal is to become one of the largest entertainment exhibitions in Europe. The European market alone is expected to reach an unbelievable $7.8 billion in the year 2003!"

<www.nime.se>

Tokyo Game Show

In October 2001 the Computer Entertainment Software Association (CESA) hosted more than 150,000 visitors at its Tokyo Game Show. Called the Makuhari Mass, it was held at the Nippon Convention Center in Chiba City. Chiba City was made famous by cyber punk guru William Gibson. Delegates from the West find the place quite exotic! It is unsure whether the event will be repeated or not, because, more and more, Japanese companies are taking care of their own promotional needs.

<www.cesa.or.jp/tgs/english.html>

6.

Game Companies

ARTIFICIAL MIND AND MOVEMENT, INC.

Artificial Mind and Movement, Inc. (A2M) develops mainly for consoles such as PSX, PS2, Dreamcast, GC, Xbox and GameBoy Advance. It also adapts some of its games for PC.

PRINCIPAL GAMES: *Jersey Devil* (PSX, PC), *Bugs Bunny Lost in Time* (PSX), *The Grinch* (PSX), *Bugs Bunny and Taz Time Buster* (PSX), *Smurf Racer* (PSX) and *Monster Inc.* (PSX).

WEBSITE: www.a2m.com

ADDRESS: A2M, 416 de Maisonneuve West, Suite 600, Montreal, Quebec, H3A 1L2, Canada

PHONE: (514) 843-4484

FAX: (514) 843-4234

EMPLOYMENT: www.a2m.com

EMAIL: info@a2m.com

ACCLAIM ENTERTAINMENT, INC.

Acclaim Entertainment Inc. develops and distributes interactive game software for console and PC. The company is best known for its Turok and NFL Quarterback Club series.

PRINCIPAL GAMES: *18 Wheeler: American Pro Trucker* (PS2, GC) *All Star Baseball 2000* (PC), *All-Star Baseball '97* (PSX), *All-Star Baseball 2002* (PS2, GC), *Amorines: Project S.W.A.R.N* (N64), *Batman & Robin* (PSX), *Dave Mirra Freestyle BMX* (GBC) *Dave Mirra BMX 2* (PS2, Xbox, GC, GBA), *ECW: Anarchy Rulz* (PSX, DC), *ECW: Hardcore Revolution* (DC, PSX, N64,), *Extreme-G 3* (PS2, GC), *F355 Challenge* (DC), *Ferrari 360 Challenge* (PS2), *Ferrari Grand Prix* (PS2), *Iggy's Wreckin'Balls* (N64), *Jeremy McGrath Supercross 2000* (DC, PSX, N64), *Jeremy McGrath's Supercross World* (PS2).

WEBSITE: www.acclaim.com

ADDRESS: Acclaim Entertainment, One Acclaim Plaza, Glen Cove, NY 11542

PHONE: (516) 656-5000
FAX: (516) 656-2040
EMPLOYMENT: www.acclaim.com/company/
    careercenter/index.html
EMAIL: Staffing@acclaim.com,
    HResources@Acclaim.Com
STOCK EXCHANGE: NASDAQ
SYMBOL: AKLM
ANNUAL REPORTS:
    www.acclaim.com/company/financial
    Information.html

ACTIVISION, INC.

Activision\, Inc. develops, publishes and distributes interactive game software for Sony, Nintendo, Sega, Microsoft and PCs. Activision is recognized as a major publisher in the industry, drawing its success from its FPS games and its brand O2.

PRINCIPAL GAMES: *QUAKE III Arena, QUAKE II, Civilization: Call To Power, MechWarrior 2, Dark Reign* and *Cabela's Big Game Hunter* for PCs; and *Tony Hawk's Pro Skater, Disney/Pixar's Toy Story 2, Tenchu, Asteroids, Space Invaders* and *Vigilante 8* for PlayStation.
WEBSITE: www.activision.com
ADDRESS: Activision, Inc., 3100 Ocean Park
    Boulevard, Santa Monica, CA 90405
PHONE: (310) 255-2000
FAX: (310) 255-2100
EMPLOYMENT: http://www.activision.com/jobs
EMAIL: hr@activision.com
STOCK EXCHANGE: NASDAQ

SYMBOL: ATVI
ANNUAL REPORTS:
    http://www.activision.com/investor/
    financial-info.html

AGANDEC, INC.

Agandec, Inc. (formerly ASCII Entertainment) is a developer and publisher of console games (PSX, PS2, N64, DC) and is best known for the games *Armored Core* and *Felony 11-79*.

PRINCIPAL GAMES: *Armored Core 2 Another Age* (PS2), *Battle Hunter* (PSX), *Chess* (PSX), *Andernal Ring* (PS2), *Evergrace* (PS2), *Fatal Fury: Mark of the Wolves* (DC), *Forever Kingdom* (PS2), *King of Fighters – Evolution* (DC), *Last Blade 2: Heart of the Samurai* (DC), *Mandal Slug X* (PSX), *Panzer Front* (PSX), *Putter Golf* (PSX), *RPG Maker* (PSX), *Sports Jam* (DC), *Strikers 1945* (PSX), *The Adventures of Cookie & Cream* (PS2), *Armored Core* (PSX), *Armored Core - Master of Arena* (PSX), *BackStreet Billiards* (PSX), *Bass Landing* (PSX), *Clock Tower II* (PSX), *Fighter Maker* (PSX), *Master of Monsters* (PSX), *R-Type Delta* (PSX), *R-Types* (PSX), *Rising Zan: The Samurai Gunman* (PSX), *Shadow Tower* (PSX), *Virtua Athlete 2000* (PSX).
GAMES IN DEVELOPMENT: *All-Star Slammin' D-Ball* (PSX), *King's Field: The Ancient City* (PS2).
WEBSITE: www.agandec.com
ADDRESS: Agandec, Inc., 1070 Stewart Drive, Suite 4,
    Sunnyvale, CA 94085
PHONE: (408) 736-0800
FAX: (408) 736-8373

ANGEL STUDIOS, INC.

Angel Studios became known primarily for the game *Midtown Madness* published by Microsoft. The studio also converted *Resident Evil 2* to Nintendo 64 for Capcom. Angel Studios develops for PS2, PCs, X-box and N64.

PRINCIPAL GAMES: *TransWorld Sufr* (PS2, X-box) *Smuggler's Run 2* (PS2), *Test Drive Off Road Wide Open* (PS2), *Midnight Club* (PS2), *Smuggler's Run* (PS2), *Resident Evil 2* (N64), *Midtown Madness 2* (PC), *Ken Griffey's Slugfest* (N64), *Sky Pirates* (PC LBE), *Midtown Madness* (PC), *Savage Quest* (Arcade PC), *MLB Featuring Ken Griffey Jr.* (N64).

WEBSITE: www.angelstudios.com

ADDRESS: Angel Studios, Inc., 5966 La Place Court, Suite 170, Carlsbad, CA 92008

PHONE: (760) 929-0700

FAX: (760) 929-0719

EMPLOYMENT: www.angelstudios.com

EMAIL: hr@angelstudios.com

ARTDINK CORPORATION, INC.

Artdink Corporation develops and distributes interactive game software. The company is best known for its *A-Train* series.

PRINCIPAL GAMES: *A-Train* (PSX), *A-Train 6* (PS2), *Buchigire Kongou* (PS2), *Lunatic Dawn Tempest* (PS2), *No One can stop M. Domino* (PSX), *Ogre Battle* (PSX), *Tail of the Sun* (PSX)

WEBSITE: www.artdink.co.jp

ADDRESS: Artdink Corporation, 22F, WBG Marive West Bldg, 2-6 Nakase, Mihama, Chiba, 261-8701, Japan

ATLUS USA

Atlus USA is a subsidiary of a Japanese company and develops interactive game software for Sony and Nintendo.

PRINCIPAL GAMES: The *Persona* series (PSX), *Snowboard Kids 1&2*(N64), *Ogre Battle* (PSX), *Tactics Ogre* (PSX), *Ogre Battle 64*, *Thousand Arms* (PSX), *Hoshigami* (PSX) and *Dodge Ball Advance* (GBA).

WEBSITE: www.atlus.com

ADDRESS: Atlus USA, 15255 Alton Parkway, Suite 100, Irvine, CA 92618

PHONE: (949) 788-0455

FAX: (949) 788-0433

EMPLOYMENT: www.atlus.com

BANDAI CO., LTD.

BANDAI Co., Ltd. is the third largest toy company in the world. It develops, publishes and distributes interactive game software based on its toy line for Sony PlayStation and PCs.

MAIN FACTS: The company produced the Tamagotchi virtual animal that was the most popular toy of 1997 and the entire series of Power Rangers action figures.

PRINCIPAL GAMES: *Gundam: Zeonic Front* (PS2), *Gundam: Journey to Jaburo* (PS2), *Gundam Battle Assault* (PSX), *Digimon World 2* (PSX), *Digimon World* (PSX), *Digimon Card Battle* (PSX).

GAMES IN DEVELOPMENT: *Digimon Rumble Arena* (PSX).

WEBSITE: www.bandaigames.com

ADDRESS: Bandai America, 5551 Katella Ave.,
    Cypress, CA 90630
PHONE: (714) 816-9500
EMPLOYMENT: http://www.bandai.com/company/
    employment/employ.html
STOCK EXCHANGE: Tokyo 1st Section
SYMBOL: #7967

BETHESDA SOFTWORKS, INC.

Bethesda Softworks, Inc. has been one of the leading
game software companies ever since its inception in
1986. It develops, publishes and distributes interactive
software games for PlayStation, PlayStation 2, X-Box,
Dreamcast and PCs.
PRINCIPAL GAMES: *Hotrod: Burnout Championship
    Drag Racing* (PC), *PBA Bowling* (PC), *Magic &
    Mayhem* (PC), *Echelon* (PC), *Sea Dogs* (PC), *IHRA
    Drag Racing* (PC, PSX), *PBA Tour Bowling 2001*
    (PC), *Gromada* (PC), *NIRA Intense Import Drag
    Racing* (PC), *The Elder Scrolls Adventures:Redguard*
    (PC), *F16:Aggressor* (PC), *PBA Tour Bowling 2* (PC),
    An Elder Scrolls Legend:Battlespire (PC), *The Elder
    Scrolls II:Daggerfall* (PC), *X-Car* (PC), *Symbiocom*
    (PC), *Zero Critical* (PC), *Skynet* (PC), *The Elder
    Scrolls:Arena* (PC).
GAMES IN DEVELOPMENT: *The Elder Scrolls III:
    Morrowind* (PC, Xbox).
WEBSITE: www.bethsoft.com
ADDRESS: Bethesda Softworks, A Division of
    ZeniMax Media, Inc., 1370 Piccard Drive,
    Suite 120, Rockville, MD 20850
PHONE: (301) 926-8300
FAX: (301) 926-8010

EMPLOYMENT: ICQ# 28848359
EMAIL: hr@bethsoft.com

BIOWARE, CORP.

BioWare Corp. is an electronics company specialized
in the design of video games for PCs and consoles. The
company was established in 1995.
PRINCIPAL GAMES: *Baldur's Gate* (PC), *BG: Tales of
    the Sword Coast* (PC), *Baldur's Gate 2* (PC), *BG2:
    Throne of Bhaal* (PC), *MDK2* (PC, DC), *MDK2:
    Armeggedon* (PS2), *Shattered Steel* (PC).
GAMES IN DEVELOPMENT: *Nerverwinter Nights*,
    Star Wars: Knight of the Old Republic.
WEBSITE: www.bioware.com
ADDRESS: BioWare Corp. #302-10508-82 Ave.,
    Edmonton, Alberta, T6E 6H2, Canada
PHONE: (780) 430-0164
FAX: (780) 439-6374
EMPLOYMENT:
    http://www.bioware.com/info/jobs.html
EMAIL: jobs@bioware.com

BIZARRE CREATIONS, INC.

Bizarre Creations, Inc. is a developer based in the
Northeast of England. Established 14 years ago, the
company first developed for Commodore 64 and
Amiga before PlayStation and the new generation
consoles arrived on the scene.
PRINCIPAL GAMES: *Formula 1* (PSX), *Formula 1:
    Championship Edition* (PSX), *Fur Fighters*
    (Dreamcast), *Fur Fighters: Viggo's Revenge* (PS2),

Metropolis Street Racer (Dreamcast), *Project Gotham Racing* (X-Box).
GAMES IN DEVELOPMENT: *Project Smokescreen.*
WEBSITE: www.bizarrecreations.com
EMPLOYMENT: www.bizarrecreations.com
EMAIL: webmaster@bizarrecreations.com

BLACK OPS ENTERTAINMENT

Black Ops Entertainment is a game developer for PlayStation, PS2, XBOX, PCs and N64. The company is best known for its first game, *Knockout Kings 2000*, produced for the N64.
PRINCIPAL GAMES: *Agile Warrior* (PC), *Black Dawn* (PSX), *Treasures of the Deep* (PSX), *Tomorrow Never Dies* (PSX), *The World is not Enough* (PSX), *NCAA March Madness 2001* (PSX), *Knockout King 2001* (PSX, PS2).
WEBSITE: www.blackops.com
EMPLOIS: www.blackops.com
EMAIL: resumes@blackops.com

BLIZZARD ENTERTAINMENT

Blizzard Entertainment develops and publishes interactive game software.
MAIN FACTS: The company's free online game service is one of the world's largest, with millions of active users. Blizzard Entertainment is a division of Havas Interactive, which is a division of Havas SA. Havas SA is a subsidiary of Vivendi SA.

PRINCIPAL GAMES: The *Warcraft* series, the *Diablo* series and *StarCraft.*
GAMES IN DEVELOPMENT: *Warcraft III: Reign of Chaos, World of Warcraft.*
WEBSITE: www.blizzard.com
ADDRESS: Blizzard Entertainment, 131 Theory, Suite 100, Irvine, CA 92612
PHONE: (949) 737-7200
EMPLOYMENT: http://www.blizzard.com/jobopp/
STOCK EXCHANGE: NYSE
SYMBOL: V (Vivendi)

BULLFROG PRODUCTIONS

Bullfrog Productions was established in 1987 by Les Edgar and Peter Molyneux. *Populous* was the first game developed by Bullfrog. In 1995 Bullfrog merged with Electronic Arts and has been one of its development studios since then.
PRINCIPAL GAMES: *Populous* (PC), *Powermonger* (PC), *Flood* (PC), *Populous 2* (PC), *Syndicate* (PC), *Theme Park* (PC), *Magic Carpet* (PC), *Theme Hospital* (PC), *Syndicate Wars* (PC), *Magic Carpet 2* (PC), *Dungeon Keeper* (PC), *Populous: The Beginning* (PC), *Theme Park World* (PS2), *Dungeon Keeper 2* (PC).
WEBSITE: www.bullfrog.co.uk
EMPLOYMENT: http://www.bullfrog.co.uk
EMAIL: Jobs.Bullfrog@ea-europe.com

BUNGIE

Bungie was first known for its Mac games. A huge level of interest for *Halo* prompted Microsoft to acquire the company and make *Halo* one of the key titles for the launch of XBox.

MAIN FACTS: During the year 2000 Bungie surprised the industry by announcing its sale to Microsoft. At the same time it announced that its new title, *Halo*, would be a major Microsoft XBox title. *Halo* has since redefined FPS console games and is a big hit... *Halo 2* is no doubt not far behind.

PRINCIPAL GAMES: *Minotaur: The Labyrinths of Crete* (Mac), *Pathways into Darkness* (Mac), *Marathon* (Mac), *Marathon 2: Durandal* (Mac), *Marathon: Infinity* (Mac), *Abuse* (Mac), *Myth: The Fallen Lords* (PC, Mac), *Myth2: Soulblighter* (PC, Mac), *Oni* (PS2, PC, Mac), *Halo* (X-Box).

WEBSITE: www.bungie.com

ADDRESS: Bungie, One Microsoft Way, Redmond, WA 98052

EMPLOYMENT: http://www.bungie.com/jobs/jobs.htm

EMAIL: jobs@bungie.com

CAPCOM

Capcom was founded in 1979 and has become one of the most well-known game developers and publishers in the industry. The company is best known for its *Megaman*, *Streetfighter* and *Resident Evil* series.

PRINCIPAL GAMES: *Dino Crisis* (DC, PSX, PC), *Devil May Cry* (PS2), *Genma Onimusha* (X-Box), *Resident Evil Code Veronica* (PS2), *Capcom vs SNK 2* (PS2).

GAME IN DEVELOPMENT: *Maximo* (PS2).

WEBSITE: www.capcom.com

ADDRESS: Capcom, 475 Oakmead Parkway, Sunnyvale, CA 94086

PHONE: (408) 774-0500

FAX: (408) 774-3995

EMPLOYMENT: http://www.capcom.com/jobs

EMAIL: resume@capcom.com

CAVEDOG ENTERTAINMENT

Cavedog Entertainment develops interactive game software for PCs.

MAIN FACTS: The company was acquired by GT Interactive, which has since become Infogrames.

PRINCIPAL GAMES: *Total Annihilation, Total Annihilation: Battle Tactics,*

WEBSITE: www.cavedog.com

ADDRESS: Cavedog Entertainment, 3855 Monte Villa Parkway, Bothell, WA 98021

EMPLOYMENT: www.cavedog.com

EMAIL: jobs@cavedog.com

CINEMAWARE

Cinemaware rose from its ashes in 2000 to resume game development for the new generation platforms and the web. The company became known in 1986 for its Commodore 64 games including *Robin Hood: Defender of the Crown* and *The Three Stooges*.

GAMES IN DEVELOPMENT: *Robin Hood: Defender of the Crown* (PS2, X-Box, PC, GBA, WAP), *Defender of the Crown: Digitally Remastered Edition* (PC, Mac),

The Three Stooges: Digitally Remastered Edition (PC, Mac) *The Three Stooges* (GBA), *Wings* (GBA),
WEBSITE: www.cinemaware.com
EMPLOYMENT:
   http://www.cinemaware.com/jobs.asp
EMAIL: hr@cinemaware.com

CLIMAX GROUP

Climax Group was founded in 1988 and is today one of England's largest developers. Climax develops for PS2, X-Box, Game Boy Advance and the GC.
PRINCIPAL GAMES: *ATV: Quad Power Racing* (PSX), *Austin Power: Mojo Rally* (DC), *Battlezone: Rise of Black Dogs* (N64), *Mille Miglia* (PS2),
GAME IN DEVELOPMENT: *Title Defense* (X-Box),
WEBSITE: www.climax.co.uk
ADDRESS: Climax Group, Fareham Heights, Standard Way, Fareham, PO16 8XT, United Kingdom
PHONE: 44 (0) 1329 827777
FAX: 44 (0) 1329 828777
EMPLOYMENT:
   http://www.climax.co.uk/jobs/index.htm
EMAIL: personnel@climax.co.uk

CODEMASTERS

Codemasters develops and publishes video games for Sony, Nintendo and Microsoft consoles and PCs. Codemasters also develops and publishes multi-player/persistent world games for on-line Internet and interactive play.
PRINCIPAL GAMES: *Colin McRae Rally* (PSX, PC), *Colin McRae Rally 2* (PSX, PC), *Insane* (PC), *Mike Tyson Boxing* (PSX, PC), *TOCA 2* (PSX, PC).
GAME IN DEVELOPMENT: *Colin McRae 3.*
WEBSITE: www.codemasters.com
ADDRESS: Codemasters, Carnegie Hall Tower, 152 West 57th Street, 21st floor, New York, NY 10019
PHONE: (212) 582-3532
FAX: (212) 582-8602
EMPLOYMENT:
   http://www.codemasters.com/jobs/index.php
EMAIL: recruitment@codemasters.com

CORE DESIGN

Core Design became known for its now famous *Lara Croft* and *Tomb Raider* series. A division of Eidos Interactive, it concentrates its development efforts on the Playstation 2 console.
PRINCIPAL GAMES: *Tomb Raider* series (PC, PSX), *Herdy Gerdy* (PS2), *Project Eden* (PS2), *Thunderhawk 3* (PS2).
GAMES IN DEVELOPMENT: *Tomb Raider Next-Generation* (PS2, PC).
WEBSITE: www.core-design.com
ADDRESS: Core Design, 2 Roundhouse Road, Pride Park, Derby, DE24 8JE, United Kingdom
PHONE: 44 (0) 1332 227800
FAX: 44 (0) 1332 227801
EMPLOYMENT: www.core-design.com
EMAIL: recruit@core-design.com

CRAVE ENTERTAINMENT

Crave Entertainment develops, publishes and distributes interactive game software for Sony, Nintendo and Sega. The company is also known for porting PC games to consoles.

PRINCIPAL GAMES: *Galerians 2* (PS2), *Shadow Madness* (PSX), *Ultimate Fighting Championship* (DC, PSX, GBC), *Starlancer* (DC), *Soldier of Fortune* (DC)

GAMES IN DEVELOPMENT: *Ultimate Fighting Championship* (X-Box)

WEBSITE: www.cravesgames.com

ADDRESS: Crave Entertainment, 19645 Rancho Way, Rancho Dominguez, CA 90220

PHONE: (310) 687-5400

FAX: (310) 661-3010

EMPLOYMENT: www.cravegames.com

EMAIL: hr-la@cravegames.com

CRAWFISH INTERACTIVE

Crawfish Interactive specializes in developing games for Game Boy Color and Game Boy Advance. It also develops for WAP, PDA and interactive TV. The company was founded in 1997.

PRINCIPAL GAMES: *X-men Mutant Academy* (GBC), *Driver* (GBC), *Ready to Rumble* (GBC), *Lego Island 2* (GBC), *Ready to Rumbal Round 2* (GBA), *Ecks vs Sever* (GBA).

WEBSITE: www.crawfish.co.uk

ADDRESS: Crawfish Interactive, 8th Floor, Green Dragon House, 64-70 High Street, Croydon, Surrey, CR0 9XN, United Kingdom

PHONE: +44 (0) 20 8686 4777

FAX: +44 (0) 20 8686 2036

EMPLOYMENT: www.crawfish.com

EMAIL: jobs@crawfish.co.uk

CRITERION GAMES

Criterion Games is a division of Criterion Software Ltd. and is an entertainment software developer known for its work on *Redline Racer* and *Trickstyle*.

PRINCIPAL GAMES: *Trickstyle* (DC, PC), *Suzuki Alstare Extreme Racing* (DC, PC), *Redline Racer* (DC), *Deep Fighter* (DC, PC) *Burnout* (PS2), *Airblade* (PS2).

WEBSITE: www.criterionstudios.com

ADDRESS: Criterion Games, Westbury Court, Buryfields, Guildford, Surrey, GU2 4YZ, United Kingdom

PHONE: +44 (0) 1483 406200

FAX: +44 (0)1483 406211

EMPLOYMENT: N/A

EMAIL: N/A

CROTEAM

Croteam was initially started as a "garage game development" company in 1993. Since then it has been involved non-stop in game development and is getting rave reviews for *Serious Sam*, an archaeological first-person 3D shooter.

PRINCIPAL GAMES: *Football Glory* (PC, Amiga), *5-A-Side Soccer* (Amiga), *Save the Earth* (Amiga), *Serious Sam* (PC), *Serious Sam: Second Encounter* (PC).

WEBSITE: www.croteam.com

CRYSTAL DYNAMICS

Crystal Dynamics is a developer of games for PCs, Playstation and PS2, N64 and X-box and is a development studio of Eidos Interactive.

PRINCIPAL GAMES: *102 Dalmatians: Puppies to the Rescue* (PSX, DC, GBC), *Blood Omen 2* (PS2, X-Box), *Gex 3: Deep Cover Gecko* (PSX), *Legacy of Kain: Soul Reaver* (DC, PC, PSX), *Mad Dash Racing* (X-Box)

ADDRESS: Crystal Dynamics, 64 Willow Place, Menlo Park, CA

PHONE: (415) 473-3400

FAX: (415) 473-3410

CYAN WORLDS, INC.

Cyan Worlds, Inc. is a developer of games for PC and creator of the No. 1 title *Myst*. *Myst* and *Riven* (the sequel to *Myst*) have sold 9 million copies throughout the world and generated more than $250 million in revenue—by far the most popular video game in PC in history.

PRINCIPAL GAMES: *Myst* (PC), *Riven* (PC)

WEBSITE: www.cyan.com

ADDRESS: Cyan Worlds, Inc., 14617 N. Newport Hwy., Mead, WA 99021-9378

PHONE: (509) 468-0807

FAX: (509) 467-2209

EMPLOYMENT:
http://www.cyan.com/jobs/index.html

EMAIL: http://www.cyan.com/jobs/jobAppl.ssi

DARKWORKS

Darkworks is a French developer of Dreamcast, PlayStation 2 and X-Box games, most famous for *Alone In The Dark: The New Nightmare*.

PRINCIPAL GAMES: *Alone in the Dark: The New Nightmare* (PS2, PSX, PC, DC).

GAMES IN DEVELOPMENT: *U.S.S. Antarctica* (PS2, X-Box).

WEBSITE: www.darkworks.com

DC STUDIOS

DC Studios has been a game developer since 1999 and has completed projects for Acclaim, Toymax, Southpeak and 3DO. DC currently develops for the Gameboy Advance, PS2, GC, Xbox, PSX, PC and Toymax's TV Games system.

PRINCIPAL GAMES: *Salt Lake 2002* (GBA), *NBA Jam 2002* (GBA), *Taxi 2* (PSX), *Army Men Advance* (GBA), *Activision TV Games* (Toymax), *Mia Hamm Soccer 64,* (N64), *NBA Jam 2001* (GBC).

WEBSITE: www.dc-studios.com

ADDRESSES:

DC Studios UK, 27 Union St, Glasgow, G1 3RB, United Kingdom
PHONE: +44 141 248 6490 / 2200
FAX: +44 141 248 8972

DC Studios Canada, 410 St Nicolas, Suite 510, Montreal, Quebec H2Y 2P5, Canada
PHONE:(514) 849-2555
FAX: (514) 849-2284

EMPLOYMENT: www.dc-studios.com

EMAIL: recruitment@dc-studios.com

DELPHINE SOFTWARE

Delphine Software is a game developer established since 1988. The company is known for its *MotoRacer* series and for the game *Darkstone*.

PRINCIPAL GAMES: *Time Travelers* (PC, Amiga, Atari), *Operation Stealth* (PC, Amiga, Atari), *Cruise for a Corpe* (PC, Amiga, Atari), *Another World* (SNES), *Sega Megadrive* (PC), *Flashback* (SNES, PC, Mac), *Fade to Black* (PSX, PC), *MotoRacer* (PSX, PC), *MotoRacer 2* (PSX, PC), *Darkstone* (PSX, PC), *MotoRacer Worldtour* (PSX), *MotoRacer 3* (PC).

WEBSITE: www.delphinesoft.com

ADDRESS: Delphine Software, 9-11 avenue Micheland, 93400 Saint-Ouen, France

EMPLOYMENT: http://www.delphinesoft.com/anglais/contact.htm#

EMAIL: emploi.programmeur@delphinesoft.com, emploi.graphiste@delphinesoft.com

DIGITAL EXTREME

Digital Extreme is a Canadian game developer known for the games *Unreal* and *Unreal Tournament*.

PRINCIPAL GAMES: *Adventure Pinball* (PC), *Extreme Pinball* (PC), *Epic Pinball* (PC), *Unreal Tournament* (PC, DC, PS2, Mac), *Unreal* (PC, Mac).

GAMES IN DEVELOPMENT: *Dark Sector* (PC), *Unreal Championship* (X-Box).

WEBSITE: www.digitalextremes.com

ADDRESS: Digital Extreme, 1807 Wonderland Rd. North, London, Ontario N6G 5C2, Canada

PHONE: (519) 657-4260

FAX: (519) 471-9972

EMPLOYMENT: http://www.digitalextremes.com

EMAIL: resume@digitalextremes.com

DIGITAL ILLUSIONS

Digital Illusions develops interactive game software for Sony, Nintendo and PCs. The company has just released *Rally Sport Challenge* for the X-Box.

PRINCIPAL GAMES: *Lacrosse, Rally Masters* (PC, PSX), *Emperor's New Groove* (GBC), *Motorhead* (PC, PSX), *Disney's Dinosaur* (PSX) and *NASCAR Heat* (PSX).

GAMES IN DEVELOPMENT: *Shrek* (PS2, GC), *Pryzm* (PS2), *V8 Challenge* (PC), *Battlefield 1942* (PC, X-Box), Undisclosed Microsoft Project (PC, X-Box).

WEBSITE: www.dice.se

EMPLOYMENT: jobs@dicecanada.com

STOCK EXCHANGE: Stockholm Stock Exchange

ANNUAL REPORTS: http://www.dice.se/en/financial_info.html

DIGITAL LEISURE

Digital Leisure publishes PC and DVD-ROM titles and interactive DVD-Videos.

PRINCIPAL GAMES: *Dragon's Lair* (PC, PS2), *Dragon's Lair II: Time Warp* (PC DVD, PS2), *Space Ace* (PC DVD), *Shadoan* (PC).

WEBSITE: www.digitalleisure.com

ADDRESS: Digital Leisure, 33 Cedar Ridge Road, Gormley, Ontario, Canada L0H 1G0

FAX: (905) 888-9440

DMA Design

DMA Design is a game developer famous for its *Grand Theft Auto* series.

PRINCIPAL GAMES: *Body Harvest* (N64), *Grand Theft Auto* (PC), *Grand Theft Auto 2* (PC, PSX, DC), *Grand Theft Auto 3* (PS2),

GAMES IN DEVELOPMENT: *Grand Theft Auto 3* (X-Box)

WEBSITE: www.dma.co.uk.com

ADDRESS: DMA Design, Second Floor, Links House, 15 Links Place, Leith, Edinburgh, EH6 7EZ, United Kingdom

PHONE: +44 (0) 131 454 2000

FAX: +44 (0) 131 454 2023

EMPLOYMENT: http://www.dma.co.uk/thefamily/

EMAIL: cv@dma-design.com

Dreamworks Interactive

DreamWorks Interactive principally develops console games based on properties belonging to its mother company, Dreamworks.

PRINCIPAL GAMES: *Clive Barker Undying* (PC, PS2), *Lost World: Jurassic Park* (PSX), *Medal of Honor* (PSX), *Medal of Honor: Underground* (PSX), *Medal of Honor: Frontline* (PS2), *Small Soldiers* (PSX).

WEBSITE: www.dreamworksgames.com

ADDRESS: Dreamworks Interactive, P.O. Box 492147, Los Angeles, CA 90049

FAX: (310) 234-7201

EMPLOYMENT: http://www.dreamworksgames.com/Contact/hr.html

EMAIL: dwijobs@ea.com

Eidos

Eidos develops, publishes and distributes interactive game software for Sony, Nintendo, Sega, Microsoft and PC. The *Tomb Raider* series launched in 1996 has already sold more than 17 million copies.

PRINCIPAL GAMES: The *Tomb Raider* series.

WEBSITE: www.eidos.com

ADDRESS: Eidos, Eidos Interactive, 651 Brannan Street 4th Floor, San Francisco, CA 94107

PHONE: (415) 547-1200

EMPLOYMENT: www.eidos.com

EMAIL: jobs@eidos.com

STOCK EXCHANGE: NASDAQ

SYMBOL: EIDSY

ANNUAL REPORTS: http://www.eidosinteractive.com/corporate/analysts.html

Electronic Arts (EA)

Electronic Arts (EA) develops, publishes and distributes interactive game software for Sony, Nintendo, Sega, Microsoft and PC.

PRINCIPAL BRANDS: EA Sports, EA Games and EA.com

PRINCIPAL TITLES (over 1 million copies sold): *FIFA Soccer, Madden NFL, NASCAR NBA, LIVE Need For Speed, NHL, Hockey, Tiger Woods and PGA Tour, Golf Road Rash, Triple Play Baseball, Wing Commander.*

WEBSITE: www.ea.com

ADDRESS: Electronic Arts, 209 Redwood Shores Parkway, Redwood City, CA 94062

PHONE: (650) 628-1500

EMPLOYMENT: http://www.ea.com/global/corporate/corporate_hatted.jsp
STOCK EXCHANGE: NASDAQ
SYMBOL: ERTS
ANNUAL REPORTS: http://www.ea.com/global/corporate/corporate_hatted.jsp

ELIXIR STUDIOS

Elixir Studios is a new video game developer becoming known for its work-in-progress, the strategy game *Republic: The Revolution*.
GAME IN DEVELOPMENT: *Republic: The Revolution* (PC).
WEBSITE: www.elixir-studios.co.uk
ADDRESS: Elixir Studios, 4th Floor, The Forum, 74-80 Camden Street, London NW1 0EG, UK
PHONE: 020 7681 0000
FAX: 020 7681 0010
EMPLOYMENT: http://www.elixir-studios.co.uk/htm/cor_careers.html
EMAIL: recruit@elixir-studios.co.uk

EMPIRE INTERACTIVE

Empire Interactive develops, publishes and distributes interactive game software for Sony, Sega and PC, and also ports some PC games to Sega.
PRINCIPAL GAMES: *Ford Racing* (PC, PSX), *The House of the Dead 2* (PC), *Victorious Boxer* (PS2), *Sheep* (PSX), *Battle of Britain* (PC).
GAMES IN DEVELOPMENT: *Endgame* (PS2), *Antz Racing* (X-Box, PS2, GBA, PC), *Ghost Master* (PC, PSX).
WEBSITE: www.empireinteractive.com
ADDRESS: Empire Interactive, 16th Floor, 580 California Street, San Francisco, CA 94104
PHONE: (415) 439 4854
FAX: (415) 439 4928
EMPLOYMENT: N/A
EMAIL: N/A

ENSEMBLE STUDIOS

Ensemble Studios made a name for itself with its real-time strategy games *Age of Empire* and *Age of Kings*. The company has beeeb part of the extended Microsoft family since May 2001.
PRINCIPAL GAMES: *Age of Empire* (PC), *Age of Kings* (PC).
GAME IN DEVELOPMENT: *Age of Mythology* (PC).
WEBSITE: www.ensemblesutdios.com
ADDRESS: Ensemble Studios, 10440 N Central Expressway, Suite 1600, Dallas, TX 75231
PHONE: (214) 378-6868
EMPLOYMENT: http://www.ensemblestudios.com/jobs.shtml
EMAIL: StudiosRecruiting@ensemblestudios.com

FACTOR 5

Factor 5 was established in Germany in 1987 but has since moved to San Rafael, California. The company develops mainly for Nintendo consoles and in fact developed MusyX, the main sound and music development tools for these consoles.

PRINCIPAL GAMES: *Star Wars: Rogue Squadron* (N64), *Star Wars Rogue Leader: Squadron* 2 (GC)

GAMES IN DEVELOPMENT: *Tornado* (GC)

WEBSITE: www.factor5.com

ADDRESS: Factor 5, 101 Lucas Valley Rd., Suite 300, San Rafael, CA 94903

PHONE: (415) 492 5900

FAX: (415) 492 5901

EMPLOYMENT: http://www.factor5.com/jobs.htm

EMAIL: contact@factor5.com

FIRAXIS GAMES

Firaxis Games develops war simulation games for PC. The company was started by Sid Meier, designer of the popular *Civilization* series. Firaxis now belongs to Electronic Arts.

PRINCIPAL GAMES: *Sid Meier's Gandtysburg! Sid Meier's Alpha Centauri, Sid Meier's Alien Crossfire, Sid Meier's Antiandam! Sid Meier's South Mountain!, Sim Golf (PC).*

WEBSITE: www.firaxis.com

ADDRESS: Firaxis Games, 11350 McCormick Rd, Executive Plaza III, Suite 1300, Hunt Valley, MD 21031

PHONE: (410) 891-3001

EMPLOYMENT: http://www.firaxis.com/jobs.cfm

FOX INTERACTIVE

Fox Interactive develops in partnership with other developers and publishes and distributes interactive game software.

PRINCIPAL GAMES: *No One lives forever* (PC), *The Simpsons Road Rage* (X-Box), *Alien vs Predator* (PC), *Alien vs Predator 2* (PC), *Croc* (PC, PSX), *Croc 2* (PC, PSX).

GAMES IN DEVELOPMENT: *No one lives forever* (PS2), *Buffy the Vampire Slayer* (X-Box).

WEBSITE: www.foxinteractive.com

ADDRESS: Fox Interactive, P.O. Box 900, Beverly Hills, CA 90213-0900

PHONE: (310) 369-4263

FAX: (310) 969-3007

EMPLOYMENT: http://www.foxinteractive.com/companyinfo/jobs.xpml

STOCK EXCHANGE: NYSE

SYMBOL: FOX

ANNUAL REPORTS: http://www.newscorp.com/feg/foxReport2000/index.html

GEARBOX SOFTWARE

Gearbox Software was established in 1999 and made a name for itself with its first project, *Half-Life:Opposing Force*, the first "expansion pack" for *Half-Life*.

PRINCIPAL GAMES: *Half-Life: Opposing Force* (PC), *Half-Life: Blue Shift* (PC), *Half-Life: Counter-Strike* (PC), *Half-Life* (PS2),

GAMES IN DEVELOPMENT: *Counter-Strike: Condition Zero.*

WEBSITE: www.gearboxsoftware.com

ADDRESS: Gearbox Software, 101 East Park Blvd.,
   Suite 1069, Plano, TX 75074
PHONE: (972) 312-8202
FAX: (972) 312-8318
EMPLOYMENT:
   http://www.gearboxsoftware.com/jobs.html
EMAIL: jobs@gearboxsoftware.com

GATHERING OF DEVELOPERS

Gathering of Developers publishes and distributes interactive game software produced by independent developers for Sony, Nintendo, Sega, Microsoft and PC.
MAIN FACTS: The company was established by a
   group of independent developers to be able to
   better compete with large-scale publishers.
   Today the company is a division of Take Two
   Interactive.
PRINCIPAL GAMES: The *Railroad Tycoon II* series (PC),
   Nocturne (PC), *Darkstone* (PC), *Age of Wonders*
   (PC), *FLY! Rune* (PC, PS2), *4X4 EVO* (PC, PS2, X-
   Box), *Rock, Heavy Mandal: F.A.K.K.2* (PC), *KISS
   Psycho Circus: The Nightmare Child* (PC), *Max
   Payne* (PC, PS2, X-Box).
WEBSITE: www.godgames.com
ADDRESS: Gathering of Developers, 2700 Fairmount
   St., Dallas, TX 75201
FAX: (214) 871-7934

GRAY MATTER STUDIOS

Gray Matter Studios was established by several former employees of Xatrix Entertainment with the help of Activision. They are responsible for the games *Kingpin* and *Redneck Rampage*. Activision recently acquired the studio.
PRINCIPAL GAME: *Return to Castle Wolfenstein* (PC).
WEBSITE: www.gmistudios.com
ADDRESS: Gray Matter Studios, 2038 Armacost Ave.,
   Los Angeles, CA 90025
PHONE: (310) 207-2899
FAX: (310) 207-1229
EMPLOYMENT: www.gmistudios.com
EMAIL: info@gmistudios.com

HEADFIRST PRODUCTIONS

Headfirst Productions is a small developer well-known for its work on *Simon the Sorcerer 3-D* and its project-in-development *Call of Cthulhu*.
PRINCIPAL GAMES: *Simon the Sorcerer* (PC), *Simon
   the Sorcerer 2* (PC), *Simon the Sorcerer 3-D* (PC).
GAMES IN DEVELOPMENT: *Call of Cthulhu* (PC),
   Battle of the Planets.
WEBSITE: www.headfirst.co.uk
ADDRESS: Headfirst Productions, Unit 3, Priory, Old
   London Road, Canwell, Sutton Coldfield, West
   Midlands B75 5SH, United Kingdom
PHONE: 44 (0) 121 308 8900
FAX: 44 (0) 121 308 8815
EMPLOYMENT: www.gmistudios.com
EMAIL: mike@headfirst.co.uk

HOTHOUSE CREATION

Hothouse Creation is a developer based in England, which has a partnership agreement with Eidos Interactive. Eidos actually owns a small part of the company. It gained a name for itself with its *Gangster* series.

PRINCIPAL GAMES: *Sky Sports Football Quiz* (PC, PSX), *Gangster 2* (PC), *Gangster* (PC), *Abomination* (PC), *Cutthroats* (PC), *Who wants to be a millionaire* (PC, PSX, DC).

WEBSITE: www.hothouse.org

ADDRESS: Hothouse Creation, 5th Floor Colston Tower, Colston Street, Bristol BS1 4XE, United Kingdom

PHONE: 44 (0) 117 901 5100

FAX: 44 (0) 117 901 5115

EMPLOYMENT: http://www.hothouse.org/english/jobs/jobs.htm

EMAIL: jobs@hothouse.org

HUMAN HEAD STUDIOS

Human Head Studios was established in 1997 and is an independent studio based in Wisconsin. The company offers all services related to video game development.

PRINCIPAL GAMES: *Blair Witch Volume 2: The Legend of Coffin Rock* (PC), *Rune* (PC, Mac), *Rune: Halls of Valhalla* (PC), *Rune: Viking Warlord* (PS2).

WEBSITE: www.humanhead.com

ADDRESS: Human Head Studios, 6325 Odana Road, Madison, WI 53719

EMPLOYMENT: http://www.humanhead.com/headhunt.htm

EMAIL: www@humanhead.com

HUMONGOUS ENTERTAINMENT

Humongous Entertainment is a division of Infogrames and specializes in the development of children's video games.

PRINCIPAL GAMES: *Backyard Baseball 2001* (PC), *Backyard Football* (PC), *Backyard Soccer* (PC), and the *Putt-Putt, Freddi Fish, Pajama Sam, SPY Fox, Fatty Bear* and *Buzzy the Knowledge Bug* series (PC).

WEBSITE: www.humongous.com

ADDRESS: Humongous Entertainment, 3855 Monte Villa Parkway, Bothell, WA 98021

PHONE: (425) 486-9258

FAX: (425) 951-1903

EMPLOYMENT: http://www.humongous.com

EMAIL: jobs@humongous.com

STOCK EXCHANGE: NASDAQ

SYMBOL: IFGM (Infograme)

ID SOFTWARE

Id Software was established by John Carmack, Andrian Carmack, John Romero and Tom Hall, the inventors of first-person games with *Wolfenstein 3-D*. Its 3-D engines are used by several other developers like Raven Software. After *Quake 2* was released, John Romero and Tom Hall left to establish Ion Storm.

PRINCIPAL GAMES: *Wolfenstein 3-D* (PC), *Doom* (PC) *Doom 2* (PC, PSX, N64), *Quake* (PC) *Quake 2* (PC, N64, DC), *Quake 3: Arena* (PC, Mac), *Quake 3: Team Arena* (PC, Mac).

Game in development: *Doom 3*.

WEBSITE: www.idsoftware.com

INFOGRAMES INC.

Infogrames is a major international producer and distributor of video games for Nintendo, Sega and Sony, of CD-ROMs for both PC and Mac, as well as for all interactive television platforms, WAP compatible terminals and onboard flight entertainment systems.

PRINCIPAL GAMES: *V Rally, Alone in the Dark, Driver* and *Duke Nukem.*

PRINCIPAL LICENSES: Warner Bros.' *Looney Tunes* for 5 years, Paramount's *Mission Impossible*, Ronaldo and the Brazilian national soccer team from Nike and *Les 24 heures du Mans*, etc.

WEBSITE: www.infogrames.com

ADDRESS: Infogrammes, 417, 5th Avenue, New York, NY 10066

PHONE: (212) 726-6938

FAX: (212) 726-4204

EMPLOYMENT: drh@fr.infogrames.com

STOCK EXCHANGE: NASDAQ

SYMBOL: IFGM

ANNUAL REPORTS: http://www.us.infogrames.com/corporate/investor_relations/

INNERLOOP STUDIOS

Innerloop Studios is a developer based in Norway. The studio is well known for its *Project IGI* game.

PRINCIPAL GAMES: *Project IGI* (PC), *Sega Extreme Sports* (DC), *Joint Strike Fighter* (PC).

GAME IN DEVELOPMENT: *Project IGI 2.*

WEBSITE: www.innerloop.com

ADDRESS: Innerloop Studios, Øvre Slottsgate #27, N-0157 Oslo, Norway

PHONE: (47) 22 47 90 00

FAX: (47) 22 47 90 09

EMPLOYMENT: http://www.innerloop.com

EMAIL: anne@innerloop.com

INTERPLAY ENTERTAINMENT CORP.

Interplay Entertainment Corp. develops, publishes and distributes interactive game software for Sony, Nintendo, Sega, Microsoft and PC.

PRINCIPAL GAMES: *Descent, Virtual Pool, Fallout, Baldur's Gate, Earthworm Jim* and many others.

WEBSITE: www.interplay.com

ADDRESS: Interplay Entertainment Corp., 16815 Von Karman Avenue, Irvine, CA 92606

PHONE: (949) 553-6655

FAX: (949) 252-2820

EMPLOYMENT: http://www.interplay.com/helpwanted.asp

STOCK EXCHANGE: NASDAQ

SYMBOL: IPLY

ANNUAL REPORTS: http://199.230.26.96/cgi-bin/ir/iply/ownership.html

IO INTERACTIVE

IO Interactive is a company based in Denmark whose developments efforts are focused on 3-D projects.

PRINCIPAL GAMES: *Hitman: Codename 47* (PC)

GAMES IN DEVELOPMENT: *Hitman 2: Silent Assassin* (PC, PS2)

WEBSITE: www.ioi.dk

ADDRESS: IO Interactive, Farvergade 2, 63 Copenhagen K, Denmark

PHONE: 45 33 73 29 00
FAX: 45 33 33 02 15
EMPLOYMENT: http://www2.ioi.dk/recruitment/
     Recruitment.shtml

ION STORM

Ion Storm was originally made up of two develop-
ment studios, but following the two flops *Daikatana*
and *Anachronox*, the Dallas studio led by John Romero
and Tom Hall was closed to make way for the Austin
studio led by Warren Spector that brought us *Deus Ex*.
PRINCIPAL GAMES: *Daikatana* (PC), *Anachronox*
     (PC), *Deus Ex* (PC, PS2).
GAMES IN DEVELOPMENT: *Deus Ex 2, Thief 3.*
WEBSITE: www.ionstorm.com
ADDRESS: Ion Storm, 8303 MoPac Expressway A210,
     Austin, TX 78759
EMPLOYMENT: www.ionstorm.com
EMAIL: HR_Austin@ionstorm.com

JELLYVISION

Jellyvision Develops interactive game software for PC.
PRINCIPAL GAMES: The *You Don't Know Jack* series.
WEBSITE: www.jellyvision.com
ADDRESS: Jellyvision, 848 W. Eastman, Suite 104,
     Chicago, IL 60622-2635
PHONE: (312) 266-0606
FAX: (312) 266-0088
EMPLOYMENT: http://www.jellyvision.com/jobs/
EMAIL: amanda@jellyvision.com

KALISTO ENTERTAINMENT

Kalisto Entertainment, based in Bordeaux, France, was
established in 1990 and has offices in Japan, the U.S.,
China and England. It specializes in video game devel-
opment and R&D technology.
PRINCIPAL GAMES: *New York Race* (PC, PS2, GBC),
     Nightmare Creature 2 (PSX, DC), *4 Wheel Thunder*
     (DC), *Dark Earth* (PC), *Nightmare Creature* (PC,
     PSX, N64), *The Fifth Element* (PC, PSX), *Ultimate
     Race Pro* (PC).
WEBSITE: www.kalisto.com
ADDRESS: Kalisto Entertainment, 600 Round Rock
     West Drive, Suite 205, Round Rock, TX 78681
PHONE: (310) 454-7647
FAX: (310) 454-6807
EMPLOYMENT: http://www.kalisto.com/us/job/
EMAIL: job@kalisto.com

KONAMI OF AMERICA

Konami of America develops, publishes and distrib-
utes interactive game software for all game consoles.
The company started in 1969 as a coin-op machine
manufacturer.
PRINCIPAL GAMES: *Mandal Gear Solid* (PSX), *Mandal
     Gear Solid 2* (PS2), *Zone of Enders* (PS2), *Silent Hill
     2* (PS2), *Silent Scope 2* (PS2), *Airforce Delta Storm*
     (X-Box).
GAMES IN DEVELOPMENT: *MLS Extratime 2002* (GC,
     X-Box, PS2).
WEBSITE: www.konami.com
ADDRESS: Konami of America, 1400 Bridge Parkway,
     Suite 101, Redwood City, CA 94065-1567

PHONE: (650) 654-5600
FAX: (650) 654-5690
EMPLOYMENT:
    http://www.konami.com/main/jobs.html

LEGEND ENTERTAINMENT
Legend Entertainment is one of Infrogrames' internal studios. Its principal task is to develop games based on the *Unreal* game engine technology.
PRINCIPAL GAMES: *Wheel of Time* (PC), *Unreal Gold* (PC), *Unreal Mission Pack: Return to Na Pali* (PC).
GAME IN DEVELOPMENT: *Unreal 2*.
WEBSITE: www.legendent.com
EMPLOYMENT:
    http://www.legendent.com/jobs/index.html

LIONHEAD STUDIOS
Lionhead Studios is an independent development company established by Peter Molyneux who was also the founder of Bullfrog Productions in 1987. Lionhead made a name for itself with its first title, *Black & White*.
PRINCIPAL GAMES: *Black & White* (PC, Mac), *Black & White: Creature Isle* (PC).
GAMES IN DEVELOPMENT: *Black & White* (PS2, X-Box), *Project Ego* (X-Box), *BC* (X-Box).
WEBSITE: www.lionhead.com
ADDRESS: Lionhead Studios, 5 Frederick Sanger Road, Surrey Research Park, Guildford, Surrey, United Kingdom
EMPLOYMENT: http://www.lionhead.com

LUCASARTS
Lucasarts is well-known for its games based on the Star Wars saga, since the company was established by George Lucas and belongs to the Lucas group. It also made a name for itself with its excellent adventure games, including *Grim Fandago, Sam and Max Hit the Road* and *Maniac Mansion: Days of the Tentacles*.
PRINCIPAL GAMES: *Dark Forces* (PC), *Jedi Knight* (PC), *X-wing vs Tie Fighter* (PC), *Star Wars Episode 1: Racer* (PC, N64, DC), *Escape from Monkey Island* (PC, Mac, PS2), *Star Wars Episode 1: Obi wan* (X-Box), *Star Wars Racer Revenge* (PS2).
GAME IN DEVELOPMENT: *Star Wars: Jedi Starfighter* (PS2),
WEBSITE: www.lucasarts.com
ADDRESS: Lucasarts, P.O. Box 10307, San Rafael, CA 94912
FAX: (415) 444-8438
EMPLOYMENT: http://www.lucasarts.com/jobs/
EMAIL: resumes@lucasarts.com

METRO3D
Metro3D develops and publishes games on several platforms: X-Box, Playstation 2, Game Boy advance and GC.
PRINCIPAL GAMES: *Dark Angel* (PS2), *Armada* (DC, PS2).
GAMES IN DEVELOPMENT: *Armada 2* (PS2, X-Box), *Shayde* (X-Box).
WEBSITE: www.metro3d.com
ADDRESS: Metro3D, 12 South First Street, 10th floor, San Jose, CA 95113
PHONE: (408) 286-2900
FAX: (408) 286-2970

EMPLOYMENT: http://www.metro3d.com/
corporate/jobs.htm
EMAIL: resume@metro3d.com

MICROÏDS

Microïds develops and publishes games on several platforms: Playstation, Playstation 2, Game Boy Advance and Game Boy Color, X-Box and PC.
PRINCIPAL GAMES: *Master Rally* (PC), *Tennis Master Serie* (PC), *Druuna* (PC), *Warrior King* (PC), *Open Kart* (PC), *Road to India* (PC), *Empire of the Ants* (PC).
GAMES IN DEVELOPMENT: *Master Rally* (PS2, X-Box), *Tennis Master Series* (PS2), *Syberia* (PC), *Apprentice Knight* (X-Box).
WEBSITE: www.microids.com
ADDRESSES:
Microïds France, Vélizy Plus,
1 bis, rue du Petit Clamart, 78140 Vélizy, France
PHONE: (33) 1 46 01 54 01
FAX: (33) 1 46 32 25 64
Microïds Canada, 87 Prince St., Suite 140, Montreal, Quebec H3C 2M7, Canada
PHONE: (514) 390-0333
FAX: (514) 526-6717
EMPLOYMENT: http://www.microid.com
EMAIL: jobs@microids.com

MICROSOFT

Microsoft develops, publishes and distributes interactive game software for PC. The corporation launched its own video game console, X-Box, in November, 2001. Microsoft also made a few interesting acquisitions in 2001, including Bungie and Ensemble Studios, the creators of *Halo* and *Age of Empire*.
PRINCIPAL GAMES AND BRAND NAMES: X-box, *Oddworld, NFL Fever 2002, Dungeon Siege, Zoo Tycoon, Sigma* and *Flight Simulator 2002*
WEBSITE: www.microsoft.com/games
ADDRESS: Microsoft, One Microsoft Way, Redmond, WA 98052
PHONE: (425) 882-8080
FAX: (425) 936-7329
EMPLOYMENT: http://www.microsoft.com/isapi/
gomscom.asp?targand=/jobs/games/
STOCK EXCHANGE: NASDAQ and NYSE
SYMBOL: MSFT
ANNUAL REPORTS:
http://www.microsoft.com/msft/ar.htm

MIDWAY

Midway Games, Inc. develops, publishes and distributes interactive game software for consoles. In 2001, Midway decided to completely stop developing arcade games to concentrate on consoles.
PRINCIPAL GAMES: *Arctic Thunder* (PS2, X-Box), *SpyHunter* (PS2), *NHL Hitz 20-02* (X-Box, PS2, GC), *Hydro Thunder* (PSX, DC, N64), *San Francisco Rush 2049* (DC, N64, GBC), *Ready to Rumble* (DC, N64, PSX, GBC), *Ready to Rumble 2* (PS2, PSX, DC, N64, GBA)
GAMES IN DEVELOPMENT: *Mortal Kombat* (X-Box, GC, GBA), *SpyHunter* (X-Box, GC).
WEBSITE: www.midway.com

ADDRESS: Midway Games, Inc., Corporate
    Headquarters, 2704 West Roscoe Street,
    Chicago, IL 60618
PHONE: (773) 961-2222
FAX: (773) 961-1791
EMPLOYMENT: www.midway.com
EMAIL: resumes@agames.com
STOCK EXCHANGE: NYSE
SYMBOL: MWY
ANNUAL REPORTS: http://www.midway.com/
    Futurandense/assets/MGArticle/Midway2000A
    Rfront.pdf?GXHC_gx_session_id_Futurandense
    ContentServer=62fb826701b5a437

MONOLITH PRODUCTION

Monolith is a well-known developer of first person shooter games and the Lithtech game engine.
PRINCIPAL GAMES: *Blood* (PC), *Blood 2* (PC), *Shogo*
    (PC), *No one lives forever* (PC, PS2), *Alien vs*
    Predator 2 (PC, PS2).
GAME IN DEVELOPMENT: *No one lives forever 2.*
WEBSITE: www.lith.com
ADDRESS: Monolith Production, 10516 NE 37th
    Circle, Kirkland, WA 98033
PHONE: (425) 739-1500
FAX: (425) 827-3901
EMPLOYMENT: http://www.lith.com/jobs/
EMAIL: jobs@lith.com

N-SPACE

n-Space is a developer that focuses on Playstation and Playstation 2 consoles and is well-known for its games under the licenses of *Duke Nukem* and *Rugrats.*
PRINCIPAL GAMES: *Danger Girl* (PSX), *Duke Nukem:*
    Land of the Babes (PSX), *Die Hard Trilogy 2* (PC,
    PSX), *Duke Nukem: Time to Kill* (PSX), *Rugrats:*
    Search for Reptar (PSX).
GAME IN DEVELOPMENT: *Duke Nukem* title (PS2).
WEBSITE: www.n-space.com
ADDRESS: n-Space, 7035 Grand National Drive,
    Orlando, FL 32819
PHONE: (407) 352-5333
FAX: (407) 352-5571
EMPLOYMENT: http://www.n-space.com/employ-
    ment.asp
EMAIL: hr@n-space.com

NAMCO

Namco develops, publishes and distributes interactive game software for consoles and arcades.
PRINCIPAL GAMES: *Tekken Tag Tournament* (PS2), *Mr.*
    Driller (PSX), *Ridge Racer 5* (PS2), *Moto GP* (PS2),
    Moto GP 2 (PS2), *Klonoa 2* (PS2), *AirBlade* (PS2),
    Time Crisis: Project Titan (PSX), *Ace Combat 4*
    (PS2), *Soul Calibur* (DC).
GAMES IN DEVELOPMENT: *Soul Calibur 2* (PS2, GC,
    X-Box), *Tekken 4* (PS2).
WEBSITE: www.namco.com
ADDRESS: Namco, 2055 Junction Avenue, San Jose,
    CA 95131
PHONE: (408) 922-0712
FAX: (408) 321-0518

EMPLOYMENT:
http://www.namco.com/jobs/jobs.php
EMAIL: jobs@namco.com
STOCK EXCHANGE: Tokyo

NAUGHTY DOG

Naughty Dog was established in 1986 under the name JAM software. A garage development company, it developed several games for Apple II, Amiga, Atari ST, PC and Genesis, but it was the release of the first Crash Bandicoot game for Playstation that put the company's name on the map.

PRINCIPAL GAMES: *Crash Bandicoot 2: Cortex Strike Back* (PS2), *Crash Bandicoot: Warped* (PSX), *Crash Team Racing* (PSX), *Jak ans Daxster* (PS2).
WEBSITE: www.naughtydog.com
ADDRESS: Naughty Dog, Santa Monica, CA
PHONE: (408) 922-0712
FAX: (408) 321-0518
EMPLOYMENT: http://www.naughtydog.com
EMAIL: ndi@naughtydog.com

NEVERSOFT ENTERTAINMENT

Neversoft was established in 1994 and is well-known for its *Tony Hawk's Pro Skater* game series.

PRINCIPAL GAMES: *Apocalypse* (PSX), *Spiderman* (DC, PSX, N64, PC), *Tony Hawk's Pro Skater* (PSX), *Tony Hawk's Pro Skater 2* (PSX, PC, DC), *Tony Hawk's Pro Skater 2x* (X-Box), *Tony Hawk's Pro Skater 3* (PS2).

GAMES IN DEVELOPMENT: *Tony Hawk's Pro Skater 3* (GC, X-Box).
WEBSITE: www.neversoft.com
ADDRESS: Neversoft Entertainment, 20335 Ventura Blvd, Suite 320, Woodland Hills, CA 91364
PHONE: (818) 610-4100
FAX: (818) 610-4101
EMPLOYMENT: http://www.neversoft.com
EMAIL: resumes@neversoft.com

NEWKIDCO

Newkidco publishes interactive game software for children based on well-known characters such as *Tom and Jerry*, *Hello Kitty*, *E.T.*, and Disney characters.

PRINCIPAL GAMES: *E.T. Interplanetary Mission* (PSX), *Hello Kitty's Cube Frenzy* (PSX, GBC), *Tigger's Honey Hunt* (PSX, N64), *Tom and Jerry: Fists of Furry* (PSX, N64)
GAMES IN DEVELOPMENT: *Little League Baseball* (PS2, GC).
WEBSITE: www.newkidco.com
ADDRESS: Newkidco, 250 West 57th Street, Suites 1020 and 1502, New York, NY 10107
PHONE: (212) 581-1555
FAX: (212) 265-1620
EMPLOYMENT:
http://www.newkidco.com/jobs.html
STOCK EXCHANGE: Toronto
SYMBOL: NKC

NINTENDO

Nintendo is a world leader in content development for interactive games. The corporation just launched its new Gamecube console this year.

PRINCIPAL BRANDS: Nintendo, Gamecube, Game Boy.

PRINCIPAL LICENSES: *Mario, Luigi, Zelda, Pokemon, Kirby.*

WEBSITE: www.nintendo.com

ADDRESS: Nintendo, 4820 150th Ave NE, Redmond, WA 98052

PHONE: (800) 633-3236

FAX: (425) 882-3585

EMPLOYMENT: http://sh.webhire.com/public/524/

STOCK EXCHANGE: Osaka and Kyoto

ANNUAL REPORTS: http://www.nintendo.com/corp/financial.html

NOVALOGIC, INC.

Novalogic Inc. develops, publishes and distributes interactive game software for consoles, PCs and the Web. The company is best known for its military simulation games.

PRINCIPAL GAMES: *Armored Fist 3* (PC), *Commanche 4* (PC), the *Delta Force* Series (PC), *Tachyon: The Fringe* (PC).

WEBSITE: www.novalogic.com

ADDRESS: Novalogic, Inc., 26010 Mureau Rd., Suite 200, Calabasas, CA 91302

PHONE: (818) 880-1997

FAX: (818) 880-1998

EMPLOYMENT: http://www.novalogic.com/Company/jobs/body_jobs.html

EMAIL: hr@novalogic.com

ODDWORLD INHABITANTS

Oddworld Inhabitants was established in 1994 by two computer and animation special effects veterans, Sherry Mckenna and Lorne Lanning. This company is known for its artistic excellence and recently launched an X-Box title, *Munch's Odysee.*

PRINCIPAL GAMES: *Oddworld: Abe's Exodus* (PSX), *Oddworld: Abe's Odysee* (PSX), *Oddworld: Munch's Odysee* (X-Box).

WEBSITE: www.oddworld.com

ADDRESS: Oddworld Inhabitants, 869 Monterey Street, San Luis Obispo, CA 93401

EMPLOYMENT: http://www.oddworld.com/cgibin/start.cgi/oddworld/company/ow_jobs.html

EMAIL: jobs@oddworld.com

ORIGIN SYSTEMS

Origin Systems has developed more than 60 video game titles for different platforms. Today the company only develops online games, and is now a subsidiary of Electronic Arts.

PRINCIPAL GAMES: *Ultima* (PC), *Wing Commander* (PC), *Privateer* (PC), *Ultima Online* (PC).

WEBSITE: www.origin.ea.com

EMPLOYMENT: http://www.origin.ea.com/jobs.html

EMAIL: jobs@origin.ea.com

OUTRAGE ENTERTAINMENT

Outrage Entertainment develops interactive game software in what was formerly the Ann Arbor office of Parallax Software, developer of *Descent, Descent 2* and *Descent Maximum*. Under the management of THQ, Parallax was split into two companies, Outrage Entertainment and Volition.

PRINCIPAL GAMES: *Descent 3* (PC), *Descent 3: Mercenary* (PC).
GAME IN DEVELOPMENT: *Rubu Tribe* (PS2).
WEBSITE: www.outrage.com
ADDRESS: Outrage Entertainment, 330 E. Liberty St., Suite 4, Ann Arbor, MI 48104-2238
PHONE: (734) 663-9120
FAX: (734) 663-670
EMPLOYMENT: http://www.outrage.com/jobs.html
EMAIL: jobs@outrage.com

PANDEMIC STUDIOS

Pandemic Studios develops interactive game software and is well-known for its games *Battlezone 2* and *Dark Reign 2*. The studio also participates in the Future Combat System with Sony Pictures Imagework to develop 3-D training games for the U.S. army. More information available at www.futurecombat.net

PRINCIPAL GAMES: *Battlezone 2* (PC), *Dark Reign 2* (PC).
WEBSITE: www.pandemicstudios.com
ADDRESS: Pandemic Studios, 1920 Main Street, Santa Monica, CA 90405
PHONE: (310) 450-5199
FAX: (310) 450-5190
EMPLOYMENT: http://www.pandemicstudios.com/

inside_recruiting_pro.htm
EMAIL: jobs@pandemicstudios.com

POLYPHONY DIGITAL

Polyphony Digital develops interactive game software and is the company that brought us the *Gran Tourismo* series, which has reached cult status in the racing game category and is a Playstation and Playstation2 bestseller.

PRINCIPAL GAMES: *Gran Tourismo* (PSX), *Gran Tourismo 2* (PSX), *Gran Tourismo 3* (PS2), *Omega Boost* (PSX).
WEBSITE: www.polyphonydigital.com

POP TOP SOFTWARE

Pop Top Software develops interactive game software and is best known for the game *Railroad Tycoon 2*.

PRINCIPAL GAMES: *Railroad Tycoon 2* (PC), *Tropico* (PC, Mac, DC).
GAME IN DEVELOPMENT: *Tropico Expansion Pack: Paradise Island*.
WEBSITE: www.poptop.com
ADDRESS: Pop Top Software, 1714 Gilsinn, Fenton, MO 63026
EMPLOYMENT:
    http://www.poptop.com/Company.htm
EMAIL: jobs@poptop.com

PRESTO STUDIOS

Presto Studios develops interactive game software and is best known for its work on *The Journeyman Project* and *Myst 3:Exile.*

PRINCIPAL GAMES: *Myst3:Exile* (PC, Mac), *Star Trek: Hidden Evil* (PC), *F13* (PC, Mac), *Gundam 0079* (PC, Mac), *The Journeyman Project 1* (PC, Mac), *The Journeyman Project 2* (PC, Mac), *The Journeyman Project 3* (PC, Mac).

Game in development: *Whacked* (X-Box).

WEBSITE: www.presto.com

ADDRESS: Presto Studios, 5414 Oberlin Drive, Suite 200, San Diego, CA 92121

PHONE: (858) 622-0500

FAX: (858) 622-0310

EMPLOYMENT: http://www.presto.com/v4/corp/jobs.asp

EMAIL: jobs@presto.com

PSEUDO INTERACTIVE

Pseudo Interactive develops interactive game software and made a name for itself with its cartoon-style game *Cel Damage* for X-Box.

PRINCIPAL GAMES: *Full Auto* (PC), *Cel Damage* (X-Box, GC)

WEBSITE: www.pseudointeractive.com

ADDRESS: Pseudo Interactive, 80 Bloor Street West, Suite 400, Toronto, Ontario M5S 2V1, Canada

PHONE: (416) 966-1142

FAX: (416) 966-2075

EMPLOYMENT: http://www.pseudointeractive.com/careers.shtml

EMAIL: jobs@pseudointeractive.com

PYRO STUDIOS

Pyro Studios develops interactive game software and became known for its strategy game series *Commandos.* Pyro Studios is a Spanish developer.

PRINCIPAL GAMES: *Commandos: Behind Enemy Lines* (PC), *Commandos: Beyond the Call of Duty* (PC), *Commandos 2* (PC, DC, PS2).

Game in development: *Commandos 2* (X-Box).

WEBSITE: www.pyrostudios.com

ADDRESS: Pyro Studios, Avda. de Burgos 16-D, 1º planta, 28036 Madrid, Spain

PHONE: 34 91 3846880

FAX: 34 91 7666474

RAGE SOFTWARE

Rage Software develops interactive game software and established itself with its games *Incoming* and *Hostile Water.*

PRINCIPAL GAMES: *B-17 Flying Fortress* (PC), *David Beckham Soccer* (PSX, GBA), *E-Racer* (PC), *Rage Rally* (PC), *Incoming* (PC, DC), *Hostile Water* (PC).

GAMES IN DEVELOPMENT: *Crash* (X-Box), *David Beckham Soccer* (PS2, X-Box), *Gunmandal* (X-Box).

WEBSITE: www.rage.com

ADDRESS: Rage Software, Martins Building, Water Street, Liverpool L2 3SP UK

PHONE: 44 (0) 151 237 2200
FAX: 44 (0) 151 237 2201
EMPLOYMENT: http://www.rage.com
EMAIL: jobs@rage.co.uk

RAINBOW STUDIOS

Rage Software develops interactive game software and made a name for itself with its *Motocross Madness* series. The company also has an animation studio for film, TV and video. The *Starship Troopers: Roughneck Chronicles* series is one of the studio's 3-D TV productions.
PRINCIPAL GAMES: *Motocross Madness* (PC), *Motocross Madness* 2 (PC), *ATV Offroad Fury* (PS2), *Splashdown* (PS2).
GAMES IN DEVELOPMENT: *Star Wars Racer Revenge: Racer 2* (PS2), *Mat Hoffman's Pro BMX 2* (PS2).
WEBSITE: www.rainbowstudios.com
ADDRESS: Rage Software, 3830 N. 7th St., Phoenix, AZ 85014
PHONE: (602) 230-1300
FAX: (602) 230-2553
EMPLOYMENT: http://www.rainbowstudios.com
EMAIL: gamejobs@rainbowstudios.com

RARE

Rare develops interactive game software exclusively for the different Nintendo platforms.
PRINCIPAL GAMES: *Donkey Kong Country, Killer Instinct, Blast Corps, GoldenEye 007, Diddy Kong Racing* and *Banjo-Kazooie*.

GAMES IN DEVELOPMENT: *Starfox Adventures* (GC), *Kameo: Elements of Power* (GC), *Donkey Kong Racing* (GC).
WEBSITE: www.rareware.com
ADDRESS: Rare, Manor Park, Nr. Twycross, Warks CV9 3QN, United Kingdom
EMPLOYMENT: http://www.rare.co.uk/the_site/recruitment/recruitment_vacancies.html
EMAIL: recruitment@rare.co.uk

RAVEN SOFTWARE

Raven Software develops interactive game software based on Id Software's technology. It was recently in the headlines with its game *Soldier of Fortune* and is currently developing the sequel to *Jedi Knight* for Lucasarts.
PRINCIPAL GAMES: *Hexen 2* (PC), *Heretic 2* (PC), *Soldier of Fortune* (PC, PS2), *Star Trek: Elite Force* (PC, PS2).
GAMES IN DEVELOPMENT: *Jedi Knight 2: Jedi Outcast* (PC), *Soldier of Fortune 2: Double Helix* (PC).
WEBSITE: www.ravensoft.com
ADDRESS: Raven Software, Three Point Place, Suite #1, Madison, WI 53719
EMPLOYMENT: http://www.ravensoft.com/jobs.html

RED LEMON STUDIOS

Red Lemon Studios has been developing video games since 1996 and was in the headlines in 1999 with the launch of its first game *Braveheart*.

PRINCIPAL GAMES: *Braveheart* (PC), *Aeronauts* (PSX), *Roswell Conspiracies* (PSX)

GAMES IN DEVELOPMENT: *Farscape* (PC, Next-Gen Console).

WEBSITE: www.redlemon.com

ADDRESS: Red Lemon Studios, 175 West George Street, Glasgow, Scotland, G2 2LB, United Kingdom

PHONE: +44 (0) 141 271 2000

FAX: +44 (0) 141 271 2001

EMPLOYMENT: http://www.redlemon.com/html/jobs_index.html

EMAIL: fiona@redlemon.com

RED STORM ENTERTAINMENT

Red Storm Entertainment develops interactive game software for consoles and PCs. The company is now a subsidiary of Ubi Soft Entertainment.

PRINCIPAL GAMES: *Ghost Recon* (PC), *Rogue Spear* (PC, PSX), *Rainbow Six* (PC, PSX, GBC), *Force 21* (PC, GBC), *Shadow Watch* (PC).

WEBSITE: www.redstorm.com

ADDRESS: Red Storm Entertainment, 2000 Aerial Center, Suite 110, Morrisville, NC 27560

PHONE: (919) 460-1776

FAX: (919) 468-3305

EMPLOYMENT: http://www.redstorm.com/employment/

EMAIL: jobs@redstorm.com

RELIC

Relic has been developing interactive game software since 1997 and caught everyone's attention in 1999 with the release if its first game *Homeworld*. Its next game *Impossible Creatures* may revolutionize video game design to some degree.

PRINCIPAL GAMES: *Homeworld* (PC), *Homeworld: Cataclysm* (PC)

GAMES IN DEVELOPMENT: *Homeworld 2, Impossible Creatures* (PC)

WEBSITE: www.relic.com

ADDRESS: Relic, 400-948 Homer St., Vancouver BC, Canada V6B 2W7

PHONE: (604) 801-6577

FAX: (604) 801-6578

EMPLOYMENT: http://www.relic.com/careers/careers.php

REMEDY ENTERTAINMENT

Remedy has been developing games since 1995 and gained notoriety in the shareware world with *Death Rally*. The company's most recent game, *Max Payne*, was one of 2001's best games. And let's not forget to mention that the company was also responsible for bringing us the benchmark 3dMark 2001 benchmark.

PRINCIPAL GAMES: *Death Rally* (PC), *Max Payne* (PC, PS2, X-Box).

WEBSITE: www.remedy-ent.com

ADDRESS: Remedy, Kappelitie 6, FIN-02200 ESPOO, Finland

PHONE: 358-9-435-5040

FAX: 358-9-435-50444

EMPLOYMENT: http://www.remedy-ent.com/
contact_info/recruitment_info.html
EMAIL: jobs@remedy.fi

RETRO STUDIOS

Retro Studios is a game video game developer whose
production efforts are focused on the Nintendo GC
console.
GAMES IN DEVELOPMENT: *Mandroid Prime* (GC),
Raven Blade (GC)
WEBSITE: www.retrostudios.com
ADDRESS: Retro Studios, 1835A Kramer Lane, Suite
100, Austin, TX 78758
FAX: (512) 493-4602
EMPLOYMENT: www.retrostudios.com
EMAIL: hr@retrostudios.com

RITUAL ENTERTAINMENT

Ritual Entertainment is the video game developer that
brought us *Sin* and *Heavy Mandal: F.A.K.K. 2*.
PRINCIPAL GAMES: *Sin* (PC), *Heavy Metal: F.A. K.K. 2*
(PC, Mac, DC), *Blair Witch Volume 3: The Elly
Kedward Tale* (PC).
WEBSITE: www.ritual.com
ADDRESS: Ritual Entertainment, 2019 N. Lamar St.,
Suite 220, Dallas, TX 75202
EMPLOYMENT: http://www.ritual.com/
inside_ritual/help_wanted.html
EMAIL: roba@ritual.com

SCI

Sci is a video game developer who came to everyone's
attention with its *Carmegeddon* series and its project-
in-development, *Titanium Angel*.
PRINCIPAL GAMES: *Carmageddon* (PC),
Carmageddon TDR 2000 (PC), *The Italian Job*
(PSX, PC), *Thunderbirds* (GBA).
GAMES IN DEVELOPMENT: *Conflict Desert Storm* (X-
Box), *GumBall 3000* (PS2), *Thunderbirds:
Operation Volcano* (PC), *Titanium Angel* (PS2).
WEBSITE: www.sci.co.uk
ADDRESS: Sci, 11 Ivory House, Plantation Wharf,
Battersea, London SW11 3TN, United Kingdom
EMPLOYMENT:
http://www.sci.co.uk/corporate/jobs.asp
EMAIL: jobs@sci.co.uk

SEGA

Sega of America develops, publishes and distributes
interactive game software and video game systems
(Dreamcast). The company announced it is retiring
from the game system market and will devote its
efforts solely to game development.
PRINCIPAL BRANDS: Sega, Dreamcast and Sega Sport.
WEBSITE: www.sega.com
ADDRESS: Sega, 650 Townsend Street, Suite 650, San
Francisco, CA 94103
EMPLOYMENT: http://www.sega.com/pc/suits/
playerJobListingviewList.jhtml
EMAIL: jobs@sega.com
ANNUAL REPORTS: http://www.sega.com/pc/suits/
investor_info.jhtml

SHINY ENTERTAINMENT INC.

Shiny Entertainment, Inc. develops interactive game software for PCs and gained notoriety with its games *Earthworm Jim*, *MDK* and *Messiah*. Shiny has also recently acquired the rights to the film *Matrix* to turn it into a game for X-Box.

PRINCIPAL GAMES: *Earthworm Jim*, *MDK* (PC), *Messiah* (PC, PSX), *Wild 9* (PSX), *RC Stunt Copter* (PSX), *Sacrifice* (PC, Mac).

GAME IN DEVELOPMENT: *The Matrix* (X-Box).

WEBSITE: www.shiny.com

ADDRESS: Shiny Entertainment, Inc., 1088 N. Coast Highway, Laguna Beach, CA 92651-1338

PHONE: (949) 494-0772

FAX: (949) 376-8343

EMPLOYMENT:
http://www.shiny.com/company/jobs.htm

EMAIL: tmorgan@shiny.com

SIERRA ON LINE INC.

Sierra On Line, Inc. develops, publishes and distributes interactive game software for consoles and PCs. After first being sold to Cendant Software, the company now belongs to the Vivendi group. Sierra first became known as a developer with its *Leisure Suit Larry*, *Space Quest* and *King Quest* series.

PRINCIPAL GAMES: *Half-Life* (PC, PS2), *You Don't Know Jack*, *Trophy Bass* (PS2), *Empire Earth* (PC), *Homeworld* (PC), *Tribes* (PC), *Tribes 2* (PC), *Swat 3* (PC), *Nascar Racing 2002* (PC).

WEBSITE: www.sierra.com

ADDRESS: Sierra On Line, Inc., 4247 S. Minnewawa Ave, Fresno, CA 93725

PHONE: (310) 649-8000

SILICON KNIGHTS INC.

Silicon Knights, Inc. develops interactive game software and first became known for its game *Blood Omen: Legacy of Kain*. Lately it has aroused interest with *Eternal Darkness*, a much awaited game for GC.

PRINCIPAL GAMES: *Blood Omen: Legacy of Kain* (PC, PSX), *Dark Legions* (PC),

Game in development: *Eternal Darkness* (GC).

WEBSITE: www.siliconknights.com

ADDRESS: Silicon Knights, Inc., 1 St. Paul Street, Suite 800, St. Catherines, Ontario L2R 7L2, Canada

PHONE: (905) 687-3334

FAX: (905) 687-4055

EMPLOYMENT: http://www.siliconknights.com/apprenticeships/index.htm

EMAIL: humanresources@siliconknights.com

SONY COMPUTER ENTERTAINMENT AMERICA INC.

Sony Computer Entertainment America, Inc. (SCEA) distributes and markets the PlayStation and PlayStation 2 game consoles and is publisher and distributor of titles for a wide range of independent developers.

WEBSITE: www.scea.com

ADDRESS: SCEA, 919 E. Hillsdale Boulevard, Foster City, CA 94404

EMPLOYMENT: http://www.sony.com/SCA/job.html
STOCK EXCHANGE: listed in 16 stock exchange companies throughout the world, including London, New York and Tokyo.
ANNUAL REPORTS: http://www.sony.co.jp/en/
SonyInfo/IR/index2.html

SQUARESOFT

Squaresoft develops and publishes interactive game software for every type of platform. Squaresoft made a name for itself with the *Final Fantasy* series whose sales topped 30 million copies.
PRINCIPAL GAMES: The *Final Fantasy* series (PSX, PS2), *Bushido Blade* (PSX) *Bushido Blade 2* (PSX), *Parasite Eve* (PSX), *Parasite Eve 2* (PSX), *Vagrant Story* (PSX).
WEBSITE: www.squaresoft.com
ADDRESS: Squaresoft, 6060 Center Drive, Suite 100, Los Angeles, CA 90045
PHONE: (310) 846-0400
FAX: (310) 846-0403
EMPLOYMENT: http://www.squaresoft.com/web/jobs/index.html
EMAIL: jobs@squaresoft.com

STORMFRONT STUDIOS

Stormfront Studios develops interactive game software and is best known for its recent game *Blood Wake* for X-Box.
PRINCIPAL GAMES: *Madden '98* (PC), *Andretti Racing* (PC), *Nascar '98* (PSX), *Nascar '99* (N64, PSX), *Nascar Revolution* (PC), *Blood Wake* (X-Box), *The Legend of Alon D'Ar* (PS2).
WEBSITE: www.stormfrontstudios.com
ADDRESS: Stormfront Studios, 4040 Civic Center Dr., Third floor, San Rafael, CA 94903
PHONE: (415) 479-2800 ext. 206
FAX: (415) 479-2880
EMPLOYMENT:
http://www.stormfrontstudios.com/frjoblin.htm
EMAIL: mdaglow@earthlink.net

STRATEGY FIRST

Strategy First develops and publishes interactive game software and is known for *Disciple: Sacred Lands*.
PRINCIPAL GAMES: *Clans* (PC), *Disciple: Sacred Lands* (PC), *Disciple 2: Dark Prophecy* (PC), *O.R.B.* (PC), *Trainz* (PC).
WEBSITE: www.strategyfirst.com
ADDRESS: Strategy First, 147 St. Paul Ouest, Suite 300, Montreal, Quebec, Canada H2Y 1Z5
EMPLOYMENT: http://www.strategyfirst.com/fr/corporatif/
EMAIL: emps@strategyfirst.com

TAKE-TWO INTERACTIVE SOFTWARE, INC.

Take-Two Interactive Software, Inc. develops, publishes and distributes interactive game software for all console models and PCs. The company publishes various games though different subsidiaries such as Rockstar Games, Gathering of Developers, Talonsoft, Joytech and a few others.

PRINCIPAL GAMES: *Grand Theft Auto 3* (PC, PS2),
    Midnight Club, Smugglers Run (PS2), *Oni* (PC, Mac,
    PS2).
GAMES IN DEVELOPMENT: *Duke Nukem Forever*
    (PC), *Hidden and Dangerous 2* (PC).
WEBSITE: www.take2games.com
ADDRESS: Take-Two Interactive Software, Inc., 575
    Broadway, New York, NY 10012
PHONE: (212) 334-6633
FAX: (212) 334-6644
STOCK EXCHANGE: NASDAQ
SYMBOL: TTWO
ANNUAL REPORTS: http://www.take2games.com/
    index.php?p=financial_info

TECMO

Tecmo is a developer and publisher of interactive
game software for consoles and arcades. It recently
demonstrated the true capacity of X-Box with the
third version of *Dead or Alive.*
PRINCIPAL GAMES: *Gallop Racer* (PSX), *Gallop Racer
    2001* (PS2*), Ninja Gaiden* (PS2), *Tecmo Bowl* (PS2),
    Dead or Alive (PSX), *Dead or Alive 2* (DC) *Dead or
    Alive 2: Hardcore* (PS2), *Dead or Alive 3* (X-Box).
Game in development: *Fatal Frame* (PS2).
WEBSITE: www.tecmoinc.com
ADDRESS: Tecmo, 21235 Hawthorne Blvd., Suite 205,
    Torrance, CA 90503
PHONE: (310) 944-5005
FAX: (310) 944-3344
EMPLOYMENT: www.tecmoinc.com
EMAIL: jobs@tecmoinc.com

TERMINAL REALITY

Terminal Reality develops interactive game software
for PC and consoles, and is best known for its games
Monster Truck Madness and *Nocturne.*
PRINCIPAL GAMES: *Monster Truck Madness 2* (PC),
    FLY! (PC), *Nocturne* (PC), *Blair Witch Volume 1:
    Rustin Parr* (PC), *4X4 Evolution* (PC, DC, PS2), *4X4
    Evo 2* (X-Box, PC).
GAMES IN DEVELOPMENT: *BloodRayne* (PC, PS2, X-
    Box, GC).
WEBSITE: www.terminalreality.com
EMPLOYMENT:
    http://www.terminalreality.com/jobs.htm
EMAIL: employment@terminalreality.com.

THE BITMAP BROTHER

The Bitmap Brother develops interactive game soft-
ware for PCs and consoles and made a name for itself
with the game *Z: Steel Soldier.*
PRINCIPAL GAMES: *Speedball 2100* (PSX), *Z: Steel
    Soldier* (PC),
GAME IN DEVELOPMENT: *World War II: D-Day To
    Berlin* (PC).
WEBSITE: www.bitmap-brothers.co.uk
EMPLOYMENT: http://www.bitmap-
    brothers.co.uk/employment/index.htm
EMAIL: employment@bitmap-brothers.co.uk

THQ

THQ Inc. develops, publishes and distributes interactive game software for consoles and PCs.

PRINCIPAL LICENSES: *Red Faction, New Legends, World Wrestling Federation, Championship Motocross, Hot Wheels/ Matchbox, Tandris, Nickelodeon* and *Power Rangers.*
WEBSITE: www.thq.com
ADDRESS: THQ, 27001 Agoura Road, Suite 325, Calabasas Hills, CA 91301
PHONE: (818) 871-5000
EMPLOYMENT: http://www.thq.com/Employment/
EMAIL: resume@thq.com
STOCK EXCHANGE: NASDAQ
SYMBOL: THQI
ANNUAL REPORTS:
http://www.thq.com/about/company.asp

TITUS

Titus develops, publishes and distributes interactive game software for consoles and PCs. Titus acquired Virgin Interactive Entertainment and is a major shareholder of Interplay.
PRINCIPAL LICENSES: *Kao The Kangaroo, Robocop, Top Gun, Barbarians, Planand monsters,* and *Downforce.*
WEBSITE: www.titus-interactive.com
ADDRESS: Titus, Parc de l'Esplanade, 12 rue Enrico Fermi, Saint-Thibault des Vignes 77462 Lagny-sur-Marne, France
EMPLOYMENT: http://www.titus-interactive.com/fr/emplois/
EMAIL: recrutement@titus.fr
STOCK EXCHANGE: Paris "Le Nouveau Marché"
SYMBOL: TITP.LN (Sicovam 5012).

ANNUAL REPORTS: http://www.titusgames.com/company/financial_infos/index.php

TOTALLY GAMES

Totally Games is a company that has a great deal of experience in the development of space combat-type games. It made a name for itself with the *X-Wing* series and *Tie Fighter,* developed for Lucasarts.
PRINCIPAL GAMES: *X-Wing* (PC), *Tie Fighter* (PC), *X-Wing vs Tie Fighter* (PC), *X-Wing Alliance* (PC).
GAME IN DEVELOPMENT: *Star Trek: Bridge Commander* (X-Box).
WEBSITE: www.totallygames.com
ADDRESS: Totally Games, P.O. Box 6248, Terra Linda, CA 94903-0248
FAX: (248) 671-0867
EMPLOYMENT:
http://www.totallygames.com/jobs/index.htm
EMAIL: HR@TotallyGames.com

TROIKA GAMES

Troika Games was established by the creators of the game *Fallout* and developed *Arcanum* as its first game.
PRINCIPAL GAMES: *Arcanum* (PC)
GAMES IN DEVELOPMENT: *Magick Obscura* (PC)
WEBSITE: www.troikagames.com
ADDRESS: Troika Games, 2680 Walnut Avenue, Suite A, Tustin, CA 92780
EMPLOYMENT:
http://www.troikagames.com/jobs.htm
EMAIL: jobs@troikagames.com

UBI SOFT ENTERTAINMENT

Ubi Soft develops, publishes and distributes interactive game software for consoles and PCs.

PRINCIPALS LICENSES: *Batman, Disney: Donald Duck, Tarzan, Aladdin, Goofy, Rayman, Monaco Grand Prix.*

WEBSITE: www.Ubi Soft.com

ADDRESSES:

USA

SAN FRANCISCO: 625 Third Street, 3rd floor, San Francisco, CA 94107

PHONE: (415) 547-4000

FAX: (415) 547-4001

NEW YORK: 45 W. 25th Street, 9th floor, New York, NY 10001

PHONE: (212) 993-3000

FAX: (212) 414-1460

CANADA

MONTREAL: 5505 Boulevard Saint-Laurent, Suite 5000, Montreal H2T 1S6, Quebec, Canada

PHONE: (514) 490-2000

FAX: (514) 490-0882

EMPLOYMENT:
http://corp.UbiSoft.com/jo_offer.htm

UDS

Based in Sweden UDS is a video game developer for several big publishers of games for both consoles and PCs.

PRINCIPAL GAMES: *World's Scariest Police Chases* (PSX), *Asterix Mega Madness* (PC, PSX), *Airfix Dogfighter* (PC), *Sno-Cross Championship Racing* (PSX, DC, PC)

GAMES IN DEVELOPMENT: *Monster Jam* (GBA), *Party Paradise* (PC), *Futurama, Core* (X-Box).

WEBSITE: www.uds.se

ADDRESS: UDS, Västgötegatan 13, 60221 Norrköping, Sweden

PHONE: +46 (0) 11 470 51 00

FAX: +46 (0) 11 123160

EMPLOYMENT: http://www.uds.se/career.html

EMAIL: marie@uds.se

VALVE SOFTWARE

Valveù Software revolutionized the "first person shooter" game with *Half-Life*. Its next title *Team Fortress 2*, as well as a sequel to *Half-Life*, are eagerly awaited.

PRINCIPAL GAMES: *Half-Life* (PC, PS2), *Team Fortress Classic* (PC).

GAME IN DEVELOPMENT: *Team Fortress 2* (PC).

WEBSITE: www.valvesoftware.com

ADDRESS: Valve Software, 520 Kirkland Way #201, Kirkland, WA 98033

PHONE: (425) 889-9642

FAX: (425) 889-9642

EMPLOYMENT: http://valvesoftware.com/jobs.htm

EMAIL: jobs@valvesoftware.com

VERANT INTERACTIVE

Verant Interactive is a developer focused on so-called "massive multiplayer games". The company made a name for itself with the game *Everquest*, a big success in the realm of online games.

PRINCIPAL GAMES: *Everquest* (PC), *Infantry* (PC), *Cosmic Rift* (PC).

GAMES IN DEVELOPMENT: *Planetside* (PC), *Sovereign* (PC), *Star Wars Galaxies* (PC).
WEBSITE: www.verant.com
ADDRESS: Verant Interactive, 8958 Terman Court, San Diego, CA 92121
EMPLOYMENT: http://65.207.168.54/candidate/

VIRCOM INTERACTIVE

Vircom is a developer of "massive multiplayer games". In 2000, Vircom became part of Cryonetworks, the online subsidiary of the French multinational company Cryo SA.
PRINCIPAL GAMES: *The 4th Coming* (PC), *The 4th Prophecy* (PC)
GAMES IN DEVELOPMENT: *Black Moon Chronicles* (PC), *Prison* (PC), *Dune Generation* (PC).
WEBSITE: www.vircom.com
ADDRESS: Vircom, 2055 Peel, Suite 200, Montreal, Quebec, H3A 1V4 Canada
PHONE: (514) 845-1666
FAX: (514) 845-6922
EMPLOYMENT:
    http://www.vircom.com/company/career.htm
EMAIL: hr@vircom.com

VIRGIN INTERACTIVE

Virgin Interactive publishes and distributes interactive game software for consoles and PCs. The company is now owned by Titus.
PRINCIPAL GAMES: *Roadster, Xena, Giants, Resident Evil* and all Titus titles for Europe.

WEBSITE: www.virgininteractive.co.uk
ADDRESS: Virgin Interactive, 74A Charlotte Street, London W1P 1LR, United Kingdom
PHONE: 44 (0) 207 551 0000
FAX: 44 (0) 207 551 0001

VIVENDI UNIVERSAL

Vivendi Universal develops, publishes and distributes interactive game software for consoles, the Internet and PCs. Because of its subsidiaries, Vivendi is now the world's No. 2 company.
SUBSIDIARIES: *Blizzard Entertainment, Flipside.com, Sierra* and *Universal Interactive Studios.*
WEBSITE: www.havasint.com
ADDRESS: Vivendi Universal, 375 Park Avenue, New York, NY 10152-0192
PHONE: (212) 572-7000
STOCK EXCHANGE: Paris and New York
SYMBOL: P: EXFP, NY: V
ANNUAL REPORTS: http://finance.vivendi.com/

VOLITION

Volition develops interactive game software for PCs and consoles. Volition is a sister company of Outrage Entertainment and a subsidiary of THQ. The company recently gained attention with the games *Summoner* and *Red Faction.*
PRINCIPAL GAMES: *Descent: Freespace* (PC), *Descent: Freespace 2* (PC), *Red Faction* (PC, PS2), *Summoner* (PC, PS2).
GAME IN DEVELOPMENT: *Summoner 2* (PS2).

WEBSITE: www.volition-inc.com
ADDRESS: Volition, 2004 Fox Drive, Suite B,
Champaign IL, 61820
PHONE: (217) 355-0320
FAX: (217) 355-0767
EMPLOYMENT: http://www.volition-inc.com/v_employment.cfm
EMAIL: personnel@volition-inc.com

WARTHOG

Warthog develops interactive game software for PCs and consoles. The company is currently working on a wide range of titles for publishers such as Infogram, New Kid co and Activision.
PRINCIPAL GAMES: *Asterix: The Gallic War* (PC, PSX), *Rally Championship Xtreme* (PC)
GAMES IN DEVELOPMENT: *Bounty Hunter* (X-Box), *Battlebots* (GC).
WEBSITE: www.warthog.co.uk
ADDRESS: Warthog, 10 Eden Place, Cheadle, Cheshire SK8 1AT, England
PHONE: 0161-610-3030
FAX: 0161-610-3033
EMPLOYMENT: www.warthog.com
EMAIL: recruitment@warthog.co.uk

WESTWOOD STUDIOS

Westwood Studios was established by Brett W. Sperry and Louis Castle. The company develops interactive game software for PCs and consoles, and is well-known for its successful *Command and Conquer* series.

Westwood Studios now belongs to Electronic Arts.
PRINCIPAL GAMES: *Command and Conquer* (PC), *Command and Conquer: Red Alert* (PC), *Command and Conquer: Tiberian Sun* (PC), *Nox* (PC), *Command and Conquer: Renegade* (PC).
GAMES IN DEVELOPMENT: *Pirates: The Legends of the Black Kat* (PS2), *Earth and Beyond Online* (PC).
WEBSITE: westwood.ea.com
ADDRESS: Westwood Studios, 2400 N Tenaya Way, Las Vegas, NV 89128
FAX: (702) 240-5835
EMPLOYMENT: westwood.ea.com
EMAIL: careers@westwood.com

Z-AXIS

Z-Axis develops interactive game software for consoles and PCs. The company collaborates with Acclaim Entertainment, Activision, Rockstar Games and Electronic Arts.
PRINCIPAL GAMES: *Dave Mira Freestyle BMX* (PC, PSX, DC), *Dave Mira Freestyle BMX 2* (X-Box, PS2, GC), *Space Invaders* (PSX), *Trasher: Skate and Destroy* (PSX), *Freestyle Motocross: McGrath vs Pastrana* (PSX).
GAMES IN DEVELOPMENT: *Dave Mira Freestyle BMX 3* (X-Box, PS2, GC), *Aggressive Inline* (X-Box, PS2, GC),
WEBSITE: www.z-axis.com
ADDRESS: Z-Axis, 21021 Corsair Blvd., Suite 200, Hayward, CA 94545
PHONE: (510) 887-7900
FAX: (510) 887-7912
EMPLOYMENT: http://www.z-axis.com/jobs.html
EMAIL: jobs@z-axis.com

ZOMBIE

Zombie develops interactive game software for consoles and PCs. The company became known for the *Spec Ops* game series.

PRINCIPAL GAMES: *Alcatraz: Prison Break* (PC), *Disney Atlantis* (PC), *Spec Ops* Series (DC, PSX, PC), *ZPC* (PC), Mac).

GAMES IN DEVELOPMENT: *Shrapnel* (PC, X-Box).

WEBSITE: www.zombie.com

ADDRESS: Zombie, 114 1/2 First Avenue South, Seattle, WA 98104

PHONE: (206) 623-9655

FAX: (206) 623-9714

EMPLOYMENT: www.zombie.com

EMAIL: jobs@zombie.com

2015

2015 develops interactive game software in the "first person shooter" style. The company recently made a name for itself with its game *Medal of Honor: Allied Assault*.

PRINCIPAL GAMES: *Sin Expansion Pack: Wages of Sin* (PC), *Medal of Honor: Allied Assault* (PC).

WEBSITE: www.2015.com

EMPLOYMENT: www.2015.com

EMAIL: jobs@2015.com

3D REALMS

3D Realms revolutionized interactivity in so-called "first person shooter" games with *Duke Nukem 3-D* which was an enormous success in 1996. Since then it's been developing *Duke Nukem Forever* and produced one of 2001's big successes, *Max Payne*.

PRINCIPAL GAMES: *Duke Nukem 3-D* (PC), *Shadow Warrior* (PC), *Balls of Steel* (PC).

GAME IN DEVELOPMENT: *Duke Nukem Forever* (PC).

WEBSITE: www.3drealms.com

ADDRESS: 3D Realms, P.O. Box 496419, Garland, TX 75049-6389

EMPLOYMENT: http://www.3drealms.com/gethired.html

3DO

3DO develops, publishes and distributes interactive game software for consoles and PCs. The company is well known for its *Army Men* series.

PRINCIPAL LICENSES: *Army Men, Might and Magic, High Heat Baseball, World Destruction League*.

WEBSITE: www.3do.com

ADDRESS: 3DO, 100 Cardinal Way, Redwood City, CA 94063

PHONE: (650) 385-3000

EMPLOYMENT: http://www.3do.com/jobs/index.html

EMAIL: resumes@3do.com

Part 2

People

1.
Creative Minds

In terms of revenue, the video game industry is now comparable to the film and music industries. Who are the creative minds who made this happen? Who turned video games into such a glamour industry? 20 years back, aspiring artists would picture themselves as rock 'n'roll stars. Today, they want to become video game designers.

Video game designers are the ones who reign over the industry. They have a cohort of followers and flatterers. Publishing companies and console manufacturers all court and pamper them.

It is true, however, that without the visionary entrepreneurs who built the publishing companies, and software and hardware technologies, their splendid imagination would not have become the tangible products we now all rave about.

Let's take a look, then, at the real people who became the stars of the industry.

They will be respectfully described here as princes, rising stars and kings!

Princes

Greg Zeschuk and Ray Muzyka

MAJOR TITLES: *Baldur's Gate* (Tales of the Sword and Shadows of Amn)
GREATEST HITS: the *Baldur's Gate* series (3.5 million copies)

One day, two family doctors from Edmonton, Dr. Greg Zeschuk and Dr. Ray Muzyka, decided to reinvent themselves and go into the video game business. They had met at Med school. But their common passion for games, computer animation and comic strips turned them into strong business partners. In just a few years, they completely revolutionized the design of interactive Role Playing Games.

They started with a few training programs in medical education. In February 1995 they launched BioWare Inc. In October 1996, they published *Shattered Steel*, first on PC, then on the Mac. 100,000 copies later, they introduced their first RPG title: *Baldur's Gate*. 1,500,000 copies were sold in no time and, soon enough, two extensions became available: *Tales of the Sword* and *Shadows of Amn*. They also came out with *MDK2* for PC, Dreamcast and PlayStation 2. Their game engine (the BioWare Infinity Engine) also became very popular. Black Isles Studios used it to develop *Torment* and *Icewind Dale*.

Their current project is even more ambitious: they want to offer their game engine along with their new game *Neverwinter Nights*, so that players can add their own adventures to the ones provided by the game. Lucas just ordered a role playing game which is going to appear in the Star Wars universe: *Knights of the Old Republic*. The good doctors have just resolved a dispute with publisher /distributor Interplay when the French Infogrames stepped in and took over the delivery of their latest baby.

<www.bioware.com>

John Carmack

Major titles: *Wolfenstein, Doom* and *Quake*

John Carmack is not a game designer *per se*. He is the founder and chief software architect of id Software (The name "id" comes from Freud's theory about psychoanalysis. The id is the part of the human psyche, which he identified as closest to instinct). John is really one the top guns of the industry! He single handedly paved the way for the coming of age of the modern game genre called First Person Shooter.

In *Wolfenstein, Doom* and *Quake,* frantic action is going on all over the place! By becoming overnight classics, the three titles gave the PC game industry quite a shot in the arm.

With *Quake*, online multiplayer games found their champion. Suddenly, a complete 3-D universe was becoming available, easy to use and agreeable to play. id Software popularized the shareware model. Clients were allowed to download a game level and get to know its content. When satisfied, they were asked to pay for subsequent levels.

In 1991, John Carmack, Adrian Carmack, John Romero and Tom Hall left their jobs at Softdisk Publishing and launched id Software. One year later Apogee published *Wolfenstein 3-D*. The game was an instant best seller. *Doom* was launched in 1993 and it sold 15 million copies! It was downloaded and shared by gamers all over the world. In 1996, *Quake* was introduced and redefined what FPS games were all about. With *Quake 2*, for the first time, as many as 32 players

113

could interact over the Internet. No one ever looked back after that: a new era had begun! The industry started to honor id Software with innumerable prizes and the company kept climbing and climbing, irresistibly.

<www.idsoftware.com>

Richard Garriot

MAJOR TITLES: *Akalabeth*, the *Ultima* series (1 to 9), *Ultima Online*

Richard Garriot is one of the most picturesque characters in the industry. The son of an astronaut, he boldly named himself "Lord British"! In 1979, he created and distributed his first game, *Akalabeth*. A publisher from California, Origin, gave him his first big break and *Ultima 1* was quickly put on the market. But the red carpet treatment really started in 1985, when *Ultima 4* was published. This was the first game to adopt a first person point of view. Notions of good and evil were also instilled into the RPG genre, giving games an emotional content, which they didn't have before. *Ultima 7* is considered to be one of the best RPGs ever created. In October 1997, *Ultima Online* marked the beginning of the Internet gaming era. Today Garriot is no longer with Origin. He is working on his next endeavor: *Lineage: The Blood Pledge*. With fans all over Korea, Taiwan and other Asian countries, it is the most popular subscriber-based online game in the world.

Hideo Kojima

MAJOR TITLES: *Metal Gear Solid 1, Metal Gear Solid 2, Zone Of the Enders* (ZOE)
GREATEST HIT: *Metal Gear Solid* (6 million copies)

Hideo Kojima is a visionary. He is the rock on which the Japanese company Konami is built. He is famous for *Metal Gear Solid 2* (MGS2). The game is sought after like crazy, particularly since the introduction of PS2. With its intuitive gameplay and its life-like graphics, the game is the best ambassador for PS2. Kojima is obsessed with details and his signature includes stylistic elements such as flow and seamlessness.

<www.mgspc.com>
<www.konami.com>

Lorne Lanning

MAJOR TITLES: *Abe's Oddysee, Abe's Exoddus, Munch's Oddysee*
GREATEST HIT: *Abe's Oddysee* (2 million copies)

Lorne Lanning put an end to his 14 year long career as a 3-D specialist in Hollywood when he decided he wanted to immerse himself in the world of interactivity. His big hope was to give freedom to his own independent, creative self. In 1994, he decided to create a company based on a virtual world, which was hilarious, yet strange and disquieting: Oddworld. Abe is the anti-hero of his first two games, *Abe's Oddysee*, and *Abe's Exoddus*. He has invented all sorts of new design tricks. For example his Alive system allows Oddworld creatures to speak. He was very successful on PlayStation and would have probably carried on from there to PS2. But as everybody knows, PS2 proved difficult to program. So he got frustrated and went directly over to Microsoft and the Xbox, which gave the Seattle giant a whole load of extra visibility. His most recent title, *Munch's Oddyssee*, was launched together with the Xbox and was successful right off.

<www.oddworld.com>

Sid Meier

MAJOR TITLES: *Railroad Tycoon, Civilization, Colonization, Civilization II, Gettysburg, Antietam, Alpha Centauri*
GREATEST HIT: *Civilization*
(4 million copies)

Sid Meier's story starts with Microprose, the company he created with Bill Stealey, a US air force pilot. He found his market niche in 1990 when he published *Railroad Tycoon*. The inspiration came from Will Wright's *SimCity*. But Meier was only flexing his muscles. He was getting ready for his most important title, *Civilization* that was to become the best strategy game of all times.

Meier demonstrated that it was possible to chose a far-ranging topic, as complex as the history of mankind, and make it accessible and entertaining. In 1996, he left Microprose and founded Firaxis. *Alpha Centauri*, another one of his projects, was also a great success. His name

on a game cover is in itself a seal of excellence: you know right off that gameplay will last for months and time will fly by, hours passing like minutes on your clock!

<www.firaxis.com>
<www.alphacentauri.com>
<www.gettysburg.ea.com>
<www.strategicgaming.com/sid/book.htm>

Shinji Mikami

MAJOR TITLES: *Resident Evils 1, 2 and 3, Dino Crisis, Devil May Cry, Resident Evil: Code Veronica*

Shinji Mikami is Capcom's genius. He invented the survival/horror genre. The impact of *Resident Evil* on the sales of Playstation One was incredible! He concocted a mix of adventure, action and puzzle games,  which raised the standards of excellence for all other developers. When most developers were happy with recycling successful recipes from the 16-bit era, simply enhancing graphics, Shinji Mikami decided to exploit the murky waters of grade B horror movies and produce the most scary interactive games of all times. The rumor spread like fire: yes, a video game could be terrifying! A new genre was born. His latest production, *Devil may cry*, became one of the best games of 2001.

Shigeru Miyamoto

MAJOR TITLES: *Donkey Kong, Mario Brothers, Super Mario Bros. I, Super Mario Bros. II, Super Mario Bros. III, Super Mario World, Super Mario 64*
GREATEST HIT: *Super Mario 64* (5.5 million copies)

Shigeru Miyamoto is one of the most powerful people in the world of console games. He invented the platform-based game and a character that has become world famous: Mario. Mario and Mario-based games are forever part of the video game culture. They are ubiquitous!

His first game, *Donkey Kong*, was an overnight success. He used scenario elements, which have become universal: side-scrolling, jumping and stomping over the enemy's head in order to score points. He developed a whole series of games which all became classics on Nintendo consoles. And all the while, the public kept asking for more. In 1995, with *Mario 64*, he brought in a new concept, the full 3-D platform game. *Zelda's Legend* was another landmark on his long trail of successes. He now devotes all his attention to the development of GameCube titles, including the rather strange looking *Pickmin*.

<www.nintendo.com>

Peter Molyneux

MAJOR TITLES: *Populous, Powermonger, Populous II, Syndicate, ThemePark, Magic Carpet, Dungeon Keeper, Black & White*
GREATEST HIT: *Populous* (4 million copies)

Peter Molyneux is one of the most successful game designers. He is the guy who invented the God Game genre.

In 1987 he had a very bright idea: give gamers the role of God! Gamers could create a world, people it with their own followers and start destroying the followers of all other rival Gods. This was a brand new sort of strategy game and the first title was: *Populous*. The majority of publishers he visited with his game said it couldn't be published because it was too different! Open-minded people at Electronic Arts saw an opportunity and decided to give it a try. They sold 4 million copies! In 1994 Molyneux's company Bullfrog came out with another game, *Theme Park*, which sold 3 million copies (it sold particularly well in Japan).

In 1995 Molyneux sold Bullfrog to Electronic Arts, making a sizable amount of money! But he did not feel quite at ease in the Electronic Arts empire. So he left Bullfrog and created a new company called Lionhead, right after he had finished *Dungeon Keeper*. He then concentrated on a new kind of game, which he described as the achievement of his lifetime: *Black and White*. It was another God game in which the forces of Good and Evil were naturally at odds. But this time they had artificial intelligence technology at their disposal.

As the gamer, you were placed in a position to educate a creature and raise it to your image, teaching it your evil or your saintly ways... This feature was immediately spotted as the most intriguing design element to have surfaced over the past few years.

<www.lionhead.com>
<www.bullfrog.co.uk>
<www.bwgame.com>
<www.black.ea.com>
<www.white.ea.com>

Yugi Naka

MAJOR TITLES: *Nights, Sonic Adventure, Phantasy Star Online*
GREATEST HIT: *Sonic Adventure* (2 million copies)

Yuji Naka is the powerful boss of the Sega Sonic Team. When he created *Sonic the Hedgehog*, he showed Nintendo that Sega could invent a popular character too!

He took everybody by surprise when he came out with a platform game, which was really much faster than the competition. With *Nights*, on Saturn, he pushed the art of design in directions that no one had explored before. He added a kind of ethereal atmosphere and showed incredible instinct for negotiating a 3-D environment.

An excellent programmer and a charismatic project manager, he delivered a number of games, which were really different from one another, such as *Chuchu Rocket* and *Samba Amigo*. In his latest creation, *Phantasy Star Online*, he mapped out totally new terri-tory, offering the first online multiplayer console game. He invented a language based on multicultural symbols. Along with the game, e-mail, chat and automatic translation services were available.

Sega is really one of the top developers in the world and the Sonic Team is right where the action is!

<www.sega.com>

Jason Rubin and Andy Gavin

MAJOR TITLES: *Crash Bandicoot 1, 2 and 3*
GREATEST HIT: *Crash Bandicoot 3* (5.7 million copies)

There was Mario and Nintendo, Sonic and Sega. But Sony didn't have a popular mascot... until *Crash Bandicoot* sold 20 million copies and became world famous. Naughty Dog's American-born character became extremely popular in Japan, which was unexpected and ... unprecedented!

When Jason Rubin and Andy Gavin announced they were ready to create a version of their mascot for Xbox, Sony made them an offer they could not refuse! Since then, the two of them have come up with *Jak & Daxter* on PS2, which was greeted with unanimous praise by the press.

Jason Rubin and Andy Gavin were 16 years old when they created *Naughty Dog*!

Joel Jewett, Mick West

MAJOR TITLES: *Tony Hawk's Pro Skater* and *Spiderman*
GREATEST HIT: *Tony Hawk's Pro Skater* (3.5 million copies)

Joel Jewett and Mick West founded Neversoft Entertainment in 1994. They invented a new game genre, a sort of mix between speed racing and radical sports, with aerial acrobatics and adrenalin rushes guaranteed. They transformed the design rule "easy to play, hard to master" into reality. Their exceptional game engine gave them a big competitive edge. *Tony Hawk's Pro Skater* became of the most prosperous licenses in the industry. Using the same game engine, they produced *Spiderman*, the first superhero game really worth mentioning.

Joel handles the business side and Mick does all the development. This team is going to go all the way to the top!

<www.neversoft.com>
<www.activision.com>
<www.activision.com/games/spiderman>

Gabe Newell

MAJOR TITLES: *Half-Life, Team Fortress*
GREATEST HIT: *Half-Life* (2,5 million units)

Gabe Newell spent 13 years inside the Systems, Applications and Technology division of Microsoft Inc., moving up from one position to another. He left the Admiral's vessel to create his own company: Valve. Two years later, in November 1998, he put his first game on the market: *Half-Life*. Published by Sierra Studios, it was an incredible success, collecting over 50 prizes including the "best PC game ever" from magazine PC Gamer.

The game combines unrelenting action with a strong, heart-wrenching storyline. Artificial intelligence is put in the hands of the enemy… so that unless you use your brainpower your chances of survival are nil!

The online version was called *Team Fortress* and it became a phenomenal success on its own. It was used by millions of gamers who thought it was really cool to get an extension for free!

<www.valvesoftware.com>
<www.gameoftheyear.com>

Scott Orr

MAJOR TITLES: The *Madden* series
GREATEST HIT: *Madden NFL 99* (2 million copies)

Scott Orr is the champ of sports games. Considering that one third of overall sales are sports games, you can well imagine why his talent is in such demand! Affiliated with Electronic Arts, he created his first *Madden* for Sega's Genesis in 1990. The *Madden* series remained at the top of the charts, probably because of its life-like design and incredible wealth of options. Orr was able to incorporate the latest developments of Artificial Intelligence and real time physics, and this has kept him one step ahead of the competition all along. Why do his fans love him and keep asking for more? Because he is very finicky, picture perfect at getting all the details right; and also because he knows how to recreate the feel and atmosphere of a popular sport.

<http://easports.ea.com>
<http://madden2001.ea.com/main.html>

David Perry

MAJOR TITLES: *Earthworm Jim, MDK, Sacrifice*

David Perry started to design and program games in 1981. He left his native Ireland for London when he was 17 and immediately started to work for a variety of companies, including Virgin.

With a major success under his arm (*Teenage Mutant Ninja Turtles)*, he moved to the US, where he received instant recognition with *Aladdin* from Disney. In 1993, he created Shiny Entertainment and came up with a mega hit: *Earthworm Jim*. The game was published for all platforms and even had its own TV show! Since then he has had one success after another, *with MDK, Messiah* and *Sacrifice*. He is one of the most famous public figures in the industry and was under the spotlight again when Shiny Entertainment won the right to produce the first game under a license everybody was trying to get: *The Matrix*.

<www.shiny.com>
<www.dperry.com>

Tim and Chris Stamper

MAJOR TITLES: *Donkey Kong Country, GoldenEye 007, Perfect Dark, Conker's Bad Fur Day*
GREATEST SUCCESS: *Donkey Kong Country* (8 million copies)

In 1982 Chris and Tim Stamper, two clever businessmen, created Ashby Computers and Graphics Limited. They went public under the name of Ultimate Play The Game. From 1983 to 1987, they produced and published over twenty successful games for the Sinclair ZX Spectrum computer and for the Commodore 64.

The two brothers created Rare, a company specializing in game development for Nintendo's NES. They created about 60 different games and quite a few of them approached the technical limits of the machine! No one, however, expected the kind of Big Bang that was heard in the game world when they published *Donkey Kong Country*.

With its new 3-D look and its fancy side-scrolling routines, Rare immediately climbed to the top of the developer box office. Nintendo bought 25% of the company's shares after which the two brothers delivered success after success: *Golden Eye, DK 64, Tooie, Perfect Dark*, and the *Banjo Kazooie* series. Rare became the best developer for Nintendo platforms. For their N64 swan song they decided to deliver the most vulgar "beer, buns and boobs" game ever! Some people may object to the hanky-panky sections in the game, but in all fairness it must be said that *Conker's Bad Fur Day* proved to be one of the best designed titles for N64. Let's hope this is what they have in mind for GameCube. An added bonus — the web site is hilarious!

<www.rareware.com>
<www.conker.com>

Hironobu Sakaguchi

Major Titles: *Final Fantasy VII, VIII, IX, X*
Greatest hit: *Final Fantasy VIII* (7 million copies)

Hironobu Sakaguchi is the CEO of Square USA. He also is the creator of one of the most popular series in history: *Final Fantasy* (called *Final Fantasy* because it was supposed to be his last game). He popularized RPG games in the US. Before PlayStation came out the RPG genre was popular almost exclusively in Japan. He is a visionary with a sense for what is aesthetically appealing. He also has a very special talent for story-telling, and for making the best of the technology he may happen to be working with. He popularized cine-matics as the cherry on the graphics pie. *Final Fantasy* set the standard for cinematography within video games. Hironobu Sakaguchi eventually decided to work for the movies and co-directed the shooting of *Final Fantasy* the film. His 3-D realism reached a level no one had ever dreamed of. He is a true multimedia artist if ever there ever was one!

<www.finalfantasy.com>
<www.squaresoft.com>

Warren Spector

MAJOR TITLES: *Ultima Underworld I-II, Wings of Glory, System Shock, Deus Ex*

Warren Spector learned his trade at TSR and Steve Jackson Games. In 1989 he was hired by Lord British himself so he could work for Origin on the *Ultima* series. He was project manager for *Ultima Underworld* in 1991 and what he did impressed John Cormak (from id Software) so much that he was asked to develop *Wolfenstein 3-D*. *Wolfenstein 3-D* marked the beginning of a new era for 3-D virtual worlds and for the advancement of 3-D in the RPG genre.

In 1995, he left Origin and started his own com-pany: Looking Glass. For all sorts of reasons, the com-pany never got anywhere. He decided to join Ion Storm's team, re-hired his ex-Looking Glass team and created a new Cyberpunk classic: *Deus Ex*. It became Ion Storm's best-seller. Warren Spector was applauded both by gamers and peers. After *Half-Life*, everybody was waiting for something new and he was the one who gave role-playing games a bit of fresh air! *Deus Ex* is clearly a game that requires a lot of mental effort on the part of gamers!

Warren Spector is now firmly in the driver's seat and, over the years to come, we can expect his creative mind to come up with striking ideas!

<www.deusex.com>
<www.ionstorm.com>
<www.origin.ea.com>

Yu Suzuki

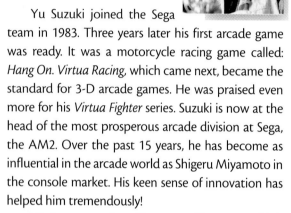

MAJOR TITLES: *Space Harrier,
Hang On, Virtua Racing, Virtua
Fighter, Shenmue*

Yu Suzuki joined the Sega
team in 1983. Three years later his first arcade game
was ready. It was a motorcycle racing game called:
Hang On. Virtua Racing, which came next, became the
standard for 3-D arcade games. He was praised even
more for his *Virtua Fighter* series. Suzuki is now at the
head of the most prosperous arcade division at Sega,
the AM2. Over the past 15 years, he has become as
influential in the arcade world as Shigeru Miyamoto in
the console market. His keen sense of innovation has
helped him tremendously!

His latest creation, *Shenmue,* offers a very high
level of immersion. The hero can move freely in a virtual world. If you want to stroll down the street, well,
go ahead and do it! Give a cat a pat on the back, buy
something at the corner store, call a friend from a public telephone booth, practice your Kung Fu routine...
do exactly what you want! You can even walk into an
arcade parlor and play with one of Suzuki's classics:
Hang On and *Space Harrier.*

<www.sega.com>

Will Wright

MAJOR TITLES: *SimCity, SimCity
2000, The Sims*
GREATEST HITS: *The Sims*
(4 million copies)

Will Wright got his start in
robotics. He then became interested in computers
and in1980, he bought an Apple II and taught himself
how to write programs. He soon found out he was
spending a lot of time on interactive games, so he
decided he wanted to create his own games!

In 1987, the first version of *Sim City* came out for
Commodore 64. Publishers didn't take the game seriously. So, with Jeff Brown, he created Maxis and published a PC version in 1989. At the beginning sales were
rather slow. Then a *Time Magazine* article got him a lot
of attention. A number of developers got really interested in this new genre. Sid Meier created and published *Railroad Tycoon* and *Civilization.* Will Wright
replied with *Sim Earth* and *Sim Ant.* Finally, *Sim City
2000* came out in 1994. It was number one on the
charts for 6 months. In 1997, he published *Sim City
3000.* Electronic Arts bought Maxis, which gave the
team an opportunity to move to the next level.

Originally, the game was a city-planning simulator. Gamers could build the houses of their dreams
and fit them into a city landscape. The game took a
new direction when characters started to settle in the
neighborhood. The focus of the game moved from
the buildings to their inhabitants. *The Sims* were born
and sales took off immediately.

Wright is working on *Sim Mars* with NASA engineers, and is also developing the online version of *The*

Sims. He also took part in the American version of *Robot Wars.* If anyone can quench our thirst for absolute control, he will!

<http://thesims.ea.com/us>

Kazunori Yamauchi

MAJOR TITLES: *Gran Turismo 1 and 2*
GREATEST HIT: *Gran Turismo 2* (3 million copies)

Let's face it, Kazunori Yamauchi reinvented the racing game! His *Gran Turismo* series first appeared on PlayStation. With a choice of 150 cars and a smart mix of action and realism, it soon won universal acclaim. Cars all have different specs. The real time physics engine works from those specs and calculates road grip accordingly. He offered an option, which everybody copied right away: the aerial race replay. With *Gran Turismo,* force-feedback driving wheels have enjoyed soaring sales!

An online version is in the works for *Gran Turismo 3.*

<www.scea.com/games/categories/racing/Gt3>

Rising stars

It is getting more and more difficult to convince a multinational firm to give you millions of dollars to make your dream come true! The industry keeps repeating that "content is king". But there are lots of good ideas. The difficulty lies in turning them into products, on time and on budget. A new generation of designers and busi-

ness leaders is coming of age and the situation they now face is radically different from what was going on only a few years back. The industry has entered a rationalization phase: pretenders must now double their efforts, put on the charm, work fast and... deliver.

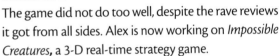

Alex Garden

In 1999, Alex Garden and his company Relic Entertainment produced *Homeworld* for Sierra Studios. The game did not do too well, despite the rave reviews it got from all sides. Alex is now working on *Impossible Creatures,* a 3-D real-time strategy game.

<www.relic.com>

Dennis Hassabis

Dennis co-created Theme Park with a famous partner, Peter Molyneux. He established his own firm in 1998 and started to develop *Republic: the Revolution,* an ambitious project that won the runner-up award for "Best Strategy Game" at E3 2001.

<www.elixir-studios.co.uk>

American McGee

American McGee was doing technical support for id Software when he decided he wanted to become a game designer. He designed a few levels for *Doom* and *Quake,* which won him a mass of followers.

In 1998, he joined Electronic Arts and produced a gothic version of *Alice in Wonderland*. The game received a lot of attention. Hollywood wants to shoot the movie version. Horror movie director Wes Craven is now working on it and the tentative release date is 2003.

<www.alice.ea.com>

Masaya Matsuura

Masaya Matsuura is one of the happy few who invented a new game genre. With *PaRappa the Rapper* and its sequel *UmJammer Lammy*, he launched the current fad for musical games. If having lots of imitators is a sure sign of flattery, well then Masaya Matsuruura is being flattered by people from all over the world!

<www.scea.com/games/
categories/stratpuzzle/parappa2>

Neil Young

Neil Young presided over the launch of Squaresoft's *Ultima Online*. In July 2001, he was back at it again, this time with *Majestic* for Electronic Arts. *Majestic* is turning the tables on gamers for good! Instead of the gamer having to control the characters, he has to react to messages actually sent to him by the various characters via e-mail, fax, or telephone. The gamer can be asked to go to different web sites and retrieve vital information... including short videos taken by hidden web cams! The more you play, the more you are being played! The whole experienced was scrapped by EA when a fraction of the initial downloaders actually finished the initial offering. A slew of ideas introduced in *Majestic* will undoubtedly find their way into a new generation of games.

<www.majestic.ea.com>

Kings

Hiroshi Yamauchi

In the good old days when Nintendo's main product was game cards, Hiroshi Yamauchi was already President. He created the Nintendo empire as we now know it. Like a true master, he runs the company with a hand of steel. Those who cross his path and want to fight it out with him learn soon enough how tough he can be. For example, he never forgave Squaresoft's decision to move its *Final Fantasy* series over to PlayStation. When Squaresoft asked if they could publish their titles on GameCube and GameBoy Advance, M. Yamauchi's answer was a fierce and final "No"!

His public comments are always terse, blunt, to the point... and they can be nasty. The Japanese press is always ready to quote a man whose words cause regular uproars and scandals. You want to know why this book does not carry his photograph? Because he hates to see pictures of himself... and I am not about to cross swords with him!

<www.nintendo.com>

Ken Kutaragi

PlayStation was Sony's biggest success since the Walkman. It accounts for 40% of their business revenues. Ken Kutaragi had been dreaming about it for 20 years. He tried like mad to convince Sony that his vision was right and he had to fight tooth and nail to get an OK on his project.

In 1982 Sony, Philips and Panasonic made an attempt to rally the market around a common standard called MSX. It was a big flop. The timing was wrong: this was exactly when the video game crisis started to hit the industry.

In 1993, Ken finally got an OK from Sony. They created Sony Computer Entertainment and Ken was named vice-president of research and development. In December 1994 his project became a real product. He was aiming at an older age group than Sega and Nintendo, but this was a well calculated risk. With 80 million PlayStations sold, he knows he was right! The PS2 is his most recent success. The PS3 is currently under development and so is the Gscube. Delivering mammoth power equivalent to 16 PS2s, it will run real time, full-screen, film quality games. Imagine Toy Story or Shrek on running on a console! Ken has been named President of Sony Computer Entertainment and no one can stop him!

<www.playstation.com>
<www.sony.com>

W. M. Hawkins III

W.M.Hawkins is one of the founding fathers of the industry. At 48, he has already spent 28 years in the business. A techno geek from his early teens onwards, he was one of the first 50 employees of Apple Inc. He left Apple in 1982 and established Electronic Arts, the biggest independent video game company in the world.

With 3DO, he was part of the giant effort made by American companies to gain a share of the console market. His technology was not successful but he managed to sell it to Panasonic. Panasonic never did anything with it! He owns 27% of 3DO.

He now has become a technology agnostic, creating games for every possible platform. He strongly believes that the future of the interactive game is on the Internet.

<www.3DO.com>

The Xbox Team

Microsoft's hopes rest on the shoulders of a team of wizards. There is Seamus Blackley, technical director; J. Allard, development manager; Ed Fries, in charge of publishing and Robbie Bach, senior vice-president for the game division, acting as general manager.

3DO represented the last American attempt at gaining a share of the console market. It failed rather miserably. But this time Microsoft seems to be poised for success: it has the human resources, the talent and the marketing clout to create market room for Xbox.

<www.xbox.com>

Ed Fries

Ed Fries started his career at Microsoft in 1985. 10 years later, he was in charge of the game division, with 700 programmers, artists and developers working for him. He is the one who hired Chris Roberts (from Digital Anvil), Bruce Shelley (from Ensemble Studios), Chris Taylor (from Gas Powered Games), Alex Garden (from Relic Entertainment) and more recently Brian Reynolds from

Big Huge Entertainment. With all these new highly talented recruits, Microsoft has become a major player in the game business.

Ed Fries adopted the same strategy to build the Xbox team… and it worked!

J. Allard

The first thing he did when Microsoft decided they wanted their share of the game market was to descend to the grassroots level and ask developers what sort of toys they wanted. J. Allard, as development manager not only provides developers with the bag of tools they need, but also is on the look-out for third party companies which will create games for Xbox. For 9 years, he developed the company's Internet strategy, pushing for the mass adoption of TCP/IP and the Web. In 1999 he decided to return to his first love: video games. He is well known for his collection of consoles, including the Odyssey, which spurred him to study computer science.

Robert J. Bach

Bach is the big boss of the Xbox team. He succeeded in seducing more than 200 independent developers, including Electronic Arts. 18 companies are going to publish games under the Microsoft trademark. From 1996 to 1998, Bach was President of the Learning, Entertainment and Productivity division of Microsoft. Before that he was Marketing Vice President for the Microsoft Office suite. He joined Microsoft in 1988, leaving his position as financial analyst at Morgan Stanley & Co. With his BA in Economics from the University of North Carolina and his MA in Business Management from Stanford, you can see that Microsoft did not really risk much when they appointed him senior vice president of the Games Division and Chief Xbox Officer.

Seamus Blackley

Seamus is considered one of the fathers of the Xbox. As chief of the Advanced Technology Group (ATG) and as Xbox Technology Officer, his mission is to allow creators to turn their dreams into reality without compromise. In his view, technology must not stand in the way of programmers, musicians or game designers. He is the kind of guy who can play the piano or talk about particle physics with equal ease and talent, so he feels very comfortable with both developers and Microsoft brass. He did work for a couple of Physics Research Centers and designed a few games for Looking Glass, writing the music and the software code. Among them were *System Shock* and *Flight Unlimited*, which eventually won prizes! He was an executive producer for Spielberg's DreamWorks when he met Bill Gates. Bill made him an offer no one could refuse. He sees Xbox as a tool to free the imagination and help artists invent a more beautiful world.

We cannot mention each and every creative mind that ever worked for the industry. But I can say one thing: putting a game on the market is a heck of a difficult task! A task fit for Hercules! So my admiration goes out to all those who were bold enough to try and strong enough to get to the finish line. If you don't see what I mean, give it a try yourself and you will get the point!

8.
Jobs

A brand new economic sector

I n 2000, according to IDSA, the American economy generated 220,000 jobs linked to the video game industry. That meant 9 billion in salaries. The growth rate is 14.9%, twice as fast as the overall economy. Salaries have gone up 17.4% and job offers 10.1%. From small companies to multinational firms, there seems to be no end to the upswing, and that translates into interesting jobs for aspiring artists, young programmers and game designers.

In the beginning video games weren't the sort of activity you could turn into a career. Passion was the key. Entrepreneurs and programmers worked in their basement, in their bedrooms or in their garages. Of course, some of the products weren't exactly professional. There were bugs here and there and quality was uneven. But the cream of the crop was able to generate a lot of money and the industry was able to grow very quickly.

In 1982 Trip Hawkins created Electronic Arts with the clear intention of rationalizing the creation process. He set up a number of design studios and coordinated them all. For the first time there was a company with a business plan and the means to meet a well-defined end.

Over the next decade the industry became a very appealing business proposition, and it is still expanding today. Publishers got organized and the administrative process of writing contracts, protecting legal rights and fighting piracy started rolling. What we have seen over the past few years: big companies buying up smaller ones, as has often occurred over the past few years, is a regular part of market consolidation

New ideas and new blood will always be welcome. The best concepts are quite often generated at the bottom of the corporate ladder, or by small, fast-foot-ed companies. *Half-Life* was created by diminutive Valve Inc., not by Havas Inc. the giant! Lara Croft was invented by Tony Gard, not by top management at Eidos.

Companies all want to scout the next Peter Molyneux, the next Carmack and the next Miyamoto. Creativity being the essence of the market, stagnation is the most frightening foe.

I have put together a list and a description of the major kinds of jobs available in the industry. Salaries may vary a lot from one company to another, or from on position to another. But if money is the primary cause for your interest in this new industrial sector, you're probably looking out the wrong window.

IGDA recently published a salary survey. You can download it at:

<www.igda.org/Endeavour/ Research/Salary/salary.htm>

Programmer/Software engineer

Computer code is the backbone of all video games. Everything depends on the software architecture and everything eventually boils down to lines of code: the 3-D engine, the real-time physics engine, the AI and whatever is needed to bring players to a game's

logical conclusion. The mission of a good software engineer is to make sure all the software components work together at the best possible speed, using the best available tools. Balancing complexity and efficiency is a very demanding task. The industry is always looking for new bright minds.

A good knowledge of C and C++ is essential. As soon as PS2 appeared on the market, programming at Assembler level became very much in demand. A good knowledge of the Windows environment and of Direct X is also part of the deal.

You must be good at math and physics, and if you know expert systems and 3-D engines, you are right on track. Remember to develop your debugging skills. Debugging is what you may end up doing in your first job as a junior.

You will move up to more gratifying tasks such as AI programming and rule-based physic engines. And after you have delivered a few games on time, you may become lead programmer or senior programmer. Some programmers will become project managers then producers, and as such, they will have to oversee all aspects of game development.

If you want to try your hand at it, here is a good opportunity: the developers of *No one lives for ever*, a big hit with critics of the PC video game market, have decided to make the source code available to the community at large.

<www.noonelivesforever.com/downloads>
<www.gamasutra.com/features/
index_programming.htm>
<www.gamedev.net/reference/start_here/>
<www.flipcode.com>

Don't rush to the Game Programming Starter Kit 5.0 right away. Start with the 125 interviews published by Marc Saltzman in his book: *Game Design / Secrets of the Sages*. These people are the most successful designers in the industry and their advice is worth a million bucks. Then try your hand at 3-D Game Studio Standard 5.12. It has a library of 3-D objects and a lot of user-friendly design routines. If you know your computer science well enough, get Microsoft's Visual C++

6.0 and polish the background images and characters you just produced. SDK's *Direct X 8.0* and the CD version of *Tricks of the Windows Game Programming Gurus* can also be added to your list. After you have practiced with them for a while, you will certainly gain a better appreciation of the professional designers who build the games you play all the time!

An insider's point of view: Daniel Martin

Daniel Martin is lead software engineer at Tiburon, an Electronic Arts studio located in Florida. He works on the *Madden Football* series and, year after year, he and his team have to outdo themselves to keep the game at the top of the charts.

After getting both a Bachelor and Masters degree in computer science, he experimented in different fields: business, research, support, multimedia, consulting, web, etc. Being a gamer all his life, he finally gave in to his true calling: developing games.

How did you get your job?

Getting in the industry may be tough, but for me it was mostly a matter of psyching myself up.

I was trained as a traditional computer scientist. In the circles where I evolved, programming games for a living was mostly viewed as a waste of time, skills, and energy. Compounding the problem was the fact that the game industry was virtually non-existent in French Canada in the early 80's.

After occupying many positions and working my way up the ladder, I came to realize that something was "missing". I was unhappy and dissatisfied, but couldn't really say why.

This really compelled me to take a hard look at the situation and decide on a course of action. The whole process took me about three years. As a result, I wrote down a mission statement: "I want to lead a top-ten game for a successful company in a team of high-skilled people I enjoy working with, where I can learn and be challenged." Then I defined an action plan: brush up specific skills, research the industry, target companies, and go to the GDC.

When all was in place, getting a job was surprisingly easy. Walking down an aisle of the GDC job fair, Tiburon's resource manager asked me "How would you like to work in Florida?" I took the entry-level position they offered me, sold nearly everything I owned and moved to the states. The rest is history!

Describe a typical day at the office

Although programmers seem to be staring at computer code day in day out, our days and tasks are varied. Depending on your level of responsibility and where you are in the development cycle, a programmer can be planning, researching, prototyping, designing, testing, debugging, coding, documenting, etc.

As a lead, a sizeable amount of your time is also devoted to management. Depending on the company, this may include code reviews, training, interviews, performance reviews, project planning, etc.

Contrary to popular belief, programmers will often spend a significant amount of time interacting with various members of the team, from artists to designers.

The only days that might be branded "typical" in my job usually occur during crunch time, which is the period just before we release a game. This is a frantic and very difficult time where everyone works long hours, often seven days a week. Here's what one of these days looks like:

I get up, and go to the office. On my way, I stop by the testers' area, and chat with my lead testers to see what important issues came up during the night shift.

I stop by the office kitchen, grab some food and head to my computers. While eating, I rebuild the game with the latest fixes, consult my mail and bug tracking system. I meet with my managers and go over our team's priorities for the day.

Then I start fixing bugs, beginning with the most urgent ones. Seniors and leads also act as "guides" to help troubleshoot different areas of the game whenever someone is stuck.

From 2 to 4 p.m. I usually work out at the gym. Then around 6 we have a team dinner. After another meeting between management and testers, the rest of the evening and part of the night is spent debugging, chatting with the testers, and helping other teammates.

What are the bright and the dark sides of your work?

Among the bright sides. First: the fans. Often I go to game stores and stand beside fans while they play and enjoy the game. There is something so gratifying about the fact that your work can generate such pure fun for people.

It also warms my heart to see people's reaction when they discover I'm one of the programmers behind *Madden*. More often than not, they become quite animated, with big bright eyes full of passion, and tell me how much they enjoy the game and recall the long hours they played.

Second: the team. Game development is hard work, harder than anything I've done before. People who stay and thrive in this industry are incredibly talented and motivated. They are gamers like me, and are passionate about it. They are the best colleagues you could ask for.

Third: the rewards. Working for one of the best game franchises within EA offers great advantages. Employees are treated to boat cruises, cinema openings, parties, lots of games, free food, bonuses, etc. The rewards always try to match the amount of effort everyone puts in.

The down sides. Shipping at least three games a year requires an incredible amount of work. Long hours, stress, crazy schedules are hard on everyone. Game development is especially hard on relationships and families — only very few people truly understand the dedication and commitment it takes to make a game.

Game development is maturing. Similar to the movie industry, games are fast becoming multi-million dollar productions. There is very little space or money left for small developers or individuals with "cool" new ideas.

Any advice to the young aspirant?

After reading what I just said, they should have a pretty good idea of what's in store for them.

Common traits in the successful programmers I work with are basically that they are all passionate, dedicated, hard working people who, despite their overwhelming abilities, have remained humble and extraordinarily efficient team players. Of course, they are all gamers at heart as well! However, this profile may change from company to company.

Still want to break into the game industry? Make a plan, develop your skills, build a demo or portfolio, target companies you like and apply for a job.

You've always wanted to work for [enter your favorite game studio name here]? If your dream position is offered and they accept you the first time around, great! However, most likely they will require [insert insane number of] years of pertinent experience, on things you either never heard of or vaguely remember.

Scale back and try again in a less skilled or totally different position. If that doesn't work, try getting in through a back door – like testing or QA. A lack of experience is your worst enemy. Break in, any way you can.

Although it took me three years to get in the industry, I could probably have shortened that delay. I rejected two previous offers at renowned studios. At the time, I wasn't willing to accept a pay cut, start at a junior level, or not work directly on the game code. Without experience, the perfect job never showed up for me. The moment I gave up all my demands, swallowed my pride and accepted to start over, I found my way into the industry.

Once you are in, the real challenge starts. You will need to excel at everything you do. You'll need to go above and beyond anything they may expect from you. Either people will notice, and you will be rewarded, or you will have acquired experience and be in a position to land a better job elsewhere.

An insider's point of view: Jake Simpson

This is how Jake describes himself: "Jake Simpson is a jobbing games programmer. He's been in this business, off and on, since the mid eighties. He's worked on everything from the Sinclair Spectrum to the Current PC, with stops on Commodore 64, Amiga, Atari ST and Gameboy along the way. He's in his mid thirties, and currently works for Maxis out on the west coast, doing interesting things with People Simulators. Before that, he worked on Arcade machines for Midway and First Person shooters for Raven Software. He's British, drinks lots of beer, and thinks Americans don't use enough U's in their spelling."

How did you get your job?

I got into the industry very young by hanging out with some of the industry types I admired, at computer shows in London. I used to talk to Jeff Minter from Lamasoft, who was my hero at the time. Here was a man in control of his own destiny, and I liked the idea of that. Of course these days it's not so easy; it's not all one man companies like it was back then. But still, unfortunately in this industry as much as any other, who you know can help. From meeting Jeff, I went to learning Assembly language by myself, coding up some small games and demos and hanging out in computer stores meeting people who were "in the industry". Whenever possible, I showed them what I had been working on, and generally tried to make myself memorable. Eventually it paid off with an offer

to work for a conversion house for a year. So I did. And that was the start for me.

Describe a typical day at the office

A typical day in the office is me getting there around 9. I tend to spend an hour going through e-mails and checking out several websites I frequent. Then I spend half an hour shutting down all the pop up windows that seem to arrive from the websites I visit. By this time, there is usually a meeting in the offing, so I'll spend time at that, or I'll get into the code I am working on. Usually it's tidying up stuff that I either didn't complete the day before, or fixing stuff I had completed but others had found bugs in. Then it's lunchtime, so it's either off doing chores, or lunch with some of the team. After lunch, I get down to it. For me, this is when the meat of what I do gets chewed. I'll try as much as I can to put on headphones, shut down Trillian (my chat program) and just get into it. If I'm in the zone, time will pass and I'll have no idea of it. By 7 I begin to get hungry, so I'll decide it's time to get something to eat. Depending on what is going on, I may go home at this point and do something in the evening (it's important to have a life beyond work!) or if I'm totally in the zone, I'll stick around and keep doing what I'm doing. Note: all through the day copious amounts of tea are being drunk. I'm British and I have to maintain some stereotypes. Besides, tea has more caffeine than coffee.

What are the bright and the dark sides of your work?

The bright sides of this job involve working with some incredibly creative people, working with people who are far smarter and more experienced than you are, so you can learn lots. You get to work on something that's big enough to appeal to the masses, yet small enough that you can see your individual impact on the project. When someone in an interview says, "Yeah, I really enjoyed game X, especially the part where..." and it's something you worked on, there is a real sense of satisfaction. You aren't just a small cog in a big machine. You get to bring entertainment to people, and express yourself in new and varying ways. Repeatedly.

The down sides often involve clueless management who often just don't "get" what you are working on. They often want carbon copies of games that have already sold, since they know they can sell that. Often they want it yesterday, and have no idea of the creative energy required to produce what we do. Then there's the work. Creating something new is a hard process. It requires time, dedication, belief in yourself, and the discipline to walk away from something that doesn't work. And that last one is particularly hard, if you've just spent a year working on it. When the end of the project draws near, crunch mode rears it's head. That's when you work 16 hours a day, 7 days a week, for about 2-3 months. All projects have this to some degree, and it's grueling. But that's part of the job. So be prepared to say goodbye to loved ones, friends, having a social life and getting any sleep when crunch time rolls around.

Any advice to the young aspirant?

Advice for aspiring game developers? Well, there's several things that come to mind. Firstly, if you want this bad enough, you will get it. It just depends on what sacrifices you are prepared to make. As with anything, there's a price to pay. But if it's what you're dreaming of, then you'll find ways to make it happen.

Practical advice: have something to show. Work on a demo, or a mod for *Quake / Unreal Tournament* or something. Nothing says "I can do this" to a prospective employer as much as having done it. Being able to comment intelligently on the development process from the perspective of having done it is a huge asset from a company's point of view. Don't expect to be driving a Ferrari overnight. We all pay our dues. It's not like John Carmack or Tim Sweeny decided one day to make a game, and a week later they were swimming in money. They paid their dues, did their research just like the rest of us. It sucks to start at the bottom, but unless your dad is financing the company, that's where you'll begin. Accept that and make sure you learn from those around you.

Play games. Play a lot of games. Learn what it is that is successful about any given game, and what isn't. Being able to describe what was good about a game both impresses at interview time, and is also a very helpful tool when developing a new game concept; it just saves time not having to re-invent the wheel.

Don't be afraid to e-mail some of the luminaries in the industry. Sure, most won't reply (they are busy people) but some might. It never hurts to have a friend in a high place. And finally, keep plugging away. Don't give up. We've all been turned down at some point for something we thought we were perfect for. Sometimes we were right, other times not. That's life. Accept it, find out why you weren't successful, and do something about it. Good luck!

Graphic Artist/Art director

Everything you see in a game, from the very beginning onwards, is the creation of a graphic artist: company logos, cinematics, the intro… they are the pieces of the iceberg you can't possibly miss. Graphic artists are there to convey the vision of the game designer. They must be super sensitive and develop a lot of flair.

No surprise, every one is expecting you to have talent! Just like programmers, graphic artists must have several arrows in their quiver. Eventually you might specialize in 3-D modeling, animation or texture design. 3-D tools are expensive but there a few free packages, like the amazing Blender.

Make no mistake, the principles underlying 3-D packages are all the same. The way they are presented or the way they are applied may be different, but that's all. 3-D Studio Max, from Montreal's Discreet Logic is the reigning champion, and you will be expected to know how to use it. Softimage, Alias/Wavefront and Lightscape share the rest of the market.

Never underestimate the power of a picture. It is often an innate talent to create a forceful image: either you have it or you don't! The same is true for animation. Having some experience with 2-D is also advisable. Photoshop and Ilustrator are the top two packages. A university course in the Arts can help a lot too, but sooner or later, you will have to know how to express yourself with a set of 3-D design tools.

<www.turbosquid.com>
<www.gamasutra.com/features/index_visual_arts.htm>

An insider's point of view: Paul Steed

Paul Steed started working in the games industry at Origin in 1991. After working on *Strike Commander*, *Privateer*, *Bioforge* and *Wing Commander III* and *IV*, he joined Iguana Entertainment and Virgin Interactive for a while before becoming a modeler and animator for id Software. He has now joined the web game company Wild Tangent as a producer.

How did you get your job?

I started my career at Origin Systems in Austin, Texas, after answering a newspaper ad for "fantasy artist wanted". I was fortunate enough to work with Richard Garriott and Chris Roberts. After being hired to sketch game design ideas, I quietly worked my way up to Art Director. The rest, as they say, is history.

Describe a typical day at the office

Get to work by 11:00, work until 13:00. Check mail. Go to lunch for an hour or so then go back to the computer. Normally, I quit around 01:00 or 02:00.

What are the bright and the dark sides of your work?

The bright side is all the women that follow me around and ambush me in my Lamborghini. Just kidding. Actually, the bright side is not doing anything else. Even though I've been making games for 10 years now, I didn't touch a mouse until I was 27. That makes me 10 years older than the average developer and much less socially challenged than my typical developer brethren. I love my job because it challenges me everyday and I appreciate how lucky I am to be in such an exciting and creative industry.

The down side is, with notoriety or fame of any sort, comes a weird familiarity expressed by complete strangers who think they know you through an interview or plan file. There's also the pressure to continually make a better game but that really isn't such a bad thing, is it?

Any advice to the young aspirant?

Just do it. Pick up a reference book, tutorial or written book like my "Modeling a character in 3DS Max" and teach yourself how to be a better 3-D artist. Don't lie around and dream about being a developer or complain about not having an opportunity. Everyone I know (including myself) who is a "known" person in the industry is self-taught. We put in hours upon hours perfecting our craft because we love what we do and strive to improve. If you wait for someone to teach you anything, then you'll be waiting a long time. If you already know a lot, then teach someone else. Sharing methods and techniques shines a light and illuminates things (good and bad) you'd otherwise never see.

Game Designer

In our interactive culture, game designers are comparable to rock stars… the same aura, the same glory! Well, maybe not exactly the same. Girls, for example, don't rave about game designers half as much!

We imagine designers to be forever playing with high-falutin' concepts and ideas. We're wrong!

The first stage, for any game, is rather simple: a few pages describing the basic concept, pointing out what makes your idea original. The emphasis will be on the USPs (unique selling points). This is called the "design treatment".

If your design treatment is accepted, then you will have to produce the reference document for your game. And this is where the job starts getting really tough. Every single second in the game will have to be described in terms of character design, screen interface, controls, game level, etc.

This document will be updated all along the production process, when design ideas are confronted with technical limits and test results. The designer must have a good attitude, lots of patience and a great ability to sell his vision to the graphic artists and the programmers on the team.

You have to be a rabid gamer... but not for fun! You must analyze the strengths and the weaknesses of your game and come to understand, from within, what works well and what doesn't. With your level editor, you will create your own maps. Nothing will work better for you than creating a couple of levels that work fine. Employers love ideas that work!

You will need passing knowledge of the standard production tools, from 3-D modeling environments to computer languages. Read books in every direction: you never know when quantum physics, astronomy or nanotechnologies may add extra interest to one of your games!

The title of the book: *Game Design: Secrets of the Sages*, may sound a bit romantic, but it contains loads and loads of expert advice from 125 game designers. This is a book you want to read!

<www.gamedev.net>
<www.gamasutra.com/features/index_game_design.htm>

A game designer may want to start working as a freelancer, or may prefer working for a well-known company. Either approach may lead to the top and turn you into a media mogul!

Here are two case studies...

An insider's point of view: American McGee

American McGee was doing technical support for id Software when he decided he wanted to become a game designer. He designed a few levels for *Doom* and *Quake*, which won him a lot of followers. In 1998, he joined Electronic Arts and produced a gothic version of Alice in Wonderland. The game received a lot of attention. Hollywood now wants to shoot the movie version.

How did you get your job?

Luck. I lived next door to John Carmack. We became friends, I was given a chance to work at id Software, took it, did well, kept moving. Have since managed to leap from challenge to challenge and have had a bit of fun along the way.

Describe a typical day at the office

The days are mixed business and creative. Some days we're out pitching projects, talking with development teams, meeting with movie studios, and forming relationships with strategic partners in the film, tv, comic, music, toy, and publishing worlds. Other days we're hunkered down in the house trying our best to ignore the outside world while we work on driving the creative process on our various projects. In either case we're usually up with the sun and working as late as we can. We're always excited by what the new day will bring and have been pleased with all the success we've had thus far.

What are the bright and the dark sides of your work?

This is a hard question to answer because there are so many bright sides and almost no down sides. I think my favorite part about what I do is that I get to be creative across so many different boundaries. I get to meet extremely talented people and figure out how to pool our collective abilities into worthwhile and rewarding projects. My biggest disappointment has been, and will probably always be, the lack of vision present in most of the "exec" types we meet at the big publishing houses, movie studios, and other "creative institutions".

Any advice to the young aspirant?

How about a favorite quote? "Dream as if you'll live forever, live as if you'll die tomorrow." Don't know who said that, but apply it to everything you do and you'll do well... and possibly die young — but happy.

The Independent approach

An insider's point of view: François Dominic Laramée

This is how Dominic Laramée describes himself: François Dominic Laramée has plagued the game industry for almost a decade, finagling his way into a variety of short-lived jobs as studio head, producer, designer and programmer, until he ran out of luck and was forced to become a (mostly starving) freelancer three years ago. He is in no way responsible for the success of the more than 20 console, PC, online and board games for which he claims unwarranted credit,  and should never have been allowed to edit Charles River Media's upcoming book *Game Design Methods* or to publish his insane ramblings in over 35 articles and book chapters. Visit his mediocre web site, but read at your own risk.

<http://pages.infinit.net/idjy>

How did you get your job?

I was a programmer first. Then, in 1992, I started a company that was doing "Play-by-mail". This is when I got involved in game design. After that, I held a few positions as development manager or production manager. And for the past three years, I have been doing freelance work in the field.

Describe a typical day at the office

For a designer, there is no such thing as a typical day. The workload may include a few hours of writing, some brainstorming, programming a prototypical version, studying board games or computer games from a variety of companies. Some time may also be spent explaining the intricacies of a game to a team of programmers, or testing a game and making sure the gameplay is as exciting on screen as it is on paper.

What are the bright and the dark sides of your work?

This is the kind of work that requires a real passion for detail. A design document can be 150 to 200 page long, and it is constantly being updated. You have to be well organized. Also, you need good communication skills to describe your design elements. And of course, if you have good ideas, which are technically feasible from a graphic or programming point of view, well… that certainly doesn't hurt! There is one key skill: being able to estimate how long it will take to accomplish this or that part of the global workload. This is really crucial.

Another thing: don't fall in love with your own ideas. 90% of what is good in a project never makes it to implementation. The difference between a game that makes money and a game that is too expensive to produce often depends on the number details the designer agrees to eliminate before it is too late.

You must master the basics of computer pro-gramming, art directing, text writing and editing. You must be able to handle the day-to-day chores of a project manager. A good designer is the guy who can be efficient at any stage or level in the production process, so he can be sure deadlines will be met.

Any advice to the young aspirant?

Get yourself a good education. Read widely. Games are moving away from the sacred "Star Trek/Alien/Lord of the Rings" circle!

Project manager/producer

It is customary to say that ideas come easily. What is difficult is to implement them. Implementation is the project manager's responsibility. He must deliver on time and on budget. No less. The job is so risky that is has been compared to jumping off a plane with a piece of string and a roll of material and sewing up a parachute on the way down!

The real challenge is to coordinate everybody's tasks smoothly. A good producer has a keen sense of what is important and what is not. He has a thorough understanding of every single task performed down the production trail. Communication skills are extremely important: eventually, the project manager is the person who will have to decide which sacred cow gets sacrificed for the sake of the almighty dollar! He also knows that he will get the ax if the project lags behind or goes over budget. This is not an easy job.

The required skills may vary from one company to another, but usually include the ability to know exactly where the project stands, at any given time; and the capacity to anticipate difficulties, so they can be solved upstream, before they change the course of the project. There is another task that project man-agers must be skillful at: keeping everybody well informed while the train is barreling down the track!

In other words, as project manager, you must be familiar with lots of games, have a good understanding of the industry and talk regularly to people in the business.

<www.gamasutra.com/features/ index_production.htm>

An insider's point of view: Denis Lacasse

Denis Lacasse got his MBA from HEC in Montreal. He worked for a while at the Montreal Computer Science Research Center, managing projects. In 1998, he landed a job at Behavior Interactive, which is now called Artificial Mind & Movement (A2M). He produced three games in three years and today, as a senior producer, is in charge of all company projects.

How did you get your job?

I had always been a gamer and I wanted to get into the industry somehow. I thought it would be a good idea to manage computer projects before I applied for jobs as a video game producer. Right after my MBA, I started doing project management for a computer science center. A few years later, I found this ad in the paper, applied for the job and that was it!

Describe a typical day at the office

There are two aspects to a producer's job. One is straight management. You plan out what needs to be done, you do quality assessment, you hold meetings with the team and deal with various priorities. You go around, meet everyone and make sure they have what they need to get the job done. And of course, you make sure the project keeps on track and on schedule.

The second aspect is dealing with people outside the company. At A2M, the producer interfaces with the publisher. The publisher, as you know, will duplicate and market the product. He is also the person who has the final say on everything. So it is very important to maintain a strong relationship with him. Our product must meet his expectations. When the project is based on a license, I must also make sure that the licensee is happy. Normally, the publisher talks to the licensee. But the producer does not want to take any chances. He does not want to see the licensee refuse the product! So he keeps the publisher and the licensee well informed and makes sure he gets their approval.

In publishing companies, the producer will also have to work with the marketing team and the consumer goods department, etc.

What are the bright and the dark sides of your work?

Delivering the product on time, that's gratifying! I know most people like to see their name in the credits. But what really turns me on is when a project is moving nicely forward and everything just rolls. When the team-spirit is bright and sunny, oh boy, does that feel good!

The down side is that I am much less of a gamer now than I was before. I don't have time any more!

Any advice to the young aspirant?

Get yourself a University degree. There are many related fields to choose from: computer science (with lots of math or 3-D design), film making, creative writing, graphic arts, etc. Get some expertise in management too; and polish your interpersonal skills.

Also, make sure you finish what you start. Any one who stops before it's over is not the person we are looking for. And finally, read a lot. Get involved with painting, sculpture, politics, foreign affairs… The wider your scope, the more valuable you are to a company like ours.

Musician

Wipeout on PS1 gave music tracks a boost. After *Wipeout*, interest in video game music took off. It is true that when games started to be published on CD-rom, lots of data became available for music files and quality increased significantly. The era of silly little tunes driving you crazy for thirty minutes was finally over! The sound track for Metroid was a little gem, I must admit.

New tools have become available for music composition. With Direct Music Producer you can compose pieces like Peter and the Wolf (if you have Prokofiev's talent!) where characters all have their own little melody. There will be a time when every single character in a game will come with a tune attached. And each of these personal tunes will fuse nicely with the general sound track. Give it a couple more years and music budgets will double or triple.

Direct Music's Producer web page:

<http://msdn.microsoft.com/library/default.asp?url=/library/enus/dmusprod/htm/directmusicproducer.asp?frame=true>

At home, you will need a PC, a sound card and a MIDI sequencer. Use a keyboard if you like to play and compose. But a keyboard is not always necessary: you can build an entire soundtrack from digital samples.

There is a whole load of software packages available. The most popular are Cubase VST, Sound Forge, Cool Edit Pro and Pro Tools. There is one called Acid that lets you perform miracles!

A classical music background will certainly help, but your potential clients will always judge you on your final product. The digital musician is a composer/arranger/technician all in one. This is a job for a one-man orchestra who loves high-tech equipment! As for the pay, it depends a lot on your negotiating skills.

<www.vgmusic.com>
<www.planetquake.com/voxfeminae>
<www.gamasutra.com/features/
index_sound_and_music.htm>

An insider's point of view: Tommy Tallarico

Tommy Tallarico is the most successful video game composer in history. Tallarico and his team have won over 20 industry awards for best video game soundtrack, and have worked on over 200 games totaling over 50 million units sold and grossing over 2 billion dollars in revenue! Tallarico was the first musician to release a video game soundtrack worldwide (Tommy Tallarico's Greatest Hits Vol. 1 – Capitol

Records). He has released five soundtrack albums since. In his spare time Tommy is the host, writer and co-producer of the worldwide weekly video game television show, The Electric Playground. Aside from being syndicated internationally, the television show airs daily in prime time on the Discovery network and MTV Canada.

<www.elecplay.com>

How did you get your job?

I'm originally from Springfield, Massachusetts. When I was a kid I always wanted to move to Southern California to be a musician (doesn't everybody!). Anyway, when I turned 21, I left Mass. and drove cross country to Southern California. The only thing I really knew out here was Hollywood, so I drove to Hollywood. I didn't have a place to stay, didn't know anybody, didn't have a job, and oh yeah, I didn't have any money!

So I showed up in Hollywood, took a look around and said, "What the hell is this!" For those of you who have been to Hollywood, you know what I'm talking about. Hollywood isn't exactly the way they portray it on TV! The only other thing I knew in California was Disneyland, so I stopped some bum on the street and asked him where Mickey Mouse lived. He directed me about 45 minutes south to Orange County. When I got to Orange County, I said "Now this is more like it!" So I picked up a newspaper and I got a job the very next day selling keyboards at the Guitar Center.

I was sleeping either in my car or on Huntington Beach at this point, so I was looking for anything I could find. I knew about music and keyboards and what the hell! The next day I started and believe it or not, the very first person to walk in the store who I waited on happened to be a producer for a new software company starting up called Virgin Mastertronic. I've loved music my whole life, I've been playing piano since I was 3 years old. My second love has always been video games. Never in my whole life did I ever think of putting my 2 loves together until that day.

I became the first tester at Virgin the next day. A tester was somebody who they paid to play games and find things wrong with them. There were only about 15 people at Virgin at the time, so they didn't need a full-time musician. When the first opportunity arose for music (*Prince of Persia* on Gameboy and *Global Gladiators* for Sega Genesis), I jumped on it.

I would sit down with the programmers and technicians every chance I got to learn about the machines. I know nothing about programming. I just know music and games. It's definitely been a plus in my career. I mean, think about it! How do you program the blues or rock 'n'roll? That's just something you feel! Anyway, I worked on *Prince of Persia* for free, on weekends and after work. The V.P. of the company was so impressed he made me the music guy!

Describe a typical day at the office

My company works on about 8 or 9 projects at a time. This is possible because most products take over a year and a half or more to be completed. So the time frame allows me to change back and forth between products. I guess the best way to describe it is by telling you what I did yesterday... So, here it goes.

I got up at around 10:30 a.m., checked and wrote some e-mails, finished composing and recording a song for the new *Scooby Doo* game, had a conference call with a new developer in Salt Lake City who I'm working with for a Sony 1st party title. We were figuring out sound design direction and the process of how we're going to deliver them the sounds. Worked on some cinematic/cut-scenes for a BMX game. Listened to and approved sound design work that my lead sound designer has been working on for a Moto X game. Recorded small crowd reactions with a bunch of friends to put into a new street basketball game. Had a conference call with Victor Lucas the executive producer of the television show I co-produce and host for Discovery and MTV (The Electric Playground). Talked about next seasons filming schedule. Made up some milestone invoices for work completed and handed them over to my father (who is my chief financial officer) for processing. Had a quick meeting with my brother (also works for me, doing PR and Marketing) about writing this interview today and 3 others that need to be done by the end of the week. Played a little *ICO*, *Grand Theft Auto*, *Devil May Cry*, *Jak & Daxter* and *Halo* before I went to bed at 3 a.m. What a life! Can't wait to do it again tomorrow!

What are the bright and the dark sides of your work?

Wow! Well there are certainly lots of bright sides! I love video games and I love music. So I get paid money to do the two things I love most! I don't consider it a job at all. It's just a way of life. I love being able to push the technology to the next level and create things that have never been done before in games. The excitement of hearing music or sound effects you've been working on finally put into the game and seeing people react favorably.

Being able to help out people trying to break into the industry is also very rewarding. I would have to say that the hardest part is trying to make everyone happy! There are so many people on these teams now it's starting to get ridiculous. And mostly every one of them is a music critic! It's funny, you can pretty much look at a piece of art in a game and tell whether or not it sucks. You can move a character on screen and tell if it feels good or not.

But put a tune in a game? Everyone has different music tastes! It's hard to find two people who agree on every single piece of music! Take country music for example. Some people love it, others can't stand it. I try telling people not to choose what kind of music they like for the game, but what type of music fits and enhances the game the best.

Any advice to the young aspirant?

I think talent and determination are the two biggest assets you could have. With enough determination you achieve/find/create luck. I would say to anyone who is serious about it to just, "Go out and do it!" Put together your best-written favorite couple of songs on CD and go to the E3 convention in Los Angeles and/or the Game Developers Conference in San Jose. Pass out CD's, make friends, learn and network with people. Take your demo and send it out to all the game companies. It's all about being in the right place. It's hard to be discovered if you're sitting in your bedroom.

I got in this industry by moving to California and starting as a games tester. The same goes for getting into any part of the industry, it's all about working your way up and who you know. If you have a genuine love for games and want to be a producer or designer, start out in the testing department... you can't really just be a producer or designer. You have to work your way up to that... If you want to be a programmer, learn C++ and Risc or Assembly language. Same if you want to be an artist, learn 3-D Studio Max.

Usually, you gotta know somebody in the industry and start out low, but one thing people don't realize is that this industry is starving for talented people right now, mostly artists and programmers. Learn your art and then take a job for whatever it pays. Hell, do it for free if you have to, just to get your foot in the door. Then once you get your chance, show them what you are made of. So that by the next project you're writing your own ticket! Experience is everything when you're job hunting in this industry. So get it any way you can! A great website to check out and find out all about the gaming industry is gamasutra. You'll find tons of interviews with gaming professionals. There are also lots of job postings every week.

<www.gamasutra.com>

Game Tester

Imagine getting paid to play your favorite games! Sounds irresistible, doesn't it? Unfortunately, professional testing is not exactly like playing. It is a lot more like hard work!

Whatever the game, the tester's role is crucial. He is the first person outside the development team who gets to take part in the creative process. Suggestions

from the tester are going to influence the whole process for the 2 years or more that will be devoted to the production.

The Alpha version is when you check the basic elements of gameplay and find the most serious bugs. You then move to the multi-player options and check the various levels.

The code for the Beta version should now be rather stable, but there is still a lot of work to be done. Everything has to be scrutinized, one step at a time. Checking if polygon collisions are correct in every nook and cranny of the game is tedious at best... but it is absolutely necessary.

Testing every aspect of a game requires a strong methodology. This is not at all like playing for fun. Think of it as a way of moving up to your next job. The nice thing about being a tester is that you can only move up!

Usually, testing is done inside the company. But some companies send their games out to a specialized firm, which conducts extensive testing. Console games never make it to the stores before a console manufacturer gives his approval. And he is pretty hard to satisfy!

<www.gamedev.net/dict>

An insider's point of view: Eric Tremblay

Eric Tremblay received a BSc degree from the University of Moncton, then did a BA in translation. He was hired as tester at Ubi Soft Montreal. First, he worked on *F1 Racing Simulator*, was promoted to team leader, worked on *Monaco Grand Prix 2* and soon found himself responsible for all testing carried out in Montreal. After a few years, he was appointed head of the quality assessment department, supervising products from Montreal, Paris, Bucharest and Shanghai. He oversees quality tests and coordinates work between the development teams and the testing teams. He is also responsible for establishing quality standards for the various platforms Ubi Soft develops products for.

How did you get your job?

I have been playing video games for I don't know how long. I really am a fan. So, when I saw that ad for a position as tester, four years ago, I went for it! I moved from tester to team leader to quality control officer to director of the quality control studio.

Describe a typical day at the office

I start pretty early. Because quality control involves teams located all over the world, I get a lot of e-mails. I start the day reading my mail and checking on a number of projects. Then I do my agenda for the day or the week. If products are nearly through with the testing process and new ones are coming in soon, I build the appropriate teams and plan out what is to be done.

I spend the day going from one team leader to another, checking how things are going. Then there may be a couple of meetings with upper management. At this time of the year, we usually hire new testers and also conduct evaluations of our current team members. Let's say we keep ourselves pretty busy.

What are the bright and the dark sides of your work?

Working in a stimulating environment, with people who are gamers just like me, is what I like best. Seeing how a game moves from beta version to final product, ready to be placed on the shelves, is quite pleasing too. Also, when I get a chance to test new consoles or any new piece of technology before it hits the stores, it makes me feel good.

The down side is that it is impossible to find all the bugs in a game and that it is impossible to correct all the bugs we discover. It is hard to admit, but if we only we had a little more time, the products would be better.

I guess the last difficult thing I have to deal with is that I do not get enough time to play!

Any advice to the young aspirant?

Love video games and be patient.

Marketing and PR

The job of the marketing department is to connect the public to a specific game and sell millions of copies. You have to live up to the buyer's expectations and build momentum towards the launch date.

The PR department makes sure a number of specialized magazines keep the public informed about the game, and sends copies to journalists, hoping to get good reviews. The icing on the cake is when you get front page coverage.

Depending on the size of the company, marketing and PR are usually done by a small team and sometimes by one person only. Some companies now outsource marketing and PR to specialized firms.

The one capacity you must have for this line of work is excellent communication skills. Whether by phone, fax, e-mail or face to face, you must be a pleasant person to talk to. If you can write press releases that are colorful and punchy, you can be sure they will be noticed and appreciated. And if you love video games, it will make the job that much more pleasant for you.

Employers will want you to have a University degree in one of the many areas available of Communications. Once inside a company, your career is pretty much set: you will start at the assistant level and move up to director.

There are two basic tendencies. Some firms ask specialized companies to promote their products. Others, and this the case with most publishers, have their own department. Remember that marketing and PR budgets are often as big as production budgets.

An insider's point of view: Melinda Mongelluzzo

Melinda Mongelluzzo started at Activision in July 1980 and quit on the same day nine years later. Since Activision was a start-up company, she did a little bit of everything including driving sub-assembly video game parts (the circuit board with the chip) from  Sunnyvale to Pittsburgh California for final assembly and shipping. After a couple of years of this, she was transferred to marketing and then to PR. She joined Accolade in August 1989 as PR manager and later Capcom in July 1995 as Senior PR manager. She was promoted to Director of Public Relations in 1997.

How did you get your job?

I started off my career in the video game industry working for Activision. I started a month after the company shipped their first four products. I guess you could say I got in on the ground floor (I was the 12th employee). I slowly worked my way into marketing and eventually into PR.

Describe a typical day at the office

E-mail is a wonderful invention, but there are days when all I do is answer e-mail. Capcom has offices in London and Japan, so the mornings can be spent talking to the London office and the afternoon talking to our parent company in Japan. Capcom is fortunate in that we have excellent products. For the most part, gone are the days of pitching a product. The biggest challenge we face is simply keeping up with the demand. Having great product is a PR person's dream.

What are the bright and the dark sides of your work?

The bright side of the job is the satisfaction of seeing the fruits of your labor appear in print. I would also add working with a great group of people, both within Capcom and the editorial community. The down side is when a reporter misrepresents your product or the views of your executive.

Any advice to the young aspirant?

The video game industry is fun, exciting and fast paced. This is an industry for anyone who loves the challenge of juggling multiple projects and products at one time. Anyone wanting to venture into this field should have strong writing and verbal skills and a love of video games.

An insider's point of view: Rob "Pickle King" Fleischer

CURRENT ACCOUNTS: *Rockstar, Take 2, Crave, Interplay, Fishtank, TDK, Mediactive.*

<rob@linnpr.com>

How did you get your job?

When I was 13 I bought my Nintendo and *Super Mario Bros.* That day I knew what I wanted to do the rest of my life: work in the videogame industry. I was a marketing major at Ithaca in NY. In December of my senior year I sent out about 150 resumes and letters to every company in the videogame industry. I got a list of marketing contacts from an early issue of Next Gen, which was about getting a job in the industry, and listed marketing contacts at just about every game company, as well as by pulling out every game company listed in the SF and Seattle yellow pages.

I sent out my resume, and to companies I really wanted to work at like Nintendo, Sony, and EA, I sent a 3 foot inflatable pickle with my resume attached to its hand. Those got me interviews easy. I ended up getting a summer job at Sony and worked in their PR department, after which I got a job at ASCII. At that point I was in the industry!

Describe a typical day at the office

9:30 AM: Get into the office. Morning: check and answer e-mails, return phone calls. Lunchtime: play games! Afternoon: make and answer calls, get people games, answer e-mails. Night: go home and play games.

What are the bright and the dark sides of your work?

Bright sides are getting to play games long before they ever come out; being able to have input into game design, like being able to say to a developer that the car is too loose on the road, and them taking you seriously; just knowing as much as we do from talking to people — knowledge is power! Other bright sides include really cool parties with games, food, and entertainment. And everyone you meet in the press and PR are for the most part very cool and interesting people.

Down sides are having to work on games that sometimes aren't so good; seeing all the politics that go on in game companies; and late nights playing games where I get really tired the next day.

Any advice to the young aspirant?

On the marketing and PR side, it is important to have great writing skills. Take some creative writing and English classes. Also, play games! If you play games and have an education, you can go a long way! Computer knowledge helps a lot as well, being able to work your way around the PC is extremely helpful and saves a lot of time. And don't give up! You need to be really ambitious... Write everyone and anyone you can and continue to follow-up until you get your foot in the door!

What about the "Pickle King" thang, can you explain it without being salacious?

In an effort to unite pickle lovers everywhere, I have taken on the responsibility of uniting people through their common love for pickles and pickled products. I, the self-proclaimed pickle king, have formed the pickle preservation society where pickle fans can go and meet one another, share recipes, pickle stories, and just plain have fun.

Pickle Power! <www.pickleking.com>

Major agencies

Chen PR: <www.chenpr.com>
Linn PR: <www.linnpr.com>
Bender Helper Impact: <www.bhimpact.com>
Highwater Group: <www.highwatergroup.com>
Edelman Public Relations Worldwide:
    <www.edelman.com>
Golin-Harris: <www.golinharris.com>
Porter-Novelli International:
    <www.porternovelli.com>
Hill and Knowlton: <www.hillandknowlton.com>
Fleischman-Hillard International Communications:
    <www.fleishman.com>
TSI Communications Worldwide:
    <www.tsicomm.com>
Access Communications: <www.accesspr.com>
Faiola Davis Public Relations: <www.fdpr.com>
Bohle Company: <www.bohle.com>
Arbuthnot Communications: <www.arbuthnot.com>

Journalist

Journalists keep hearing the same old cliché about their job: they get to do what they love most and get paid for it too! No one believes them when they say they are just back from E3, and are completely pooped!

There are a number of reasons why journalists live under pressure: deadlines are deadly! Writing critiques and in-depth articles can take a lot of time and while you are typing, there is this load of games you must report on and haven't had time to play yet! You must conduct interviews, looking for the scoop of your life! Now add the fact that most journalists work freelance, and there you are: can you handle stress well enough to feel comfortable on the job?

You may have a literature degree and indeed, it will look good on your C.V., but the day-to-day activities of a journalist are light years away from writing poetry!

Point number 1 is to write quickly and correctly. You may be the fastest gamer in the West, but if you can't convey your ideas clearly and concisely, forget it! You do need to know the industry from inside out. Getting in touch with marketing execs and PR reps will require your best communication skills.

Do you know the game called musical chairs? You better be good at it! Everything moves so fast in the publishing business. If you keep your head up and handle stress better than most, you will become the editor-in-chief you've always wanted to be. But it takes a lot of discipline!

An insider's point of view: Zoe Flower

Zoe Flower is a freelance entertainment journalist and independent broadcast producer. She has studied Computer Science, Applied Design and both 2-D and 3-D animation. She maintains an ongoing love affair with the videogame industry. A monthly column for *Official Play-Station Magazine* provides her with a sounding board for her opinions, while maintaining close ties to the industry and community. Zoe spends her spare time with friends and family, or flipping over the handlebars of her hard tail Rocky Mountain. She loves to read, play videogames, and collect DVDs. Her ultimate goal is to be a comic book character or international spy.

<www.zoeflower.com>

How did you get your job?

I had to use brute force! I had studied Computer Science and Animation before starting my own business as the owner of a network based PC arcade. I was fortunate enough to have a videogame television series being produced in my home town. As fate would have it, they approached me about using the arcade as a set for the show. Before long, I was speaking regularly with the producers and they learned of my knowledge and passion for games. Being female, they felt I would be a good fit for their program and asked me to contribute on and off camera to their project. I never imagined I would have an opportunity to be a television correspondent, but I gradually warmed up to the idea.

Through the many seasons of production, I made contacts and pushed my opinions out into the games industry. These opinions became the basis for my work as a print columnist. Obviously, writing skills were an essential so I am glad I studied my literature and grammar courses so intensely!

Describe a typical day at the office

There really is no typical day at the office for me. That's what I love about my job! One day, you are playing videogames for 8 hours straight, the next you are on the phone tracking down stories or responding to letters from readers or viewers. At some point, I've got to sit down and write something, and I usually camp out in front of my laptop on the couch as I seek inspiration for an article. Then there is the travel to various press events to see the latest products. It truly is a varied and flexible work environment. Lately, I've been traveling the States as a spokesperson for videogames, speaking on radio

and television about the social impact of games and the state of the industry. The opportunities are just endless!

What are the bright and the dark sides of your work?

The bright side to the job is the flexibility, the creativity and the pace at which you've got to keep up with it all! There is a wealth of opportunity once you're established, and I never get over how exciting it is to pass my opinions onto the hundreds of thousands of gaming enthusiasts. I love the feedback and the relationships that come out of my work.

On the down side, it can be difficult to make the first connection, or it can take a great deal of dedication without pay to finally get a shot. Luck played a big factor in my introduction to the games business. As a freelance journalist, money can be a problem. For those wanting stability and security in their work, freelancing is not the way to go. If you like a little risk and want to set your own hours, then you may not be bothered by the fact that occasionally, you'll be groveling for cheques from your contractors.

Receiving free product is another big bonus, but it can be time consuming work to keep up with contacts and strong relationships with all the publishers on the market. And if the games industry experiences a slump, you can bet you will too. Still, it seems worth it at times like this!

Any advice to the young aspirant?

For anyone looking to get into videogame journalism, whether print or broadcast, there are a few tidbits of advice I have. Obviously, you need to know games. Not just today's games, but the history of the industry. Try to learn as much as possible about how games are made and who makes them. Once you have a wealth of knowledge, think about how you would convey this knowledge to the average person. As a journalist, you need to speak as an authority, but without isolating the beginner or average reader. Writing skills are supremely important. Being a confident writer with a unique voice will garner attention. Try to build a portfolio of articles that doesn't read like the regular copy of your favorite magazine. Finally, be professional in your approach. Don't email all the editors of a magazine and harass them with your work, or tell them all the videogames you've played and completed. They want writers who have the ability to represent a professional news source. Your communication skills will say a lot about your abilities. And don't give up! It doesn't always happen overnight!

An insider's point of view: Marc Saltzman

Marc Saltzman has reported on the bourgeoning high-tech industry for the past five years as a freelance journalist, author, lecturer, consultant, and radio and TV personality. His specialties lie in video games, computers, the Internet, telecommunications, digital music initiatives and consumer electronics. Beginning in May of  2001, Marc became a technology correspondent for CNN, the Cable News Network. Marc also appears regularly on many national TV shows in Canada as a gaming guru, World Wide Web pioneer and computer specialist. Marc enjoys delivering seminars on the ever-changing world of high-tech (as far as Hong Kong!) and on how to best break into the interactive entertainment industry. Marc has also moderated a panel at the 2001 Electronic Entertainment Expo (E3) on this same topic.

How did you get your job?

To be perfectly honest, I was a computer game junkie and was fed up spending $70 on each game. So, I approached the Canada Computes! family of newspapers and asked if they wanted a gaming expert. They agreed to take a look at my work and then I realized I did not study journalism (or even English, for that matter!) in university, but decided to go for it, anyway. I called up gaming companies in the U.S. and asked for a review sample of their top games and then wrote my opinions on them.

The next thing I knew, my freelance writing skyrocketed—I began writing for larger publications with millions of readers (including *USA Today*, the *LA Times*, *Newsweek*, *Yahoo! magazine*, *Playboy*, *Maxim*) and I began authoring books on the video game industry (the last one is *Game Design: Secrets of the Sages*, Third Edition. I also got more involved in radio work (I host two shows in Toronto) and appear on many TV stations as a technology correspondent (CNN, CTV, Global, CBC, and more).

Describe a typical day at the office

Usually, I get up around 8 or 9 unless I'm traveling (then it's 5 or 6 a.m.) and begin writing articles on my PC in my home office. If there's research to be done (that is, more than just playing the game), I usually scour the Net, interview company execs via e-mail or over the phone, and so forth. Couriers arrive at my house about 4 to 5 times a day with the latest video games, peripherals, consumer electronics, etc. Of course I need time to play with these games n' gadgets, so I usually do that in the afternoon after I've written for a few hours in the AM (when I'm more "fresh"). Also, I travel quite a bit (every other week or so) visiting game companies around the world to see what they're working on. Lastly, if I'm doing a radio or TV interview, I usually leave to go to the TV or radio station for the shoot or they come to my home office.

What are the bright and the dark sides of your work?

I think the bright sides to the job are obvious – I get to do what I love and get paid to do it. I also enjoy sharing my enthusiasm for the video game industry so I get to reach millions of readers (or viewers or listeners) to share my passion. Other fringe benefits include free games, hardware and other goodies (clothing, gifts, etc.), traveling the world on someone else's dime and, in most cases, getting paid in American funds but living in Canada since most of the magazines and newspapers I write for are in the U.S.

In my opinion, there are not too many down sides to the job, except for the fact people think it's easy. Sure, I'm writing about video games but that doesn't mean it can be sloppy, inaccurate or late. I have three to four deadlines a day and must write well and make sure I know the product inside and out. Considering there are over three thousand games released each year between all the platforms, this isn't an easy endeavor!

Any advice to the young aspirant?

My advice is to find something you absolutely love (fashion, sports, technology, health, cars, etc.) and then break down as many doors as possible looking for work. I always saying breaking into this field is 70% "chutzpah" (drive), 15% timing and 15% talent. Once you're there, obviously you need to be good at what you do to stay. You'd be surprised how many awesome writers are out there but are too shy or nervous about calling or e-mailing an editor. Who cares about rejection! There are thousands of outlets for your writing and you must go to them, they won't come to you. Also, working from home isn't for everyone. There are countless distractions and no boss to look over your shoulder so you better be disciplined! And be prepared to play more games than you can handle! Bandaids not included...

An insider's point of view: Shaun Conlin

This self-professed Game Geek is published in about 30 newspaper and web sites in the USA and abroad.

How did you get your job?

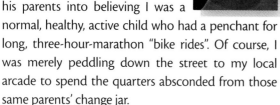

For as long as I can remember, I was one of those kids who fooled his parents into believing I was a normal, healthy, active child who had a penchant for long, three-hour-marathon "bike rides". Of course, I was merely peddling down the street to my local arcade to spend the quarters absconded from those same parents' change jar.

Somewhere between then and now came the incursion of the "Politically Correct". I smiled smugly when pop-psychologists replaced the term "lazy" with socially-soft terms like "disinterested, disenfranchised and unmotivated"; to me it was a veritable license to sit around and do as little as possible while appearing to be the end result of society's inadequacies.

Back in 1993, I stumbled into my first writing gig: a weekly traffic safety column penned for my local community newspaper; and was astounded that someone would actually pay me money to blather.

Shortly thereafter, as an eternal fan of "cool free stuff", I immediately set about carving a niche for myself as a "gamer in the know", authoring a new column, "The Game Geek", for that same community paper. Realizing that writing for one rinky-dink rag could not a career geek make, I began reselling, syndicating that Game Geek column concept to whatever paper was willing to pick it up. There was a considerable amount of leg work and Kraft dinner involved with this, but syndication had a snowball effect: the more papers that ran with my column, the easier it was to convince other papers that the column was viable and that my abilities as a games writer were testifiably creditable.

This also made for an easy "in" into glossy magazines and onto reputable web sites.

Of course, it didn't take me much longer to start authoring a weekly GadgetGeek column full of high tech gizmo and gear reviews... cool free stuff and all that.

My game and gadget reviews, features and editorials now appear in numerous big city dailies and magazines and countless subsidiary publications throughout North America.

And I'm lazy.

Describe a typical day at the office

It starts with coffee. I stumble downstairs and slosh through an assortment of half bashed boxes and FedEx envelopes before finally plopping down at the ol' slacker station (I mean workstation), there in my basement. Check e-mail. Respond to some of it. File a lot of it for later response, some of which is dated 1997. Go back upstairs and get more coffee. Come back down and try to figure out which deadline for which paper is most overdue and see if I can't reword something I wrote three months ago to sound fresh and "timely". Sneak in a few quick rounds of Unreal Tournament.

Go back upstairs and get more coffee. Note to self: move coffee machine downstairs.

Make some phone calls. Wait for callbacks and/or the timely arrival of a high resolution graphic for a product review I'm trying to file. Play *Unreal Tourney* (shortcut "Therapy") in the meantime. Image will invariably arrive three days too late or on time except decidedly "low" rez. Get off butt, walk over to recliner, and get back on butt. Play a videogame. Decide that said game should probably be compared to *Unreal Tournament* so jump into another death match. Nope, can't compare *Project Gotham Racing* to *Unreal Tournament*, but at least I did my research. Find cheats for *Project Gotham Racing* so I can get to the sweet stuff forthwith.

Bang off a thoughtful article about something. Whatever. Go back upstairs; get another coffee. Put it in the microwave because the Cuisinart shut itself off a while ago. Feed the kids lunch while wife goes to gym. Exercise? What's that? Open front door and haul in more couriered boxes and FedEx envelopes. Toss them down the stairwell for later sloshing. Write an article in head while changing diaper. Make it the most brilliant piece of literature ever written and then promptly forget it all whilst pondering the effectiveness of *Penaten*. Watch wife come in the door all buffed and cheery. Linger a while. Admire the full sized windows parading maximum daylight then excuse oneself as the keyboard awaits… in the basement with the m-dash windows.

Back downstairs. Pick up sloshables along the way; the ones that rattle and tinkle probably weren't very good products anyway. Open remaining boxes. Stack games (if any) neatly in pile of other neatly piled games that fell over in a jumbled heap in 1998. First one to get under foot is the next to be reviewed. Find hammer. Open box with high tech gizmo awaiting inside. Hit product with hammer. Write a flattering or scathing review based on results. Listen dutifully as wife bellows down the stairs, berating you for leaving a cold cup of coffee in the microwave and agree with her that maybe the coffee machine should be moved downstairs and yes, you should have thought of that a long time ago.

Do follow up phone calls clearly defining the urgency for high-resolution product shots and throw in a clear definition of "high resolution" for good measure. Act jaded and expect nothing to come of it. Play a videogame. Pause game and launch another round of *Unreal Tournament* with every intention of keeping it brief. Don't. Where'd the day go?

What are the bright and the dark sides of your work?

– Bright: Cool Free Stuff

- Down: Cool Free stuff is more-or-less inedible and cannot be exchanged for dental work or stack of diapers.
- Bright: All-you-can-handle complimentary booze at "media events".
- Down: Can't handle as much complimentary booze as I used to and doesn't that seem like a waste?
- Bright: Hanging with esteemed colleagues at "media events" in a grand back-patting ceremony reserved for the cool-free-stuff-and-complimentary-booze crowd.
- Down: The next day with a wee headache and a duffle bag overstuffed with press releases and swag that seems way too heavy considering the wee headache, which, let's face it, ain't so "wee" anymore considering the aforementioned handling inability.
- Bright: Be your own boss!
- Down: Boss is a deadbeat who won't even give you a holiday or a dental plan.
- Bright: Work from home, always near the wife and kids.
- Down: Think about it.

Any advice to the young aspirant?

Are you nuts? Have you seen the number of gaming websites and magazines vaporizing before your very eyes? The serious shrinkage of your local newspaper that probably hacked it's "technology" section back when Amazon posted it's first losses?

Writing about high tech leisure products may seem like a cool job except there's no real money in it; or the money that is in it is very hard to find. So it's not really a "job", more like a "career objective for the adamantly unmotivated"... It's still pretty cool, though.

Don't do it kid. Marc Saltzman got all the good gigs and the rest of us share what's left. That and you really should take better care of your teeth and even free booze has its price.

Retailer

This may not be the most glamorous job in the industry but it certainly is an essential link in the production chain. No one is closer to the public than the retailer. He is the interface between the general public and the game companies.

Distribution channels have undergone a few changes over the years. It used to be small specialised stores for hard core gamers only. But games like *Deer Hunter* have attracted thousands and thousands of casual gamers. And where do members of the general public go shopping? At places like Wall-Mart or Sears. Big department stores have a strong marketing clout and a major buying advantage. Small retailers know they can't beat their prices so they compensate by offering personalized service.

As a retailer you need to know how the industry works and you must have a very good knowledge of the public's expectations. Are you getting a lot of questions about a game soon to be released? Is there a buzz about a specific title? Since you are going to be the person who decides what games go on the shelf, knowing whether they will be best sellers or not is essential. You must know what the clientele wants today but also anticipate what it is going to ask for in the near future. It's called having a feel for market tendencies! You must be very familiar with the arcane world of accounting and financing. And experience with different types of businesses is a definite plus.

I want to pay a special homage here to Jean, the owner of a retail shop called Maxi-Mario in Montreal. One day he booted out a couple of shop lifters he had caught red handed. They came back three days later, shot him down and ran away with 2 Dreamcast consoles and a handful of games. His death didn't make the headlines, but to me, it came as a real shock. He would have been the first person to deny the relationship between violence in video games and violence in the street. His clientele lost a wonderful adviser, a real gamer at heart, and the community lost a fine businessman. I lost a friend.

Tycoons

If your intention is to launch a company and strike it big right away, sorry, you are about 20 years late! The first millionaires in the industry made their money during the early boom, when it took days to produce a video game, not years and when costs were only a fraction of what they are today. Risks weren't as big and if your contract was good, it is true you could make a fortune and watch bankers give you their best smile.

To create a company back then, all it took was a few PCs, talented friends, a good garage and bingo! you were in business. Distributors weren't even necessary. Richard Garriot and Dave Perry delivered their first games by mail. They wrapped them up in paper bags, with just a few xeroxed pages for a manual.

Having your own company was a great advantage. Take Peter Molyneux and *Populous* for example. Had he been a game designer at Electronic Arts, rather than Bullfrog's President, he would have made a lot less money.

A developer's business will be successful if the person in charge has flair in choosing the right platform and the right publisher.

As always, being passionate about a job well done is a key to success. You must love games and feel responsible for each and every decision you make during the production process.

And when the time has come, it is also a good thing to know whom to sell your business to.

Is it still possible to become rich and famous? Hard to tell… On the one hand the industry is consolidating, investing in protracted best selling series, not on exotic, brand new concepts. On the other hand, the pendulum is also known to swing in the other direction and *Myst*, *Half-Life* and *The Sims* are there to tell us that well produced innovative products can go all the way to the top!

There is still a lot of money to be made. If not by individuals, certainly by small teams. And small teams are quite trendy these days. Quite a few star designers have left the major company they were working for only to recreate a much smaller unit and enjoy the kind of atmosphere they lived in when they first started. The most famous example is Peter Molyneux who sold his company to Electronic Arts, then started Lionhead and came out with *Black and White*.

So here is at least one way to success: you join a famous company, you work on a few of its best titles, then, using your good name in the business to raise to venture capital, you create your own small firm.

Is the "lone genius approach" a token of the past? Is it impossible for new Miyamotos to step up and stun the world? Here again it's impossible to say for sure. The fact is that collective creation has never proved to be any better than individual creative efforts. Games that made history were the brainchildren of designers who knew exactly what they wanted. And who were very successful at selling their vision to the entire production team.

Come to think of it, this is what happens with every creative enterprise, regardless of the sector.

<www.gamesbiz.net>
<www.gamasutra.com/features/
index_business_and_legal.htm>

An insider's point of view: W.M. (Trip) Hawkins III

W.M. Hawkins is one of the founding fathers of the industry. At 48, he has already spent 28 years in the business. A techno geek from his early teens onwards, he was one of the first 50 employees of Apple Inc. He left Apple in 1982 and established  Electronic Arts, the biggest independent video game company in the world. With 3DO, he was part of the industrial efforts made by American companies to gain a presence on the console market. His bid was not successful but he managed to sell 3DO to Panasonic. Panasonic never did anything with it! He now owns 27% of 3DO, has become a technology agnostic, creating games for every possible platforms. He strongly believes that the future of the interactive game is on the Internet.

How did you get your job?

I loved games as a child and recognized that computers would become the Medium of Doing. I decided in 1975 that I would start a game software company in 1982. In 1982, I founded EA, after having helped build Apple for four years from its infancy.

Describe a typical day at the office

Getting in early, looking for harbor seals in the slough while I fetch my coffee. Then plowing through 100 e-mails and having several informal meetings and a few formal ones. Making phone calls from the car. It's always dark when I leave, unless the sun is coming up.

What are the bright and the dark sides of your work?

The best part is working with creative, fun people to invent new games. The worst part is dealing with the usual business realities including tough markets, fierce competitors, and fussy technologies.

Any advice to the young aspirant?

Get a great education. Figure out where you want to work and then offer to work there initially for free. That is what I did. My first gig was doing market research in 1977 on the Fairchild Channel F game system — it was the world's first cartridge game system.

An insider's point of view: Dave Perry

David Perry started to design and program games in 1981. He left his native Ireland for London when he was 17 and immediately started to work for a variety of companies, including Virgin. With a major success under his arm (*Teenage Mutant Ninja Turtles*), he moved to the US, where he received instant recognition with *Aladdin* from Disney. In 1993, he created Shiny Entertainment and came up with a mega hit: *Earthworm Jim*. The game was published for all platforms and it even had its own TV show! Since then he has enjoyed one success after another with *MDK*, *Messiah* and *Sacrifice*. He is one of the most famous public figures in the industry, and came under the spotlight again when Shiny Entertainment won the right to produce the first game under a license everybody was trying to get: *The Matrix*.

How did you get your job?

I started by writing simple programs for books. Soon I was writing chapters, then my own book. I was enjoying it so much, I left school and took a job in England making professional games.

Describe a typical day at the office

I spend 1/3 of my day running *Shiny*, 1/3 of my day in e-mail and 1/3 of my day in design. Usually a day does not end until I am too tired to continue. Even after 20 years in the business, the late nights never seem to end.

What are the bright and the dark sides of your work?

It's really great to have gamers come up at Shows and tell you about their experiences with games you helped make. It's also great to help people into the industry and then meet them at a show when they are now working for a video game company.

Any advice to the young aspirant?

Go to my website. I am doing all I can to help... Suggestions are welcome.

<www.dperry.com>

An insider's point of view: Gabe Newell

Gabe Newell spent 13 years inside the systems, applications and technology division of Microsoft Inc., moving up from one position to another. He left the Admiral's vessel to create his own company: Valve. Two years later, in November 1998, he put his first game on the market: *Half-Life*. Published by Sierra Studios, it was an incredible success, winning over 50 prizes including the "best PC game ever" from magazine PC Gamer. The online version was called  *Team Fortress* and became a phenomenal success on its own. It was used by millions of gamers who thought if was really cool to get an extension for free!

How did you get your job?

I worked with Michael Abrash at Microsoft. When Abrash went to id Software, Mike Harrington and I began talking with id about starting a games company of our own that would build on top of the *Quake* engine. We went down to visit them in Texas, and we left with the source code to *Quake* and a new game company.

Describe a typical day at the office

Given my role in the company, I don't really have a typical day.

What are the bright and the dark sides of your work?

The best part of working in the games business is the actual building of a game. Being part of an exciting, skilled team building something that nobody else has built before is a complete blast. The down sides of the business are that there are a lot of people and institutions in the industry that get in the way of that.

Any advice to the young aspirant?

I'd strongly suggest starting off by participating in one of the mod efforts. It's a great way to get practical experience, it focuses your attention academically if you are still in school, and it brings you to the attention of the game industry in a way that really shows what you can do.

An insider's point of view: Ray Muzyka

In February 1995, Dr. Greg Zeschuk and Dr. Ray Muzyka launched BioWare Inc. In October 1996, they published *Shattered Steel*, first on PC, then on the Mac. 100,000 copies later, they introduced their first RPG title: *Baldur's Gate*. 1,500,000 copies were sold in no time. Soon two extensions became available: *Tales of the Sword* and *Shadows of Amn*. They also came out with *MDK2* for PC, Dreamcast and PlayStation 2. Their game engine (the BioWare Infinity Engine) also became very popular. Black Isles Studios used it to develop *Torment* and *Icewind Dale*. Lucas just ordered a role playing game from BioWare that is going to appear in the Star Wars universe: *Knights of the Old Republic*.

How did you get your job?

My joint CEO Greg Zeschuk and I have an interesting story in this regard. We are trained as medical doctors originally (graduating in 1992 from the University of Alberta, Faculty of Medicine). We decided to form BioWare Corp. back in 1994/1995 (incorporating in 1995) after having worked on some medical education software (we did the programming and art for a couple of relatively simple programs in 1993/94) for students while we were finishing our internships/residencies in 1993/94. We had run into some really talented programmers and artists working on what later was released as *Shattered Steel* in October 1996, our first game. *Baldur's Gate* was our next game and we started work on this in January 1996 because we had always enjoyed playing role-playing games in the early 1980's. In essence, the reason I got into the industry is because I have always loved video games, particularly RPGs!

Describe a typical day at the office

It's hard to describe a "typical day" for me. Such things don't exist. Every day is completely different. Some days are spent looking at "biz stuff" e.g. legal contracts or finances (I have an MBA). I recently graduated from the executive MBA program of the Richard Ivey School of Business, University of Western Ontario. Some are spent in Human Resources or planning meetings, and many are spent focused on product develop-

ment. Both Greg and I are joint CEO's and co-executive producers on all of BioWare's projects. And other days are spent playing our own games. All of our employees really believe in playing all of our own games to ensure we find and resolve as many bugs as possible.

What are the bright and the dark sides of your work?

The bright side of the job for me I think is related to the great people working at BioWare. They are a very smart, creative and hardworking group of people that make BioWare a fun and stimulating place to work. The only down side I can think of is the long hours, but at least the work is interesting and fun!

Any advice to the young aspirant?

Much depends on what field the young aspirant aspires to. If it is design or writing, then a degree in writing and perhaps computer science would be helpful. Similarly, for programmers, a BSc, MSc or PhD in computer science or computer engineering would be an asset. There are also many good diplomas and degree programs for artists and animators. So, education is a great starting point, which we really value at BioWare. Experience is also a plus, though for us not always essential. We like hiring young graduates who have lots of enthusiasm and talent and we are happy to provide a good working environment where people can get the experience.

An insider's point of view: Lorne Lanning

Lorne Lanning put an end to his 14 year long career as a 3-D specialist in Hollywood when he decided he wanted to immerse himself in the world of interactivity. In 1994, he created a company based on a virtual world, which was hilarious, yet strange and disquieting: Oddworld. Abe is the anti-hero of his first two games, *Abe's Oddysee*, and *Abe's Exoddus*. Lanning has invented all sorts of new design tricks. For example, his Alive system allows Oddworld creatures to speak. His most recent title, *Munch's Oddyssee*, was launched together with Xbox and was an immediate success.

How did you get your job?

Actually, I created it by convincing Sherry McKenna that if she helped me create a business plan, then I could figure out a way to get some chump to cough up a few million bucks. Hence, Oddworld was born and I got a job in the games business.

Describe a typical day at the office

I come to work in the morning, say "hi" to all the admin people as I pass them on my way to check with my assistant to see if anyone wants to kill me today. Then, I walk to my office and try to avoid anyone I gave directions to the previous evening. Once in my office, I immediately chug down a plate of vitamins and 2 ounces of wheat grass (compliments of Sherry McKenna). I then start to read my e-mail and see if there is anything burning on the production floor that needs immediate attention. If that's okay, I look over the e-mails and see if anything is on fire outside of the studio. If not, I complete my e-mails and get started with checking up on the latest production elements

that need feedback. Who I'll be spending more time with depends on the point of production. Early on in a production most of the time is spent with programmers and production designers. Later on my time is spent mostly with game designers and computer graphics folks.

Come lunch time I leave the office with Sherry and catch up on business aspects taking place outside the company and with the publisher. When Sherry finally gets sick of hearing my shit... we return to the office. The rest of the day is focused on making sure that my mind is dumped into the appropriate department so that nobody is falling behind because of me.

What are the bright and the dark sides of your work?

Oh god, where do I begin! We could write a book on this subject. I guess the most blatant dark side is having to deal with HR when there are personnel issues. Firing someone is never fun, neither is having to accomodate someone's hardships in the various forms that they occur.

The bright side is of course the work itself. The content. The stories and the characters and the actual gameplay. Watching it all come to life after so many weeks/months/even years of planning. Most of the time when it comes together it's quite uplifting. Sometimes it's horrific if things aren't turning out as you had hoped.

It's also wonderful to see artistically inclined people (including programmers) get pushed to do something they didn't think they could achieve. In many ways I see this as a fundamental part of my job. It's to lead people and give them the circumstances, the environment, and the direction to allow them to create things they may not have thought themselves capable of. Especially when the teams are well rounded. It's great to see people get more excited because the strength of a good team is making each individual's work get stronger and more impressive.

Any advice to the young aspirant?

You need to develop a strong work ethic, strive for excellence, and take pride in your work. Which means always pushing to do great work (even when others say there isn't enough time, money, etc.) and not being satisfied with mediocrity. If you want to make games and think you can do it in the context of a 9 to 5 job... think again. Any work you've ever admired has been the result of other peoples very hard work. Long hours and heavy stress are par for the course if you want to create strong work that stands out from the herd.

Also, go for quality-of-work over quantity-of-money... every time. When you do this you'll find that you'll wind up making more money in the long run anyway. I've seen a lot of people get full of themselves and think they're worth more than they actually are. Each time, it seems to direct them towards short term goals and mediocre careers. They take better paying jobs which most often require them to produce lower quality work. This temptation will always be there, don't fall for it. If you have friends who fall for it, then it's time to find new friends. You don't want their mediocre influence around you.

Oh, and be humble. Puff up with arrogance and it will be the beginning of your downfall.

Where do you see this new artform going?

Over the next 20 years games will exceed anyone's present imagination. The market, the competition, and the laws of computer power will generate incalculable advances that cannot be predicted. Within 10 years some games will have reached new heights in ways that will have superseded motion pictures in terms of emotional connection and dramatic immersion. Virtual life forms, massive multi-participant worlds, voice recognition, and the nature of free markets will create a synthetic landscape that will become far more appealing (to many) than our overpopulated world. These new highly addictive and synthetic landscapes will create social and psychological repercussions that may cause us to seriously consider whether we want to participate in the "real world" or the "virtual world". We'll see more and more people consciously choosing to live Matrix-like existences that will make William Gibson novels seem tame and conservative. Cost of living alone will drive this population implosion.

An insider's point of view: Warren Spector

Warren Spector learned his trade at TSR and Steve Jackson Games. In 1989, he was hired by Lord British himself so he could work for Origin on the *Ultima* series. He was project manager for *Ultima Underworld* in 1991 and what he did impressed John Cormak (from id Software) so much that he was asked to develop *Wolfenstein 3-D*. *Wolfensteinn 3-D* marked the beginning of a new era for 3-D virtual worlds and for the advancement of 3-D in the RPG genre. In 1995, he left Origin and started his own company: Looking Glass. For all sorts of reasons the company never got anywhere. He decided to join Ion Storm's team. He re-hired his ex-Looking Glass team and created a new Cyberpunk classic: *Deus Ex*. It became Ion Storm's best-seller. Warren Spector was praised by both gamers and his peers, and is now firmly in the driver's seat. In years to come we can expect his creative mind to come up with some striking ideas!

How did you get your job?

Like most folks in the game business, I started out as a gamer. Years of my life were spent playing pen and paper games like *Dungeons & Dragons*, *Call of Chthulhu*, *Runequest* and other RPGs, to say nothing of board games like *Ogre*, *GEV* and pretty much the entire Avalon Hill catalog! My hobby became my profession when I got a call from a friend who worked at Steve Jackson Games, a paper game developer in Austin, Texas, asking if I wanted a minimum wage job as an assistant editor. The choice was starvation as a university professor (I was THIS close to a PhD in media studies) or near-starvation as a game developer. Wasn't much of a choice, really. That SJG job led to a position with TSR, the folks who made *Dungeons & Dragons*.

But after five or six years in the paper game business, I realized the action was all in electronic games, not just professionally but personally as well. I was an obsessive computer and videogame player by then. Out of the blue, I got a call from an ex-Steve Jackson Games employee asking if I wanted a job as an associate producer with *Origin* and I was pretty much on the next plane. So, really, it was all kind of luck and hap-penstance. I had the right combination of skills, interests, connections and timing to take advantage of it when lightning struck...

Describe a typical day at the office

There ARE no typical days in this business. That's true no matter what position you hold, but it's even more true for me, given how I've structured this studio and my life. Basically, my role these days is Studio Director. That's a very different role than Project Director or Designer but it's the role I've chosen for myself. Nowadays, I'm more interested in championing a particular kind of game, the immersive simulation, and in helping some younger creative guys step up into leadership roles. Basically, I'm playing a real-world game called *Sim-Game-Studio...* and with real money!

But to answer your question, I spend a lot of time in e-mail, fielding questions and requests from team members, publisher and press. I pass along problems to the folks best suited to fix them (which can be frustrating when you think you're the best person to deal with a problem but you know you can't take the time!). I look over people's shoulders to make sure games are coming along the way they should. I go over schedules with producers and talk with designers about game systems and mission specs. I evaluate maps and missions to make sure they're up to snuff. I do some interviews. I go over budgets with the finance folks. I interview potential hires. The scary thing about my job is that I often come into the office with no set, specific goals — I just come in and wait for the day's problems to come to me. That just about ensures that no two days unfold in exactly the same way!

What are the bright and the dark sides of your work?

The bright side is getting to work in a field that is still figuring out what it's capable of. We're creating a new medium every day when we come to work. The bright side is getting to work in a creative field with some of the smartest, most creative collaborators you can imagine. The bright side is getting to make games and getting paid for it, for crying out loud!

The down side? Well, there can be some hellaciously long hours, which can be tough on family and friends and health... And it's often frustrating having to deal with technology that changes hourly (seems that way sometimes...). But, really, making games for a living is pretty darn cool!

Any advice to the young aspirant?

Make sure you really love games and want to turn your hobby into a profession. Everything changes when you're doing something for a living. Get a good education and don't limit yourself to the technology aspect of game development. To make games you have to be a Renaissance person. You'd be amazed the breadth of knowledge that's come in handy over the years! You don't have to go to school to get an education (though it helps), but make sure you're not just sitting in the dark playing games all the time, assuming that's all that's necessary to get a job in the game biz. I could write a book on this subject but since that's not going to happen any time soon, check out the International Game Developers Association website. There's a newbie section there that has advice, links and everything an aspirant could want to know. I used to answer questions like this at some length, now I

don't have to. The IGDA's doing a great job of answering it better than I ever could.

<www.igda.org/Endeavors/
Outreach/Students-Newbies/
students-newbies.htm>

A degree, yes or no?

My answer to the question is a little biased: in 1997, I created one of the first video game curricula, and set up a full-fledged professional training school in Montreal. In this industry, continuing education is absolutely necessary. Things change too fast. Operational knowledge has to be re-cycled regularly.

<www.nad.qc.ca>

Forget about having a life for a while…

The Game Designers Association has taken concrete steps towards improving education and training. Their web site states: "The IGDA has created an education committee. Its mandate is to achieve goals, outlined below, providing real benefits to academia, industry and students by:

- Helping universities provide developers with better trained, better qualified entry-level staff and contributing to a common critical and functional language of game development.
- Ensuring that the curricula offered by educational institutions (trade and academic) is relevant to real world development processes, the industry and the state of the art.
- Raising industry and academic awareness and understanding of games as an art form and game development as a profession.

Check their list of universities and trade schools with courses and/or degree programs in gaming".

<www.igda.com>
<www.igda.org/Endeavors/Outreach/
Students-Newbies/
students-newbies_schools.htm>.

Modifications (mods)

In 1993, id Software introduced a new multi-player game called *Doom*, which changed the game scene for ever. Its key characteristic was that any gamer could add levels to the game. At the time, weapon modifications and character changes became the norm. Three year later, when *Quake* was launched, it came with its own computer language called Quake-C. And this is when the "mod" fad really took off.

When the WWW protocol became available on the Internet, the fad spread even more. Gamers kept exchanging files. If you were capable of creating a fascinating mod, it was soon passed from one computer to the next, the world over. Software tools became both easier to use and more powerful. The community of mod artists was very friendly and lots of fun.

Today the community has grown exponentially. With the tools that come bundled with the games you buy, you can create completely new games. *Unreal* offers its own level editor and *Half-Life* is used as an editor by thousands of amateur developers. Web sites such as *PlanetQuake* and *PlanetHalfLife* offer more tools than you can handle. Sites like these are breeding grounds for talented developers and quite a few game companies log on to spot out future employees. Half of *Half-Life*'s team was recruited that way! Game demos have become business cards today, and the hot sites where "mod" makers get together are the sites where aspiring artists want to be seen.

<www.planetquake.com>
<www.planethalflife.com>
<http://gamedesign.net>

Eventually, you could graduate to the next level and participate in the yearly Independent Games Festival competition (IGF) organized by the Game Network. Each year, the competition gives out $15,000 in cash prizes for the best games, as determined by the IGF jury.

<www.gamanetwork.com>

Aspiring young turks

Be forewarned: your girl friend is going to leave you, your complexion is going to change to a much paler hue, your parents are going to complain they never see you any more, your dog may bite you next time you finally crash at home…

Am I exaggerating? Just a wee bit. If you are not passionate about your job, you are going to fall behind very quickly. Think of this as a key to happiness: the finer the line between job and pleasure, the better you can get.

Imagine yourself as a responsible person… Kind of difficult, isn't it? Imagine yourself as taking Continuing Ed Courses on a recurring basis… Rather tough, eh?

Well, you have to love your job so much that even having to become responsible and taking courses won't stop you from saying you will never change for any other job in the world! That's how dedicated you've got to be!

This overview has revealed but the tip of the iceberg. There are many other kinds of jobs in the industry. You'll probably get to know them while you're on the job. They may include: 2-D/3-D artist, Art Lead, Artificial Intelligence Developer and Programmer, Business Development Manager, Development Lead and Manager, Executive Producer, Program manager, Product Manager and Planner, Release Program Manager, Retail Merchandising Manager, Software Design Lead, Software Design Engineer and on and on…

<www.gamejobs.com>
<www.sloperama.com/advice>

The IGDA newbie and student links page is an excellent place to start a field trip in the more remote sectors of the industry.

<www.igda.org/
Endeavors/Outreach/
Students-Newbies/
studentsnewbies_links.
htm#job>

9.

Rules do change and so do gamers

The media

There is a strong difference between the way popular newspapers treat video games and the way specialized magazines see them. I remember once, the same week this year, there was an article about video games in a science magazine and one in the most widely read newspaper in Montreal. The title in the science magazine read: Beyond reality: how real-time physics and video games can work together. The article made it clear that video games are now part of applied sciences. Meanwhile, the front page of the newspaper carried the following title: 80 year old granny dead: teens charged with murder. Priest says films and video games are to blame.

The popular press tends to neglect how video games have affected society. Unless some killer on the loose has created havoc somewhere and then blames video games for his act, they barely pay attention. But when this happens, the IRA lobby steps in, a handful of psychologists and sociologists are interviewed and a local politician usually puts the blame on video games... We rarely see the press talk about education or awareness. Most of the time the media will deplore the fact that violence is now everywhere on TV, in the movies and in video games. Why do they leave out one of the most popular hobbies in society? It is hard to say, and hard to excuse! When a movie is launched or when an art gallery opens with a new exhibit, the press coverage is usually more substantial. A video game, which will sell 3 million copies and sway the imagination of gamers for several months, barely gets any write-ups.

Specialized magazines do an excellent job. They follow the announcement, launch, sales and design advances of each new game. They help build awareness in the community.

But there has been some sad news too. First, *Daily Radar* closed shop and its journalists went on the dole, victims of the dotcom crash. They had a wicked tongue, they were witty and fast, the best in the business. Before that, *PCXL* magazine had also gone down and another team of independent minds was lost... Without them, video game coverage has now lost some of its luster and flash. *Next Generation* also disappeared and so did *Fastest Game News Online* and *Myvideogames*. Call it consolidation!

The black sheep of culture

In 2001 92% of all American citizens aged 2 to 17 (i.e. 59 million) consider themselves gamers.

<www.mediaandthefamily.org/
research/vgrc/2001-2.shtml>

When the National Institute on Media and the Family handed in its report card on the video game industry, the industry itself got an A-, the Arcade sector got a D, the retailers got a D (because they hadn't enforced the evaluation code properly). So, all categories considered, the average grade for 2001 is a C.

The Institute makes a few recommendations to the industry..."The industry should continue their efforts to educate the public about game ratings. The retail and rental stores who have committed to policies preventing the sale or rental of adult games to children and teens should actively enforce them. The arcade industry should improve the implementation and enforcement of its rating system. Parents need to become more knowledgeable about the games their children are playing and should exert greater supervision."

As you can see, the Institute favors education over repression.

The cyber athletes are coming!

Today professional athletes can be spotted right away: they look like a mass of muscle in a Kevlar envelope, making a load of money! But athletes are no longer what they used to be. Try and picture a cyber athlete: no visible muscles, a six-pack and a set of caffeine tablets!

Yet some of these geek athletes are world stars and they make more money in a week than their parents in a year!

The Cyber Athlete Professional League

The Cyber Athlete Professional League was founded in 1997 and is holding multiplayer tournaments in the United States, Europe and Asia. The tournament offers lots and lots of prize money to competing champions. They do *Quake* and a number of other games. In 2001 they shared a purse of $300,000. 15 CPL events took place around the world. Among the sponsors were Microsoft, Intel, Gateway and Logitech.

In December 2001, teams from Seattle, Boston, Sweden, Chile, Malaysia, and a number of other nations converged on Dallas for the first ever World Championships with a grand prize of $150,000 to be divided by the winning teams. The event marked the largest tournament in video game history with it's 85 to 150 identical computers, part of a segregated Local Area Network managed by the CPL. Due to difficulties establishing a fair competition environment on the Internet, the Cyber athlete Professional League tournaments are all LAN-based. Reasons include latency, ping variance, ineffective player identification, inadequate server locations and differences in hardware. The Cyber athlete Amateur League (CAL) does run amateur competitions and CPL qualifiers online.

Visit CAL at:

<www.caleague.com>

Peripheral manufacturers such as Saitek or Madkatz also sign cyber athletes under their label. Madcatz for example, spends $100,000 promoting its line of joysticks in competitive events. You want to know a sure sign that the profession is growing? Well, a number of champions now show up at competitions with their own agent!

The *Quake* 2000 and 2001 champion is Jonathan "Fatality" Wendel, now aged 20. He pocketed $100,000 in 2000 and in 2001. He has become the ultimate geek athlete mutant.

<www.cyberathlete.com>

The cyber athlete phenomenon first surfaced in *Rolling Stone Magazine* in 1997. They published an article about a 22 year old woman named Stevie Case. In a now legendary contest, she had beaten John Romero, one of the creators of *Doom* and *Quake*. John fell on the field of honour and also fell... madly in love with the young lady. The media went gaga over the fact that on a testosterone battlefield, the winner was loaded with estrogen! Stevie Case quickly became a star and sat for a Playboy shoot session. She now runs her own web site.

<www.stevana.com>

Angel Munoz is the founding father of CPL. He approached budding star Stevie Case and asked her to become the first cyber athlete in his organisation. Today, there are 2000 people on the list of those who attempt to turn their passion into a lucrative professional occupation. And the number is growing.

Microsoft, with its MSN Gaming zone and 12 million registered gamers worldwide, is a pioneer in online tournaments. Every week the company organises 800 tournaments based on its line of PC games and online games. The Marquee Events offer prize money for the winners. At the tournament which marked the launch of *Rise of Rom*, an extension for *Age of Empires*, there were more than 3000 participants in the online competition.

The Virtual Golf Association (VGA) has attracted more than 12,000 members. When Microsoft launched *Links 2001*, the winning cyber golfer walked away with $200,000 in his pocket!

<http://zone.msn.com>

The Quake III Arena Championship

At QuakeCon 2001, id Software staged the first NVIDA *Quake III: Arena* Championships. Of a total of $50,000 in bursaries, the champion was offered $30,000. Rounds involved 512 players at a time. They competed in an environment created with *Quake III Arena Pro Map Pack*. The event started as a gaming community get-together in 1996. This year 3000 competitors are expected to sign up.

<www.quakecon.org>

Is it a sport, yes or no?

Can playing video games be considered a sport? The definition of a sport is vague enough to cover all sorts of activities. Maybe we should consider video game tournaments as we do chess tournaments. Video games and chess are sports for the mind!

Concentration, endurance, excellent hand/eye co-ordination, a strategic approach and hours of practise are required in almost every sport. And all of these human faculties are compulsory prerequisites to playing video games at the professional level. So video games and sport do have a lot in common.

Some Olympians might argue that playing video games, even at the professional level, is hardly a sport at all. Should we tell them about the purchasing power of all gamers combined? Aren't sports a matter of money and prestige as well as athletic ability?

The crux of the matter may simply be that playing well has now become a way to become rich and famous. Some parents give their kids a lot of support when they engage in a popular sport. But would they consider for one second the fact that kids who want to become professional cyber athletes stand a better chance of financing their way through University than an athlete?

Solo PFS games often serve as warm-up sessions before an online tournament. The gamer gets all juiced up, then when he feels ready, he moves on to a multiplayer game and faces hordes of barbarians with licenses to kill.

LAN parties have developed into a subculture where teams fight each other without shame or mercy. On Local Area Networks, virtual gangs do their best to beat the heck out of each other. Both teams will get bruised in the process, but in the end, there will be only one "hottest digital gang in town".

When Ian Garvey was an eighth grader, he was a smart, soft spoken class representative. He didn't do sports much. But, with a Gameboy in hand, he did beat thirty-one opponents flat and became the US Pokemon champion. What he likes most about *Pokemon* are the strategic aspects. He does not enjoy the trigger trance and frenzy so typical of FPS gaming.

In the video game sector, setting records is not really new. Every year, Twin Galaxies publishes a book listing all records. The company also maintains a web site about it. Of course, these records are there to be beaten and game maniacs read the Hall of fame regularly to see where they stand. Gamers who have decided to be the best can get pretty obsessive about setting records.

<www.twingalaxies.com>
<http://www.twingalaxies.com/cgiperl/wgg_nominees.pl>

Samsung is backing the World Cyber Games. The first World Cyber Games were held in 2000. Based on the Olympics model, the World Cyber Games will take place in major cities around the world as of 2003.

Another place you can read about professional gamers and gaming records is Computer Sports. How about an ESPN pay per view direct TV show broadcasting a *Quake* competition?

<www.worldcybergames.org>
<www.csports.net>

Women and video games

Now we are getting down to the nitty gritty! It looks like half the population of this planet wants to participate in the interactive revolution. But they are not getting their fair share of it at the moment. IDSA says that among the 145 million American gamers, 43% are women. But what kind of gamers are they? Tea and cookie ladies?

In a sector where marketing reigns supreme, you don't have to be a politically correct male to notice that females are given a pretty pumped up image. For the testosterone gangs, female chest measurements are often used as the icing on the cake.

According to a California group called Children Now, video games even have a negative influence on little girls. The group analysed 10 of the most popular games for Dreamcast, Playstation and Nintendo 64 and discovered that 54% of games using female characters had given them disproportionate physical attributes and sexually provocative behaviors.

To be precise, 38% of all female characters would prance around, showing off their bodies, 23% showed of a lot of cleavage, 31% had bare thighs, 15% had bare buttocks and 32% had bare belly buttons. 38% flaunted oversized breasts, and 46% much too narrow waists. In other words, video games and popular magazines behave pretty much the same way, idealizing a very specific image of women!

My own family is a good example of the kind of change which is currently taking place in how women relate to video games.

Three years ago my wife used to say there is nothing human about PCs or the Internet and wanted to have nothing to do with either. But now that she has become Yahoo's queen of bridge, people gather to kibitz her games (watch her play). She has developed friendships with people all over the planet.

My daughter on the other hand, has become so good at *Quake online* that her male opponents simply can't believe it was a female who kicked their collective butts. They check out her photograph on her clan site, and come back for more, some stating that they hope to give her a lesson and put her back in her place! Only to bite the dust again… Way to go kid!

According to IDSA, half of the 35 million online gamers are women. But the majority spend their time on card games, quizzes and lotteries, most of which are free.

There is no reason why males and females could not share interactive activities on the Net. Even if you consider old psychological clichés about differences between the sexes such as "women like places to be neat" and yes, with

Tetris they can place every shape in the proper order; or "guys love to pull things apart" and with FPS games, they blast every animate and inanimate object.

But despite these very basic differences, games like *Everquest* indicate a new trend. Women and men love the game for the same reasons. They love heroic fantasy and they love the atmosphere!

Women usually think that the way they are represented in games is rather childish. There are female oriented sites now which offer different "skins" for female characters. This helps female players identify more easily with their roles in the game.

They cannot identify with the poor princess waiting for the knight to save them. Games must reflect their expectations and respect their values. Adventure and RPG games understand this and are very popular with females players.

Of course, there are hardcore female gamers who identify with the PMS clan. The PMS clan name comes from "pre-menstrual syndrome", but was adapted to mean "Psycho Men-Slayers". These pioneer women have since disbanded, but they have spurred a new generation of female gamers who celebrate their favourite form of leisure

The way women are characterized in video games is no different than in other media

on several web sites. These young women get together to create skins with which they will identify best and then store them for future games.

KT aka Nasty Girl belongs to a very large online gaming clan called *Gods Forsaken Gothic Force*. Don't let the name scare you, girls like her simply like to play online action games. She has worked as a leader in two different chapters of the clan: the *Soldier of Fortune* and the *Tom Clancy* series. The clan now has over 200 members and is still growing.

<www.gfclansite.com>

This is how she sees her experience as a woman:
> My experiences with online gaming began one Saturday morning when I was looking for a game to download and play. I ran across a game demo called *Soldier of Fortune*. So I downloaded it, set it up and went right online to play, after a short time playing the single player mode. My first experience was pretty much the same as any woman's when they go online to play an action game. First I'm asked, "Are you really a girl?" I was a bit shocked a first that I was being asked this, and of course replied, "Yes." I played until I was good enough to win games and began to get known as one of few female players who played online. For some reason, the

It must be all Lara Croft's fault !

male population cannot understand why or how a female could ever be good at a computer game or even be interested in playing. I have been playing for almost two years now and I still get asked if I am really a girl.

I have been harassed a few times verbally by men who use sexual innuendoes. I do not let it get me down. Only a tiny minority behave that way. I simply play the rest of the game to win and take every opportunity to take out the offender. We females need to be confident that we are capable of playing these games and being just as good as the guys are, if not better then many. I believe women have every right to play online and play as females.

My experience
in the last
2 years

has taught me that 90% of all the online guys who win or lose against us enjoy having us women playing with them. I have formed good friendships with many of the guys who play the games I do. I am respected and even protected by them. They are generally a very accepting bunch. I have to admit I have to be cautious when I'm on a winning streak: I better not rub it in. When I lose I still have to be extra humble, after all they still think its a man's world. But all in all, they take their beating like a man. Once they get to know you, they accept you and treat you with the utmost respect. Over all, I found the males who play on line to be no different then the women in their treatment of each other. I actually get treated special by most of the guys and get a very warm welcome when I join a game. I am happy to be just a regular player...and in most cases I am. On an average evening of playing I am just like anyone else. We are there to play, laugh and kick some ass. Generally, I like to test my skills online rather then play against artificial intelligence in a single player mode. I love the graphics and the beauty of the game and am totally amazed at how real it can be at times.

Being a person who loves a good adventure, gaming has taught me a lot about computers and I would not give it up for anything. An evening of gaming is a great way to unwind and shut out the world. I love the adventure and get totally caught up in it at times. The riddles to solve and the beasts to slay are just too much fun to pass up.

Many times, when playing on line on public game servers, I have seen the guys type in, "My wife is sitting beside me watching and she thinks it's so great you play..." Women need to tell their men to... move over! And take control of the mouse and keyboard and go shoot it out with the rest of us. I think most women don't realize how easy it is and feel they will be shunned. Take it from me, its not like that at all. I am told over and over how cool it is that I play. Over the last year I have seen some of the wives who used to just watch get into playing as much as me. I just happen to be one female that gave it a shot and stuck with it. Nothing makes me happier then to kill off the male species one at a time in a simulated war zone. The grenades fly through the air with as much grace as birds in flight. But... you have to remember to take cover under more then an umbrella, because the mess a grenade leaves won't come out in the next wash! Nothing is more exciting than loading up a new game and exploring the levels that were created by such talented people in the gaming industry.

Hilary Doda, a game designer at Dream Pod 9, the company responsible for the *Heavy Gear* series, has a lots of experience in the field. She started playing at the early age of 8. She can bear witness to the fact that attitudes have not changed much. Here is what she has to say to the industry and also to males gamers who want to befriend the female population:

"We want to be treated like humans beings. We want to be greeted with the same kind of curtsey and professional attitude men take for granted. We want games that reflect our reality. And no this does not mean Barbie RPGs. We want games that are open to us and recognize our contributions. We do not want clans that assume we are not capable of understanding what's going on. We want to feel welcome in the stores, in the clans and in the games online."

Today, sophisticated female gamers want to be heroines, spies, scientists, hired-killers and goddesses. Nothing but normal! The only obstacle in their way is age-old sexism. Otherwise, there is absolutely no mental or psychological barriers… They can and will excel at interactive games.

<www.dp9.com>
<www.grrlgamer.com>
<www.womengamers.com>
<www.planetquake.com/qwf>
<www.gamegal.com>
<www.gamegirlz.com>
<www.qgirlz.com>
<www.girlzclon.com>

Illegal copying

The US Trade Representative (USTR) identified Ukraine as one of the countries where there is absolutely no control over the production and export

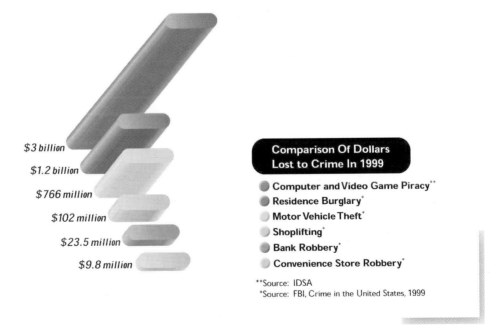

$3 billion
$1.2 billion
$766 million
$102 million
$23.5 million
$9.8 million

Comparison Of Dollars Lost to Crime In 1999

● Computer and Video Game Piracy**
● Residence Burglary*
○ Motor Vehicle Theft*
○ Shoplifting*
● Bank Robbery*
○ Convenience Store Robbery*

**Source: IDSA
*Source: FBI, Crime in the United States, 1999

Game piracy is costing the industry a fortune

of illegal copies. They have asked the Ukrainian government to join the international community, respect copyright laws and clamp down on illegal copying.

There are 16 countries that do not respect international copyright agreements. Among them are Egypt, India, South Korea, Malaysia, the Philippines, Thailand, Russia, Paraguay and Taiwan. China must be added to the sad list: the concept of intellectual property is quite alien to its culture. In these countries, nine copies out of ten are illegal. An estimated $3 billion is lost every year.

Losses incurred over the Internet in the US, Canada, Mexico and the European Union should also be added to the $3 billion. Just imagine the rage and frustration of a publisher who discovers illegal copies of his game are available on the Internet even before the commercial product is shipped to stores!

In February 2001, twelve publishers and developers took 4 warez (or rom) Web sites to court. The sites had hundreds of titles ready to be downloaded for free. The lawsuit wanted the sites closed and asked for $150,000 in compensation per game.

Warez activists believe access to information should be free. By extending this principle to copyrighted material, they hit every single element in the production chain. This issue went public when the Napster controversy broke out. Content creators and innovators all want to be able to eat once in a while! And the same is true of producers, publishers and investors! Everybody needs to add value down the chain and thus generate profits.

Illegal copies are a major problem, but they are not the only problem. Online con artists have also plagued the video game industry. Those hackers use their talents to cheat and acquire super powers in online version of games like *Quake, Ages of Empire* or *Phantasy Star*. There is a rather lengthy list of cheats. Among them are super speeds to avoid bullets, and special codes to make you invincible. Clean gamers are obviously frustrated by this.

Home pirates hurt the developers they admire as gamers

Hackers not only create cheats, they make them available on the Net, undermining the very essence of the virtual worlds which developers have spent millions to create. Online versions, which most the time are free, represent an extra cost for developers. If they have to create a private police force to patrol the Net 24 hours a day, it is going to put a serious dent in their revenues. Genuine gamers have started to create a militia of game citizens to fight off intruders. They may even turn the war against hackers into a game!

For MMOG owners, permanent surveillance must be part of the online process: paying customers want to keep the integrity of the games they pay for. The game must be equal for all. There may be a business opportunity there for Pinkerton Online!

In the battle between online cops and online villains, technology and its various tools are becoming more and more complex and more and more easily available.

Online cheaters are a pain in the proverbial butt !

Part 3

Platforms and Games

10.

All Sorts of Games!

2001 Computer Game Sales by Genre
Ranked by Units Sold
(Source: NPD TechWorld™)

Strategy 25.4%
Arcade 3.4%
Adventure 4.3%
Simulation 5.6%
Driving 5.6%
Child 14.2%
Sports 8.1%
Role Playing 8.8%
Family 11.5%
Action 10.1%

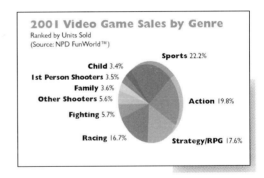

2001 Video Game Sales by Genre
Ranked by Units Sold
(Source: NPD FunWorld™)

Child 3.4%
1st Person Shooters 3.5%
Family 3.6%
Other Shooters 5.6%
Fighting 5.7%
Sports 22.2%
Action 19.8%
Racing 16.7%
Strategy/RPG 17.6%

Game genres

Action

Action games rely on hand/eye coordination, more than on story line. The pace is usually very fast. FPS games like *Half-Life, Quake* and *Unreal* are the most popular action games. *Soul Caliber* or platform games like the *Oddworld Abe's* series and the now classic *Tomb Raider* also belong to the category.

Adventure

In adventure games, the story line is paramount. All along your quest, you must solve riddles and explore all sorts of castles, rooms and settings. The narrative is predetermined and unfolds one step at a time. As you progress along the track, you interact with characters and use the objects in your inventory as well as you can. Among the best example of the genre are *Grim Fandango* by Lucas Arts and *The Longest Journey* by Funcom.

Puzzles and table-top games

This category addresses games which have been around for quite a while, like solitaire and bridge, checkers, chess, Monopoly, etc. *Tetris* and *Bust-a-Move* were born as video games but also fall into this category.

Role Playing Games

Role Playing Games are a bit like Adventure games but the emphasis is placed on the characters. The story does not have to be linear. Your interactions with other characters you meet on your way can greatly influence the way the story will unfold. There can be a lot of action too, as in *Diablo*. The current trend is towards online RPGs. Best examples are *Everquest* and *Ultima Online*.

Text-based adventure games

Text-based games are the dinosaurs of adventure games. *You Don't Know Jack* is one of the last representatives of a tradition going back to Lucas's *Habitat* and Infocom's *Zork*.

Educational

Educational games rely on interactivity to teach children various concepts and skills. Lucas Arts, with its *Star Wars* franchise, Disney and its innumerable toon characters, Humongus with *Putt-Putt* and Havas

with *Adibou* are the major companies creating games in that category.

Simulations

Simulations give you a first person perspective on how to fly planes, drive cars or steer submarines. They reproduce an element of reality as well as they can. Total immersion inside that element is what they want to achieve. Simulations of vast and complex ensembles also exists. *SimCity* simulates an urban area, *Populous* manages a variety of communities. With *The Sims*, you create human beings and watch them interact.

Sports

Sports games are realistic versions of popular team sports. Action is all over the place. You can build strategies from the point of view of one individual player or of a whole team. Sports game are very popular in PC format or as platform games. Official organizations (NFL, NBA, NHL, etc.) license out their names to specific developers. Other sports games bear the names of famous stars (*Madden, Tiger Woods*, etc.).

Strategy

Strategy games are all about logical thinking and resource planning. It is not necessarily how fast you react that matters, but how well you manage communities or unexpected events. Organization is the key. Tactics are all in the hands of the player. The old school is represented by *Civilization*, while the new trend (real time strategy) is exemplified by *Starcraft* and *Age of Empires*.

Games without a category

From time to time games appear which can't be classified in any specific category. They seem to pop out of nowhere. The rhythm and dance game *Parappa the Rapper* is a good example. So are *Rez* and *Seaman*, two gems from Sega.

Game Perspectives

Many games adopt a different perspective, a different camera angle, depending what part of the game you are in. Eventually gamers will be able to choose what angle they want to see the game from. Seamlessness between viewpoints will always be a problem. Right now game genres are associated with the angle which best suit a particular game.

First person

This the perspective adopted in most shooting games like *Quake*. In these 3-D games you see the action through the eyes of your character. Simulation games also adopt a first person angle.

Third person

Since the arrival of 3-D games, this is a very popular camera angle. It allows the gamer to see the hero in action and trace him (or her) wherever she goes. *Tomb Raider* popularized this visual approach. *Mario 64, Zelda, Crash, Metal Gear Solid, Resident Evil*, and platform games generally, are played from a third person angle. RPGs, sports games and adventure games also work that way.

Top view

This is nothing fancy! The camera angle is right above the action. *Galaxian, Centipede* and *Frogger*, from the golden age of Arcade games, were the first to adopt this point of view. Today only a few nostalgic Japanese game still use it.

Isometric view

This angle is more or less equivalent to the top-view, except that it adds depth. You see from above and also get a view of what lies ahead. This kind or perspective creates a feeling of total immersion. *Civilization* and *Starcraft* are the best examples: they allow you to have a wider view of your troops and immediately see where everybody is. *Diablo, Baldur's Gate* and *The Sims* also allow you to see all the characters and their local environment.

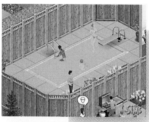

Side view

In the eighties and nineties *Mario* and *Sonic* turned this perspective into a classic. Because of the limits it imposes on gameplay and on the general look and feel of a game, it is becoming less and less common. A few recent games like *Abe's Oddworld* and *Worms* have given this perspective a radical brush-up. Somehow it fits rather well with the on-going action.

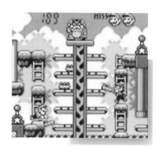

11.

Console games

There are games for all tastes and for all seasons! Trying to prove that one game is superior to another is a childish and pretty limiting endeavor. Pleasure is way too subjective. As any developer can tell you, the quantity of effort does not always equal the quality of experience.

One of the advantages of the capitalist system is that sales do send a clear message. True enough, some excellent games do not find their public. The amounts of money spent in promotional campaigns often make a huge difference. And yet, *Deer Hunter* did not need all the hoopla to achieve popular success with very little marketing. The casual gamer can have an impact!

There can be quite a difference between what reviewers think of a game, and what happens on the market. It is refreshing to see that gamers make their own opinion. Specialists, stare at the tree and won't see the forest! So my advice is in doubt, rent before you buy!

In this section of the book, I will talk about best sellers. But I will also mention games, which have highlighted the console's advantages. I will finally indicate my favorite games per platform. There may be cases when your favorite game is missing in action. With around 3000 games published each year, it's nothing but normal!

In case you are in the money and are already equipped with 4 consoles and a loaded PC, think of the next 3-D card you could get; think about the Dolby 5.1 audio you could add; and update your processor speed to 1 Gig Hz or more.

Then again, if you are broke, go out on the Internet and download 50 of the best PC demos.

<http://gigex.com/top50.asp>

And if you still have a few dollars left, well, here are the games! Go ahead! Rent or buy! Read the official guides and yes, have a look at the cheats too, but remember: "Easy victory yields no triumph or glory!"

Playstation One

The Playstation One has captured more than 47% of the console market. To date, 88 million units have been sold (30 millions in the US alone) and so have around 700 millions games. There is a PS1 in every three other household in America. There are over 1,000 titles to choose from. The average owner is 23 years old and one third is over 24.

The PS one is not a new console. But with its 5" portable screen it has the best resolution on the market. You can hook it to your car's lighter socket and let the teens play away in the back while you do the driving. There are vibrant colors and the refreshment rate is impeccable. The loudspeakers are quite convincing and the headphone outlet is a blessing for parents!

The new PS One will extend the PS1 life cycle

2001 Best sellers

The PS1 made RPG games popular in the US. *Final Fantasy 9* was an arch success. *Spiderman* is just too cool. You must try it. There are all kinds of excellent games:
- War games like *Medal of Honor Underground*.
- Survival games like *Dino Crisis 2*.
- Fighting games such as *WWF Smackdown 2*.
- Extreme driving with *Driver 2*.
- Skateboarding with *Tony Hawk Pro Skater 2* and *3*.
- There is also *Spyro Year of the Dragon*, *Rayman 2* and *Crash Bandicoot Warped*.
- Sports games like *Madden NFL 2001* and a platform game *Frogger 2* are still riding high among the top 10.

Grand Turismo 2 (late 1999) and *Tekken 3* (1998) continued to sell well in the new century. Classics never die!

My favorite PS1 games

Fear Effect 2: Femmes Fatales!

Mature titles are not going to appear in any significant number on the PS1. So if you haven't graduated to the PS2, where mature material abound, this game is your best choice! The game's visuals are splendid; the controls, very much in the *Resident Evil* tradition, are user friendly, precise, and well defined. The heroin is a smashing beauty, equally successful at making war and at making love! She has a new female companion. Skipping from one heroin to the next is one of the delights of the game. Of course killer robots, thugs and monsters of all shapes and sizes are going to make life a little difficult for you... But you will have at a number of fancy weapons at your disposal, among which a high-voltage rod that delivers mega volts and mega jolts! On your way, you can expect mathematical riddles and pattern-matching problems to pop up. And yes, you will have to collect a number of power objects before you can access higher levels. The four CDs are full with action and cinematics. All in all, *Fear Effect 2* this is a very original and very rewarding game.

<www.eidosinteractive.com/games/embed.html?gmid=81>

MLB 2002: Batter up!

In real life, professional teams don't always meet up to our expectations! So why don't you turn yourself into a manager and make sure your team becomes a solid winner? With *MLB 2002* you can act as a player or you can be the manager. Every aspect of game management is covered. Signing contracts, fishing for new recruits in the minor leagues... They're all there! Eight different game modes are available, plus an all-star game and of course the World Series. With such complete control over the players, you can put together an impressive line-up and then and only then show up for a game. The TV-like angles are quite realistic and the rules controlling the AI component are based on the expertise of the best players and the best managers in Major League baseball. There are over 300 motion captures and 250 gestures for which baseball stars are famous. A whole lot of virtual tobacco chewing in sight!

<www.989sports.com>

Birth of a game genre

Companies love to recycle their catalogue of great oldies. And the public keeps asking for more. With the *Final Fantasy Chronicles*, RPG game fans have a lot to rejoice about.

Final Fantasy IV first appeared on the Super Nintendo and it paved to way for the RPG game trend in America. But when *Final Fantasy VII* was launched, the trend turned into a craze. Its cinematics were awesome. They showed how things had changed in just a few years.

Bundled with *Final Fantasy VII* comes *Chrono Trigger*, another arch classic. Get yourself the *Official Brady Game Guide* and see how intricate these games are and how difficult it is to design right. The complexity of these two games is incredible. Ever since these two games came out, PS1 gamers have been their solid fans.

<www.squaresoft.com>
<www.bradygames.com>

What's up Doc?

For *Time Buster*, *Bugs Bunny* invited a famous guest: the *Tasmanian Devil*.

A2M played its competitors a good trick: it was first to introduce dual control. But not on a split screen, no Sir! Two characters are controlled by each of the two players, in the same environment. It made player cooperation as easy as pie. Cool hack! There is typical *Looney Toons* humor in the 30 odd levels. And there is a stunning variety of game styles. Characters like Yosemite Sam, Elmer Fudd and my favorite, Daffy Duck, pop in and strut their stuff now and then.

It is also possible to play solo, but then you have to move from one character to the next and use their talents to the best. Quite inspirational!

<www.a2m.com>
<www.infogrames.net/games/
bugstaz_timebusters_psx>

Neo-classic 2-D

Capcom created fantastic franchises. *Resident Evil*, *Street Fighter* and the *Mega Man* series, a legend in itself. More than 20 titles have been published since. *X5* uses the same old 2-D recipe. As you move up the various levels you fight the boss off and can incorporate his personal powers. This is pre 3-D gameplay: so simple, so fluid, and so pleasurable! *Mega Man* and *Zero* can now duck and avoid attacks, adding lots of fun, but the essence of the game comes from the final challenge and the special items you pick up on the way.

<www.capcom.com/megaman.htm>

A wheelie is not enough!

For the radical bikers among you, here is the game that will at last match your skills: *Matt Hoffman's Pro BMX*. *Pro BMX* uses Tony Hawk's incredible skateboard engine. The controls let you nail one radical move after the other, at full speed. The BMX pros pictured in the game all have their favorite routines and their variations are quite convincing. There are spectacular falls too! Think twice before you try those tricks in real life! The sound track is particularly well done. The Treatment Plant and La Habra are my favorite levels. But the best news is the level editor. You can design your own BMX courses and dare your friends to race against you! Way cool!

<www.activision.com/games/ mathoffman/index.asp>

Give them an eye

Time Crisis: Project Titan
X-Men: Mutant Academy 2
Tales of Destiny 2
Metal Slug X
Dance Dance Revolution.

Old timers

Tekken 3 is my favorite classic among fighting games. *Abe's Oddysee* and *Abe's Exoddus* and the two Oddworld titles, are superb, original and smart. *CTR* is the kart version of the excellent *Crash Bandicoot* series: here is a family game that's lots of fun! *Spiderman* is the best title among super hero games.

Developers have now turned their eyes on the new 128 bit consoles. But with 80 million PS1s out there, we can still expect a few surprises!

Nintendo 64

In December 2000, Nintendo sales were ranked 1 to 6 in the top 10. In December 2001, there were only 3 left in the 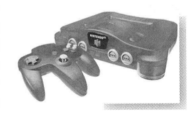 top 10, two of them being *Pokemon* titles: N64 was on its way out and GameCube was on the horizon.

The N64 installed base reached 30 million. In 2000 only, the *Pokemon* franchise cashed in $15 billions. If you don't know the *Pokemons* yet, you must be living on a different planet! The *Pokemons* have their own

2001 hits

With a 36.4% market share, Nintendo owns the world's best known characters. *Mario Tennis* and *Party 2 & 3, Donkey Kong 64, Zelda: Majora's Mask, Kirby and Banjo-Tooie* all had a new version this year. The impeccable *Perfect Dark* continued to galvanize gamers. In the Sports game category *WWF No Mercy, Madden NFL 2001, Excite Bike* and the ubiquitous *Tony Hawk* have had their hordes of fans. RPG amateurs have had *Mario Paper, Ogre Battle* and *Harvest Moon* to feast on. Younger kids have enjoyed *The Rugrats in Paris, Scooby-Doo, Pokemon Puzzle League,* and *Hey you Pikachu!*

Super Mario 64, Mario Kart 64 and Super Smash Brothers once again exemplified title longevity. Old as they are, they still find themselves among the top 10. The year ended with a final fireworks show called *Conker's Bad Fur Day*, by from developer "extraordinaire" Rare Ltd. All in all, with 60 new games, what an incredible year it was for Nintendo!

powers. Kids collect them and train them for future fights. Because the media have described them as a world phenomenon, we tend to forget how innovative and efficient they are as a game. Nintendo was smart enough to create entire dynasties of GameBoy and N64, cross-console, characters. Parents may have stopped trying to make sense out of them long ago, yet if learning math or modern languages was as fascinating as playing *Pokemon,* the world could count on a new generation of geniuses!

My N64 favorites

Banjo-Tooie: colossal, gigantic, out of this world!

The original game quickly stood out as one of the best platform games. The bear, the bird, and their quick wit are back! Rare inc. has added a number of other characters you can all control. Depending on what level you are on, you will be a T-Rex, a marble statue, or a washing machine. You have 40 moves at your disposal. You can play as Banjo or as Kazooie. There is a 4-player mode and even *a Golden Eye*-like shooter! Banjo-Tooie definitely has better controls and better camera angles than the original title.

Platform game amateurs are going to love it. The *Official Brady Strategy Guide* is available.

<www.banjo-tooie.com>
<www.bradygame.com>

Conker's bad fur day: Parents, keep out!

This game is a sure sign that Doomsday is coming! The best N64 developers have decided it was time to go out on a binge and let their wild animal side come out! The game starts with a mock imitation of Kubrick's movie Clockwork Orange. Characters piss, vomit, and fart at every corner of the game! Because of its rampant sexual and scatological innuendoes, it has been categorized for a "mature" audience (meaning aged 17 and above). But the "M" rating could also be due to the fact that it takes a lot of brain power to play with any kind of success.

There is a context-sensitive gameplay system, whereby all necessary objects or motions become available precisely when needed. Pissing on you opponents (Press "Z" for a full fountain dose!) or setting your farts on fire do require particular circumstances! You can play all the levels in solo mode, but you can also explore seven multi-player modes. There is one little game inspired by the opening scene in *Saving Private Ryan* that I highly recommend.

<www.conker.com>
<www.rareware.com>

Mario paper: let's go to RPG school!

The N64 never was especially graced with good RPG games... And suddenly, now that it has reached old age, out comes a superior game in that category: *Paper Mario!* IT is a direct offspring of Super *Mario RPG*. The characters are in 2-D, set in a 3-D like environment. As usual, Mario has to rescue the Princess from the slashing claws of Bowser. As with every RPG game, you have to keep an eye on your statistics. Several second roles assist Mario in his quest. Indeed, the game has got a "kiddy" look and feel, but this is exactly what our young ones want and this will help them get started along the rather convoluted paths of RPG games.

<www.papermario.com>

The Force is with Rogue Squadron!

Reviewers and gamers had given *Rogue Squadron* a very warm welcome! Factor 5, the developer, decided to go at it again… They came out with *Battle for Naboo*. If you like interstellar fights, you are going to love this game. You first have to save your captain and then, off you go to outer space! Fifteen missions will take you to very colorful environments. As you collect medals on the field of honor, you will experiment a variety of airborne battleships. The honorable N64 shines in all its glory. There is one level which takes place over shivering cold water ways: believe me, you are going to love it! Enjoy the soundtrack; the whole Star Wars atmosphere is very perceptible. *Battle for Naboo* is exactly the kind of action game N64 owners needed.

<www.lucasarts.com/products/naboo>

Majora's Mask: when minutes count!

In three days, the Moon is going to crash on the surface of the earth. Every minute you spend at the game is like one hour in the scenario's timeline. Thank God, you have a magical ocarina that you can play on to zip across time and come back to day one if you have to. You can save your most valuable power objects but you can't stop and save where you're at in the game. So *Majora's Mask* becomes a matter of smart time management. Pretty soon, you are caught in a frantic quest, plunging headlong into the adventure. Controls are very intuitive and you forget about them quickly. By donning a variety of masks, you will muster up the powers you need to solve riddles and fight off intruders. *Majora's Mask* is a masterpiece for the entire family.

<www.radiozelda.com>

Stadium 2: Nintendo does it again!

Pokemon *Stadium 2* harps on a traditional theme once again. But things are getting a bit easier. Remember the Pokemons you trained with so much care in your Game Boy compatible games? Thanks to the Game Transfer Pack you are going to be able to move them over to your N64. They will fight against one another and improve their status towards the four Stadium cup tournaments. There are 249 Pokemons available and you can learn about them at

Pokemon Academy, which is included with the game. Four opponents can fight at a time, in a 3-D stadium full with special effects. No surprise the franchise keeps going and going!

<www.pokemonstadium.com>
<www.pokemon.com>

Tony Haw's Pro Skater 2: last call for the N64!

Let's face it, N64 is at the end of its life cycle. But the old venerable is still kicking! For 2001, *Tony Hawk's Pro Skater 2* is one of the best games. You can select from among 13 skateboard pros or create your own athlete. Eight racetracks are provided, but you can design your own with the 3-D editor. You can play in solo mode or against your friends, listening to *Anthrax* and *Rage against the Machine*! The platform may be obsolete, but the game is nearly perfect!

<www.activisiono2.com/tony_hawk>

Give these game a try

Pokemon Puzzle League
Ogre Battle 64: Person of Lordly Caliber
WWF No Mercy
Spider-Man
Indiana Jones, and the Infernal Machine.+

Old timers

Super Smash Bros., with five millions de copies sold, is the perfect family game. *Golden Eye* is still fascinating. *Super Mario 64* started the 3-D revolution on consoles. The three of them are irresistible!

Sega's Dreamcast

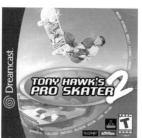

2001 hits

2000-2001 was a rock 'n'roll year for Sega. Lots of ups and downs. Still, two games for the Dreamcast stood out as truly original: *Jet Grind Radio* and *Shenmue*. The Dreamcast is still the only console to offer multi-payer games over the Internet.

Go see how well you drive compared to the *Speed Devils*. Or try your luck at *Quake III Arena*, *NFL 2K1* and *NBA 2K1*. You have got to try your skills at *Virtual Tennis*, *World Series Baseball 2K1*, and *Dave Mirra BMX*. And finally, for RPG amateurs, *Grandia* and *Skies of Arcadia* are really tops too.

If you like racing games, there are many to choose from: *Sega GT*, *San Francisco Rush 2049*, *Test Drive: V-Rally* and *Le Mans*. Sega made a big success with the arcade game *18-Wheeler Pro Trucker*. There is also *Crazy Taxi* and *Ready to Rumble*, apparently forever in the top 10. The Dreamcast has muscle to show off and quality titles to brag about: *Soul Calibur*, *MDK 2*, *Resident Evil: Code Veronica*, *Rayman 2*, *Tony Hawk 2*, *Hidden and Dangerous*, *Power Stone 2*, *Ecco the Dolphin*, *DOA 2*, *Rainbow 6* and *Fantasy Star Online*. *Phantasy Star* is the only RPG title available both on console and on the Internet. Sega published almost 150 titles in 2000 and an extra 100 in 2001.

Dreamcast games I loved

Jet Grind Radio: Tag it!

The game in itself is a good reason to buy a Dreamcast. Sega created a universe in which controlling animated cartoon characters is lots of fun. The moves are so realistic that you feel like you are controlling real people. You are wearing overdrive magnetic-motor skating shoes and act like a tag artist spraying the walls of Tokyo with vivid colors and shapes. Your competitors come from local street gangs, but they are the least of your problems when the powers that be use their tanks, helicopters, and heavily armed paratroopers to get to you. The ending is way cool since you have to fight a diabolical plan by Mafia thugs to control everybody's mind with a very special tune called *Pact with the Devil*. The sound track is rich with a variety of musical styles. You can grab a spray can and create your own tags or start collecting tags by your favorite artist. One control knob for jumps and one for tags, and bingo, you can plunge into a game that has incredible depth! Pure Japanese imagination! Definitely one the best games for the Dreamcast!

<www.sega.com/games/
dreamcast/post_dreamcastgame.jhtml?
PRODID=177>

Phantasy Star Online: high-tech phantasm!

With *Phantasy Star Online*, Sega pioneered console-based multi-player online gaming. A symbol system allows players to exchange understandable, cross-cultural messages. You can choose from nine characters and three professions. Line up a four-member team and things will kick into gear for you and your newfound friends. But beware! When the time comes to share your treasure into equal parts, your teammates may not behave as the honest human beings you thought they were! Human nature tends to take over and diplomacy goes out of the window, to be replaced by pure greed! Sega is definitely one of the best game developer in the world and this game stands as a living proof!

<www.sega.com/sega/game/
pso_launch.jhtml#>

Version 2.0 offers six new fighting modes, plenty of new power objects and added protection against hackers. Its costs $15 to get unlimited access to PSO2. The new Ultimate mode dramatically hikes up the level of difficulty. The solo mode is more balanced and the new Deathmatch will allow you to use

all of your combat skills, regardless of the levels other players are at. The Go Go Ball soccer mode is a little simplistic, but its cinematics are fun. You can import your character from version 1.0 into version 2.0. Try the free version, then move on to PSO2.

<www.sega.com>
<www.sega.com/community/profiles/member-shipselect.jhtml>

Skies of Arcadia: A gift from the sky!

With *Skies of Arcadia*, RPG game lovers now have a top game to rave about. The game is so good you will probably want to stop in mid quest and admire a job well done! The myths and legends in that universe are quite complex and the characters have a nice, attaching personality. Pirates in flying ships, islands floating in the sky... the environment is extremely beautiful. At every turn, a new wonder pops up. Special effects are spectacular and battles in mid-air leave you breathless. Armed with 70 different weapons, you will have 36 incantations to master. Moreover, there is a myriad of mini-games, sub-quests, and secrets to discover. RPG amateurs, go get that game and enjoy!

<www.sega.com/sega/game/
skies_launch.jhtml>

Sonic Adventure 2: Sonic boom!

10 years ago, *Sonic* revolutionized console games by introducing super-high speed, extremely vivid colors and attitude to boot! The Sega scream was heard around the world. With *Sonic Adventure 2*, Sega delivers top quality for the hedgehog's last run on a Sega console. The game runs at 60 frames per second. Gameplay is excellent, as ever, allowing you to move through the levels quickly. Challenges are increasingly difficult but level design is so well done that you always know what you have to do. The game offers three genres in one! You can choose shooting style, adventure style, or regular console style; the three merge very nicely. Other modes are available, such as "boss attack", "kart", "chao", and "versus". After you have gone through the official ending of the game you can access yet another level. Sonic team geniuses have lots of tricks up their sleeves. This is accessible interactive entertainment at its best.

<www.sega.com/sega/game/
sonic2_launch.jhtml>
<www.sonicteam.com/sonicadv2/
sonic_e.html>

Grandia 2: A grand RPG

Ubi Soft is a fast growing company. *Grandia 2* can explain why! Ryudo, the hero, has a quick tongue. He sets the pace and tone of the game. Among the top quality aspects are the game engine, the graphics, the sound track, and the interface. Fights are held in a mode that is sort of halfway between real time and traditional: turn based characters. Putting a different spin on the traditional RPGs, fights are not random. They are clearly marked out with icons. The attribute buying system allows a la carte distribution, which is rather original. The special effects coming with the incantations are really splendid; they all fit in very nicely with the highly detailed environment. Absolutely smashing!

<www.grandia2.com>

Ooga Booga: way out there!

Dreamcast console production has now stopped, but *Ooga Booga* carries on with Sega's amazing off-center game tradition. *Ooga Booga*, the goddess, organizes competitions in a magic Polynesian island. Champions from four different tribes are sent in and you are one of them! There are three tournaments. The visu-

als are kept simple, allowing for fast pan-out sequences. The levels are designed with the multi-user mode in mind. The Boar Polo mode is extremely funny. The multi-player online mode is implemented with real talent. Thumb candy at it's best!

<www.sega.com>

Alien Front Online: Everybody say Yeah!

Alien Front Online is a typical shooting game. You are from planet Earth, sitting at the controls of a tank and you try to fight off space aliens. Or you can play those space scums too! The solo mode offers 20 missions and is quite exciting as such. But the game's originality comes from its 8-player mode. For the first time on a console game, you can speak directly into a microphone inserted in the joystick. Thank you Sega for the idea! You have 5 to 10 seconds to express yourself. One message is dispatched at a time. New weapons become available as you move from one level to the next. Practice off line before going on the Internet, or else you may face severe public punishment. Innovative and fun!

WSK2K2: Sega steps up to the plate and swings!

WSB2K1 had superior visuals, but the gameplay was not as good. Sega reworked 2K1 entirely and the result is impressive. Flaws, glitches, and bugs have disappeared. There is a one-on-one online playing mode, plus five other modes. You can manage your season and your franchise; statistics play an active role. Because of the official WSB license, the baseball stadium and the baseball stars are pictured with extreme precision.

You have total control over the infield players, something that was not possible in 2K1, clearly a design mistake in a professional game. Players on the mound have a full array of vicious throws and they seem to know every batter's bad habits and shortcomings! With *WSB2K2*, Sega now has a solid baseball game. It will hold its ground when sport juggernauts such as Electronic Arts launch their games on PS2, GameCube, and Xbox.

Worms World Party Bite the dust, you lowly worm!

Gameplay is at the center of the interactive experience, yet it is very easy to forget it be swayed by technology. *Worms* is one of these games which has gained very wide acceptance without any of the usual 3-D bells and whistles. The con-

cept is new and, yes, incredibly efficient. You don't need to be an expert to enjoy this strategy game. All you have is a team of four worms and a full array of bazookas, earthquakes, and sheep you can use to destroy the enemy. In 45 seconds, each worm can do a lot of damage! This is a can of worms you will open with joy!

Bass Fishing: lots of outdoor fun and no black flies!

Ok, time for a pause. Get yourself a beer, turn on the TV set, and let's go fishing! Sega was the first company to introduce video outdoor activities to the arcade world. Make fun of the outdoor games if you want, but the market has a different view: *Bass Fishing* is very popular. Keep an open mind and try something different. Surprise, it is lots of fun!

Options will let you choose the time of day, the temperature, the bait, etc. You can use a scanner to "see" below your boat and cast your line on the best spots only. The cyber fishing rod is totally realistic. The only thing missing is fresh water pressing against your waist! Definitely the best game in its category.

Shenmue: Watch out, revolution in the making!

In *Shenmue*, you can freely stroll around and do as you wish. Rio, the main character wants to avenge his father's death. You are there to help him. He is attacked by a horde of martial arts specialists. There are two combat modes. One is inspired from *Dragon's Lair*, the other is a light version of *Virtua Fighter*. The orchestral music is perfectly in synch with the action. *Shenmue* made history by offering heightened freedom of movement in a virtual world.

<www.shenmue.com>

Metropolis Street Racer: C'mon, step on it!

Metropolis Street Racer is in a class of its own. The 3-D graphics will immediately jump at you. Complete city districts from London, Tokyo and San Francisco have been reproduced up to the minutest detail. You'll play in real time, depending on the time zone you are in. Each city has its own radio stations. You can create your own CDs. These new design elements are impressive in themselves, but make no mistake, the most impressive aspect is the game engine itself. There are more than 40 car models to choose from, and 13 car manufacturers altogether. The learning curve is smooth and you can go a long way before you hit expert level. Get this game, all of you Dreamcast buffs and race fans out there!

<www.sega.com>

Scare dare!

More and more gamers will admit (with a little coaxing) that they got scared playing video games. If you don't believe them, try the *Resident Evil* series. This is the best you can get in the way of survival/horror games. And *Code Veronica* is the best game of the series so far.

The game integrates exploration, armed survival, and problem solving in the most majestic way. Every element in the game is there to make you feel more and more isolated. So turn the light down, and let yourself be engrossed in the atmosphere. Terror is right around the corner…

The Dreamcast version comes on 2 CDs. You can expect about 25 hours of uninterrupted fright!

Resident Evil 2 and *Resident Evil 3* are excellent too, but start with *Code Veronica*. Welcome to the universe where goose bumps and chills are served hot and steamy!

And justice for all at junior high!

If you are like me, you must be pretty upset about the level of everyday violence in our school system. It does crank up expectations for unnecessary horror in our video games, as if we didn't get enough on TV already. In *Project Justice*, Capcom chose a typical schoolyard for its background. The amazing 2-D expertise the developer possesses has been elegantly transferred in this 3-D fighting game graced with wild attacks and rather unique anime style characters. You can create teams of three fighters. The deeper you get into the game, the more dangerous and imaginative the attacks will get. The game is unpretentious, easy going and fun... just like what junior high-school yards should be!

<www.capcom.com>

Trigger-happy!

It is not easy to design successful first person shooters for the console market. When *Golden Eye* first came out, most of its success came from the fact that the controls were very easy to get used too.

Though you still use the keyboard and the Dreamcast mouse for games like this, you will easily get into this one with your trusty game pad.

With *Outtrigger*, you can at all times select first-person or third-person camera angle. This arcade conversion is handled with flair. You have several modes to choose from: solo, four-player and even six-player mode in the online version. Form your own party of friends and challenge other wannabe hot shots on the web. If you want to experience better immersion, deselect the Control Assist option. You can create your own character by selecting properties from a base of four possible configurations in terms of weapons and skills. As you move forward into the game, you will be able to up the ante in every category. The frame rate is stable at 60 fps. Special effects are delivered with talent. The learning curve is cool and the bosses you have to fight out are quite challenging.

The 40 solo missions are well designed. With its exceptional graphics and online multiplayer mode this title is quite a respectable first person shooter.

<www.sega.com>

Does what ever a spider can!

The Dreamcast version is the best of all versions to date. For the first time, a super hero game conveys the feeling of having super powers you can actually use. You can climb walls, cast your web, lift heavy objects, jump from one sky-scraper to the next and swing like a pro at the end of your spider thread. Villains beware! Stan Lee, the comics strips legend does the voice over and the original song theme is there to boot! While we are waiting for the film... *Spiderman, Spiderman!*

<www.neversoft.com/spiderman/index.htm>
<www.activision.com/games/spiderman>

It's a mad, mad world!

Crazy Taxi 1 was a hit the minute it came out. The scenario is simple: you take a passenger aboard and drive him to destination as fast as you can. Special shorts-cuts, lots of fun driving tricks, mini-games, and interesting visuals made it an instant crowd pleaser.

Crazy Taxi 2 is a little more demanding. So if this is your first time with this award winning game, start with version 1. Old fans can jump into version 2 right away.

In *Crazy Taxi 2*, the action takes place in busy New York City. You can load several passengers at a time and increase your revenue. You can drive right over buildings for better efficiency and extra pay! You can play all sorts of mini-games: Crazy Golf is particularly interesting.

Rocking band Offspring is back at the wheel of the soundtrack. The multi-player and the online modes have disappeared. Give yourself a treat and go crazy in the Big Apple!

<www.sega.com/sega/game/
crazytaxi2_launch.jhtml#>

Just as good as at the arcade thrill!

Daytona USA allows teams of 4 to compete against one another. This is as close as you can get to a full arcade experience. There are tons of options, superb graphics, 10 circuits to race on and 5 playing modes. The solo mode is quite acceptable, but the online version is the one you want to try: you can lose your three opponents in the fog, display race results, download driver statistics and create phantom cars to train on before entering competition. You can personalize your car and your game pad response. You can replay every race and learn from your mistakes. The sensation of speed is exceptionally well rendered. Even without the online mode, the game would be a smashing hit! So you know what to do: ready, set, go!

<www.sega.com/
post_gamegame.jhtml?PRODID=748>

House of the Dead 2: Typing skills required!

Here is another inventive, original and wacky game from Sega. In our Internet age, we all have to improve our typing skills. Why not do it in a fun way? This is basically what *House of the Dead 2* is all about. Those zombies are so hungry to get a bite out of you that you will quickly improve your typing skills, only to dodge them better! By typing the words right on top of them, you can send them back directly to hell.

The keyboard you play *Quake Arena* with is going to be your best weapon! You intellectual giant you!

The whole thing is rather weird, but on the whole, it is quite fun and efficient way to bring your typing skills up to par! I am a peaceful kind of guy, but I must admit that those pesky zombies really deserve to be fed a lead bullet breakfast.

<www.sega.com/games/dreamcast/ post_dreamcastgame.jhtml?PRODID=680>

Other titles you can give a try

NBA 2K2
NFL 2K2
World Series Baseball 2K2
Last Blade 2: Heart of the Samurai
Soldier of Fortune

My favorites

I still consider *Soul Calibur* as THE best fighting game on console. *Virtual On*, with its giant Mechs, is also a blast to play with. The *Ready Rumble 2* series is fun, efficient, simple, and brings in a bit of fresh air to the genre. *Worms Armageddon* is hilarious and dangerously addictive!

SONY'S PS2

Fueled by the most controversial launch of history, the PS2 made the Guinness book of records with 500,000 units sold on the very first day. In its first year, Sony sold over 10 million units, three of them in the US. The 25 million mark is now behind them.

2001 biggest hits

Electronic Arts titles such *SSX, Madden, NHL* and *FIFA 2001* are brilliant. *Dead or Alive* and *Tekken Tag* are fine new generation fighting games. *Quake III, Unreal Tournament* and *Red Faction* are very elegant first person shooters. *Sky Odyssey* is an interesting flight simulator and *Armored Core 2* is a strong Mech game. It is pleasant to see that *Theme Park Roller Coaster* works fine on a console. *Starfighter, ATV Offroad Fury, Twisted Metal Black, Dynasty Warrior, Kessen* and *Smuggler's Run* are fast paced and very well designed. If you want to have a good give idea of what the PS2 can do, *Grand Turismo 3* and *Metal Gear Solid 2: Sons of liberty* are probably the best titles to look at.

PS2 games I loved

The PS2 finally delivers!

The title that was supposed to show what the PS2 really had to offer was finally offered to the wide-eyed crowds. The sort of craze taking place now and then around a specific game is perfectly justified in the case of *Gran Turismo 3: A-Spec.* I know some people who have decided to take their vacation playing it! Good bye blue sky! The most difficult thing for these maniacs will be to stop playing, take care of the basic bodily function, have a bite, and rest some!

In the beginning, and some would still argue that it is still the case, Dreamcast titles were better looking than the first PS2 titles. People started to question all the hype, which was passed around when the PS2 was released. Big Chief Ken Kutaragi remained firm, repeating gamers would see for themselves, as soon as good developers would get to work. Quite insulting for the lowly third party developers, wasn't it? Well anyway, the inside job must have helped, because it turned out Ken was right: *Gran Turismo 3: A-Spec*, is the best interactive 3-D game!

Gran Turismo 2, produced by Sony's star developer Polyphony Digital, had sold 11 millions copies. Beating that mark is not going to be easy! The title was first meant to be published on the PS1, but finally, it came out on the PS2 in April 2001. Over the first 48 hours, 1 million copies were sold in Japan.

GT3 is a driving simulator. Cars are reproduced with particular attention. Car accidents, however, do not show realistic impacts; the reason is simple: car manufacturers objected to having their pet products look bad after a spill. It was either that or no license!

More than 150 models are available, from the most exotic one to the most standard. There are two race modes: arcade and simulation. The race replay option now has several camera angles you can choose from and if you try them out you will quickly notice that pleasure and practice can grow together!

In the arcade mode, you have to defeat five AI opponents race after race to climb up the ladder, which is a complete game in itself… You can play solo or with a friend. But if want, you can use the i.Link socket and connect up to six different PS2s for a unique experience indeed. You can also look at the race from a spectator's point of view. The Broadcast option will offer you to choose from several TV camera angles! Amazing!

The simulation mode takes you through a real adventure. You will get better and better, spending your race earnings in technical improvements to your car. The learning curve is pretty steep. You can spend a lot of time getting to the top, where the best cars will become available.

GT3 has really got the looks! The game is just too beautiful! Notice the lighting effects, the distortions occurring in the reflected light because of the heat. Watch the dust clouds rising from the dirt tracks. The light rays at sunset and the reflections on cars passing by create a very specific ambiance… And look what happens when the track gets wet! Amazing! Wide screen TV owners can display the game in 16:9 anamorphic format.

The sound track has been treated with equal care. Cars have their individual engine roars, rev ups and purrs; and the tires have their own screech! If you want to feel fully immersed, turn off the music and listen to the public shouting in the wind!

GT3 is the sort of game you will have fun playing with the first time you try. "Wow!" and "Cool!" is what you are going to hear. GT3 is more than a classic. It is a new stage in the development of video game.

<www.scea.com/games/categories/racing/Gt3>

The most awaited video game in history

The console war is going to rage on without mercy. Three days before the Xbox was launched, Sony released its blockbuster title: *Metal Gear Solid 2*. With 20 million PS2 consoles and six million original copies out there, Sony obviously wanted to kick its rivals in the shins.

Hideo Kojima is a visionary. He is the rock on which Japanese company Konami is built. He is famous for *Metal Gear Solid 2 (MGS2)*. The game is sought after like crazy, particularly since the introduction of the PS2. With its intuitive gameplay and its life like graphics, the game is the best ambassador for the PS2. Kojima is obsessed with details and his signature includes stylistic elements such as flow and seamlessness.

The first thing not to do is to read the instruction manual. I want you to enjoy every bit of surprise. This is interactive art at its best. No self-respecting gamer can do without it! There is a new signature series *Official Brady Strategy Guide* that is absolutely smashing!

<http://ps2.ign.com/news/33019.html>
<www.konami.com/main/games/mgs2>

The king is dead, long live the king!

From the first game on, the *Final Fantasy* series became a standard. Gamers will never forget the hours they spent in their quests. They will never forget the cinematics, the most beautiful in the entire industry.

Characters change from one game to the other, which is unusual in a series. But who cares? The game has been so successful that event the complete flop of the movie version didn't affect the sales. *FF VII* sold seven million copies! And in Japan, in two days, two million copies left the stores when *FF X* was released!

When the game is played in real time, the image resolution is usually different from when cinematics are played. That difference, which has always affected our sense of immersion, is now becoming less and less visible. There will be a time when real time images and cinematics will look exactly the same: no more abrupt resolution changes and no more "suspension of disbelief".

The visual effects and numerous bosses are still very impressive. One thing is entirely new: you can introduce new characters during your fights. Teams are usually made out of three people, but now, with a single push of shoulder button L1, you can access your reserve and select an extra character. This is a great advantage. It has considerable strategic consequences. Weapon and item inventory management is made a lot simpler: even if a new character steps in at the very end of a fight, he can have his share of the booty when victory finally comes.

Squaresoft has announced that *FF X* would be the last single player of the dynasty: everything is being moved over to the Web for *Final Fantasy XI*. So take *FF X* as the swan's cry of one of the most beloved game franchise.

Here again, a good look at signature series Brady's official guide will help you take better advantage of all the game's potential.

<www.squaresoft.com/playonline/games-frameset.html>
<www.bradygames.com>

Thugs wanted!

If all violence could take place in cyberspace, society as a whole would certainly be better off. Humor and derision have always been a tool by which artist (and now game designers) pass sarcastic comments on our society.

Grand Theft Auto 3 is a new generation game, which introduces us to the untamed and taboo world of criminal behavior. The purpose of the game is to steal cars and get noticed by the mob kingpins. You can do it in great number of ways. Of course, you will have to drive at top speed, rub fenders and elbow your way as if you were a stock-car expert; but don't worry for your vehicle: it is a strong and sturdy as any on the circuit! If you want to win, you have to be the meanest bully of them all! *Grand Auto Theft 3* depicts a cruel world indeed! You will have to drive, shoot, explore, and adopt an attitude the way you would in an RPG game.

The action takes place in three different parts of Liberty City. Each one has specific feel and atmosphere. In each mission, you are faced with a variety of characters. Cinematics move the story forward in seamless fashion. You are free to explore as much as you want. As you do so, you will fall into pretty hectic situations... There are weapons, powers, and secret tunnels to discover. The AI component is very powerful. The soundtrack of your career as a criminal is provided by nine different radio stations. Excellent professional actors lend them their voice and the result is very convincing. Elements in the game all fit in very nicely. This is one of the best games in the year.

<www.rockstargames.com/grandtheftauto3>

Jak and Dexter: The best 3-D platform game ever?

Crash Bandicoot humorous designers have had incredible success. Their marsupial star has sold 20 million copies worldwide. Pushing the platform genre to the next level, they have come out with *The Precursor Legacy.*

Graphics are great. The gameplay is a good example of what it should always be. The title, as such, is not revolutionary. But it puts together all the best elements in the genre and it eliminates many of the defects that drove us crazy before. Game rules and objectives are explained quite clearly: you always know what you have to do. Controls are extremely intuitive and the reactions are immediate. Camera angles change

and flow nicely. Character animation is top quality, which adds to the pleasure of discovery. *Jak and Dexter* is absolutely brilliant.

<www.scea.com/games/categories/
actionadvent/jakanddaxter>
<www.naughtydog.com>

NBA Street: Hip-Hop sport!

Electronic Arts Vancouver studio, who developed the incredible snowboard game *SSX Big*, is back with a new title: *NBA Street.* You don't have to come from a ghetto to get a street basket ball education! It has nothing to do with the professional game. Two teams of three players compete. As in *SSX Big*, a number of tricks and acrobatics ups the fun factor. The Hip-Hop intro puts you right in the mood. In the City Circuit mode you can build your dream team and compete with the best three NBA players or with players from the street. As you start winning games, you'll get to travel around the US for other games to play.

In the Hold the Court mode, there is a function allowing you to create new players, teams, and fields, giving the game an RPG approach. The more you win, the better your players become. Try the easy level first, get into the hang of it, and then try the intermediate level where the AI component is already quite efficient.

The fact than only six players are in the field, rather than the usual ten, must have helped the graphics team to create excellent renditions for the basketball players. The acrobatics will leave you breathless.

The background setting is full of details, giving the whole game a very realistic appearance. The soundtrack fits well with the competitive atmosphere.

Controls are intuitive. The acrobatics are triggered by different combinations of the four top shoulder buttons of the game pad. The game breaker option allows you to deliver the opponent team a real blow. Tension builds unavoidably till the end of the game. Honestly, the game is more than exciting, it is nerve-racking and lots of fun! *NBA Street* is a complete success.

<http://nbastreet.ea.com>

Devil May Cry: hellish efficiency!

I love Capcom! This company has given us superb titles such as *Street Fighter, Mega Man* and *Resident Evil*. In 2001, *Onimusha* caused quite a surprise, but *Devil May Cry* is the one that will really sock it to you! At the PS2 presentation by Sony, during E3, it had caused enthusiastic roars and comments from all gamers present.

This action game is like a sustained adrenalin rush! There are guns, swords, combos and enemies of all sorts and shapes. The camera angle is always the same, but the controls are so efficient that with the automatic cross-hair system, interactivity is at its best. Our hero, Dante can shoot in every direction as he walks, jumps, runs and does his own acrobatics! He can even shoot enemies as they are up in air, writhing under his

fire. The game is going to draw comments like "Wow! So cool!" There is a superb *Official Brady strategy guide* available for *Devil May Cry*.

<www.capcom.com/devilmaycry>
<www.bradygames.com>

Silent Hill 2: Freak out city!

Horror games for platforms have found a new master! With *Silent Hill*, claustrophobia, hyperrealism and the evil eye are everywhere. The screen exudes with cold sweat and anguish. Meet James, the hero, gets a message from his wife who passed away three years before.... Silent Hill is the city where the action and gore is staged. Just as with the original, action, riddles and exploration are part of the scenario. The story unfolds as if we were in a nightmare. There is a ubiquitous haze, which becomes almost a character per se... It is very realistic and yet eerie and out of this world.

Moving about town is made easy, thanks to the intuitive controls. I was impressed by the cinematics. The soundtrack adds to the feeling of immersion. The game is addressed to a mature audience. Konami brings the horror/survival genre to yet another level. Be warned: this is a disturbing little tale.

<www.konami.com/silenthill2>

SSX Big: back to the board!

It is always a joy when a game that seems to come out of nowhere becomes an instant classic!

SSX Big was developed by EA Canada. The game is all about speed and acrobatics on the snowboard. It was the best title available when the PS2 was launched. Graphics are exceptionally good. Replay value is fantastic. It does not have much in common with regular snowboarding. Imagine your Mount Local invaded by hyper aggressive champions who love to push and shove you around till you lose it… while you're doing exactly the same! A regular barrel of laughs!

The race starts with 24 participants, all more or less mentally deranged. Your mission is to bomb down the trail and make it to the finish line among the first three competitors! Of course, there are shortcuts you can take and blows you can give. But don't worry about a broken leg! You can experiment with daredevil jumps that would leave pros panting! The acrobatics mode is just as much fun as the race mode. Trail design is what make SSX Big such an incredible game. Trails are long, detailed and pre-loaded. With the PS2, background images suddenly coming out of nowhere are things of the past. Way cool!

SSX Tricky is the latest version and is stronger than ever. It is more beautiful and as agreeable than the original. The experience is big. The game still doesn't have much to do with real snowboarding and this is what's so cool about it! The stunts are not realistic, they are tricky!

<www.ea.com/exphat.jsp?destURL=ssx.ea.com>

Tekken Tag Tournament

Tekken is the most popular console series in the US. If you want to have an idea of what Tag Tournament is, see it as Tekken 3 on steroids! Characters are drawn with more polygons. Image resolution is higher and the environment as a whole is definitely superior.

The new trick is the Tag mode. Press a button and an extra fighter will jump into the fray. You have thirty opponents to defeat. Background images and special effects are very realistic. There are plenty of secret elements to discover, more than in any other fighting game. No one can say Namco shuns innovation: the company was bold enough to add the infamous Tekken Bowling mode. Pinch me somebody!

<www.namco.com>

Onimusha: Warlords/ The soul of the warrior

With Onimusha: Warlords, Capcom, the master of horror games, is now directing its efforts towards the PS2. The intro scene will just blow you: five minutes of the best 3-D I have ever seen.

The action takes place in feudal Japan, during the 16th

century. But the story about the samurai who has to rescue the princess transcends time. Capcom did announce that this was their most imposing production ever. Let's admit they spent their money wisely. Characters are designed with great details. Takeshi Kaneshiro, the Japanese martial arts star, lent his professional moves to the main character, Samenosuke. The background is rich with convincing animated additions like flying bats, moving shadows and weather changes, enhancing the immersion effect.

Just like in *Resident Evil*, there is a good balance between physical action and problem solving, except there is more action in *Onimusha*. The Gods in the game will give you all sorts of weapons plus a special gimmick allowing you to store the energy coming from your enemy's soul; plus quartz crystals for you to tame Nature's elements and use them in your favor. You will also have a female fighter friend at your disposal. She will help you save Samenosuke from a number of pitfalls. It is violent and superb. A must.

<www.capcom.com/onimusha_teaser.htm>

Ring of Red: 3-D strategy games

Strategy games represents 27% of PC game sales, but on consoles, for all sorts of reasons, the genre is almost non-existent (2%). Konami decided to turn that wind around and create *Ring of Red*, the best console strategy game ever. The learning curve is steeper than on a platform game. I don't think it will turn hundreds of thousands of console gamers into strategy game fans. But if you are into strategy games, you must give it a try.

The action takes place in a parallel world where Japan has just fought off alien invaders. With steam-propelled Mech robots. The fighting system is more immersive than in a classic PC game because you are drawn into the action. You can influence the outcome of the battle thanks to a user friendly interface. You can pay attention to every aspect of the action. A unique and engrossing experience!

<www.konami.com/main/home_frame.html>

Rayman 2: The French dynasty carries on!

Rayman 2 Revolution follows on the steps of the N64 version published at the end of 1999. The game was then successfully adapted to the PS1, the Dreamcast and the PC platform. As always, the graphics are spectacular. But the most striking aspect is the very inventive level design. There is also some new material like three multi-player mini games with two levels to discover. There is a remarkable new addition: a radar which helps you pick up drops of light on your way. The sound track and the sound effects deserve to be heard on a home movie system.

Using the extra memory offered by the DVD format, Ubi Soft was able to add French, Spanish, German and Italian versions of the game. One day, all games will be designed that way... *Rayman 2* is top of the line, period.

<www.raymanworld.com>

Star Wars Starfighter: The Force is with this one!

Beautiful! And with action galore! Space combat fans were expecting something like that on the PS2, and they finally got it! At 60 frames per second, space ships, backgrounds, lighting, explosions and other special effects are given excellent treatment by the game engine. Each of the three characters has their own spaceships. You will have adapt to their different combat style. The 14 missions have several levels of difficulty. If you complete them with success, you will have access to a few extra levels, which are really worth it. The firing system is very instinctive. The zoom function makes shooting enemies all the more pleasant! *Starfighter* is an elegant continuation for *Battle for Naboo*. Overall a solid title, which no Star Wars fan will want to miss.

<www.lucasarts.com/products/starfighter>

ATV Offroad Fury: Full throttle!

ATV Offroad Fury is the first game to come out of Sony's studio that really pushes the PS2's capabilities to the limit. The expertise they gained while developing *Motocross Madness* is apparent. *ATV Offroad Fury* is a good example of mental backlash. It is so well designed that it could give you the impulse to buy a four-wheel drive, and rip the environment with a big smile on your face!

The outdoor environment is huge. You can personalize your vehicle quite easily. The four-player mode is a success. Controls are intuitive and efficient and the AI component adds to the competitive aspect of the game. As one can expect in a PS2 game, there are beautiful sunsets and delightful fall colors up the trees. There is a button to let you take a peek behind, adding to the sense of speed and urgency. The game has twenty race tracks plus a "freestyle stunt" option, which adds days of gameplay. The music score includes tunes by bands such as Soundgarden, Primus, Alice in Chains and Antrax. This gives you an idea of the kind of gamer Sony is aiming at.

<www.scea.com/games/categories/racing/atv>

Dark Cloud: a snappy mix

There is now a tendency among game designers to create hybrids by mixing game genres. *Dark Clouds* borrows from every-where, creating a unique experi-ence where the end product is superior to the sum of the parts. The role-playing influence comes from *Zelda* and from Squaresoft's epics. As you explore the dungeons randomly, you will acquire the hundred items you need for your battles against the bosses. The fighting system does the job accordingly. There is a nice variety of environments to play in. Your allies are gifted with powers you'll be very happy to take advantage of. Your hero's world has been destroyed and you must help him rebuild it. Hopefully, the game offers you Georama, a design tool for new environments. You can create new environments from a ? top view perspective, but you can run them in full 3-D. Impressive indeed! The temperature will change during the game and this will affect your game. With more than fifty hours of gameplay, *Dark Cloud* will take you through a highly imaginative adventure.

<www.scea.com/games/categories/
roleplaying/darkcloud>

Shadow of Destiny: Change your destiny!

On consoles, adventure games are far and few apart. So the appearance of *Shadow of Destiny* on the PS2 comes as a surprise. But what's more, it is a fascinating title! How often have you wished you could come back in time, experience a precise event once again, but acting differently? This is what the game is all about.

The challenge is to change your karma and pre-vent your own death. Whether you go back in time for a few hours or a few centuries doesn't make any differ-ence: everything you do can affect your future. This is the kind of notion that makes the game really interest-ing. The story line is so well knit that whatever you choose to do, you will be drawn to one of five prede-termined endings. The numerous backgrounds are impressive. Shadows from different light angles move in real time, adding a nice touch. The cinematics are played by the game engine so that the story can unfold with seamless elegance. This title did not get much of a promotional campaign and yet it ranks among the most convincing game.

<www.kcetokyo.com/som/english/top/
e_shadow1.html>

Zone of the Ender: Screaming metal

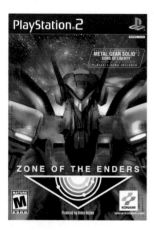

It is no surprise if the first playable demo for Metal Gear Solid 2 is included in the *Zone of the Ender* DVD. Hideo Kojima is responsible for both titles. *Zone of the Ender (ZOE)* is an excellent robot combat game in full 3-D Anime style. Controls are intuitive and help turn battles into sheer pleasure. The structure is simple: you must move from one zone to the next, shooting down your opponents in very impressive environments. There is a variety of weapons and of attacks. Holding your enemy at arm's length is an option, which comes with a variety of strategies. The camera is the most striking element in the game: the analog control button is simple and efficient, allowing the camera angles to flow nicely with the action. Hop on a robot and fight like a... machine!

<www.konami.co.jp/kcej/products/zoe/english/index.html>

MDK2 Armageddon: original, cool and bloody funny

The original version was created by the pranksters from Shiny, of *Earthworm Jim* fame. Gamers loved it but the general public didn't catch on to it. In *MDK2*, the difficulty level is now adjustable, so this factor can't be used as an excuse any more. The game is now in the hands of Bioware, the Canadian company, which *Baldur's Gate* made famous. Under their direction, *MDK2* did not become an RPG, but it certainly grew in size and scope. The PS2 is a good support for the outer world atmosphere expressed in the superb 3-D visuals. Humor is constant and the characters have kept the same quick tongue. This is a unique, bizarre and entertaining title.

<www.bioware.com/mdk2/mdk2game.shtml>
<www.shiny.com/games/mdk/index.htm>

Super Bombad Racing: you big headed alien!

Ever since *Mario Kart* was published, licenses owners all feel compelled to produce a go-kart race version. Star Wars owners did just that and adapted their pod race to the sub-genre.

This Lucas Arts game is very well crafted. All the right elements are there. Success lies in the skilful combination of good kart and good pilot. You have to find the good shortcuts and all the special items, and, of course, you have to drive like a pro.

The various modes can be played solo, with up to four players, or in teams. The races are run in nine environments from *The Phantom Menace*. To keep you on edge, there are gravity effects and two dozen gadgets available. What makes this game so agreeable to play is that you can race out against your pals and show that your driving skills are backed by the Force!

<www.lucasarts.com/products/bombad/lecindex.html>

Dead or Alive 2

This incarnation of *Dead or Alive, Hardcore*, is the most impressive in the series. It's got everything a fighting game fan could dream of. In this new version, You will find two new hidden characters, many more combat moves, a grand total of 15 levels, twice as many costumes, better graphics and up to ten playing modes. The graphics engine has improved in every way: twice as many polygons available, graceful body moves and an incredible array of real time lighting effects.

Each of the fighters has new moves and combos. The fighting engine is brilliant. The characters are wild and engage in ferocious battles. If you haven't played *DOA* yet, try the latest edition; it is one of the best fighting games on the market.

<http://64.70.202.85/home.http>

Gauntlet: Dark Legacy

Playing a favorite arcade game at home is always a thrill. Fans of the Gauntlet classic series are in for a treat. In *Dark Legacy* the feeling of urgency that was so present in the arcade version is now replaced by an exploration in *Diablo* style. This is the most accomplished version so far. The action is a lot more intense, with new characters and new incantations tied to a fairly simple level strategy.

Attack and spell combos are quite sophisticated. Special effects are spectacular. The levels are pretty complex and include an exciting multi-player mode where 4 opponents can fight at a time. The characters own enough attributes and attacks to keep gamers on the alert. Gauntlet's legendary voice is back, bringing you back to the arcade version. This heroic fantasy saga will haunt you for eternity, at least!

<www.midway.com>

Klonoa 2:Lunatea's Veil: a little gem!

The first version, on the PS1, was excellent. With *Kloana 2*, Namco has just created an amazingly low profile title.

Kloana's looks, for the American macho men, may look a bit on the softy side, so some of them may simply fail to notice. The 3-D graphics and the gameplay go really well together. You never look around, not knowing what to do. The camera angle never gets in the way. Kloana grabs her enemies and uses them as projectiles or as props to jump over obstacles. It is simple, it is efficient. The riddles are fun to solve and as you move up in the game, they will become more and more sophisticated. The aesthetics are superb. Jet Grind Radio's 2-D/3-D cell shading look is put to good use. This is exactly what happens when old time gameplay is happily married to the bells and whistles of new technology. Please to not miss this ever pleasing game!

<www.namco.com/usa_index.html>

Twisted Metal Black: Reckless driving!

As our four-wheel drive fans know only too well, rough rides can be a real ball! With video games there is no limit: you can drive like a total maniac. *Twisted Metal* had opened the gates some and now with *Twisted Metal Black,* boy, the gates are flung open! Watch out, though, this is not a game for kids! It is inspired by the atmosphere of the scariest horror movies... and it works! The basic theme is this: a bunch of crackpots have escaped from the asylum and they are determined to settle their feuds once and for all. How? By entering a tournament where ugly, twisted hot rods and vehicles of all sorts will race! The solo modes (story, the challenges and endurance) are nicely put together. You can also work them out on a cooperative basis. But the best of the best is the multi-player mode. The levels are huge, with lots of innovative stuff and their design is fantastic. You can destroy just about everything and you're given the proper weapons too! The special effects will get you! You will speed through like you never have before. The controls are extremely precise. This title demonstrates what the PS2 is really capable of. The web site is totally crazy and just too cool!

<www.scea.com/games/categories/shooter/tmb/>

Red Faction: with a pick and a shovel!

Red Faction is a top-quality shooting game with lots of personality. The environments are destructible thanks to the Geo-Mod house technology. Cosmetic, but cool! Real time physics is applied to wind, and water, and to the bits and pieces flying off. The AI aspects are just as good. There is a strong multi-player mode, where Geo-Mod can be used creatively. The level editor's gameplay is top-notch and definitely the game's best asset. Inventive and fresh!

<www.redfaction.com>
<www.thq.fr>

Music Generator 2: DJ Gamer!

This is a piece of engineering software that will turn you into a DJ and a composer in no time. I can't promises you will get a contract for your new album and I can't promise Mistress Barbara will admire your work. But I can tell you that trying it out is a pleasure worth the entrance ticket! MTV's *Music Generator 2* will make you an overnight composer out of you. This piece of software compares favorably with professional tools on the market. You can create your own music from included samples then move on to your psychedelic video-clip! Several music genres are offered: house, trance, break beat, indie, garage, pop and R&B. The samples and melodies can be edited so that you can personalize your compositions. Don't tell you pals, just play what you worked on. They will ask you where you got this killer groove. Put your sunglasses and say, with a blasé look on your face: "Just my latest hit, call me DJ gamer".

Nascar Heat 2002: race frenzy!

Companies that have launched car racing games at the same time as *Grand Turismo 3* are taking a big risk: their product may be ignored. In the case of *Nascar Heat* and *Tokyo Xtreme*, that would be too bad. Both titles have got everything they need to attract racing fans. Nascar races are very popular in the US. With 19 race-tracks and 25 pilots, the license is pretty well covered. You can add your own specifications to your speedscar or you can hop in and drive away. Four different camera angles are offered, which is nice to have. *Nascar Heat 2002* is a good, solid game to have on the PS2.

<www.infogrames.com>

Tokyo Xtreme Racer Zero

This racing game is a totally different thing. The theme is quite original. It will stir up the macho man in you as you enter a series of illegal races bang in the heart of Tokyo. You can personalize the look of your car. You will face 400 opponents as you explore the city; enough to keep you busy for years! As soon as you defeat members of the *13 Devils* gang, new sections of town will become available. The refresh rate is nice and smooth and the 3-D environments are pleasing to the eye. The king's fool of all racing games on the PS2.

<http://208.179.202.5/TXR0/index.html>

MX 2002: Watch you neck!

The last motorcycle game that was any good was Excite 64 and that was a long way back! *MX 2002* offers a strong game engine, good AI opponents and brilliant level design. The most important thing in this kind of game is the controls and, here, they've nailed it! The real time physics engine draws good power from the processor of the PS2. The added acrobatics are a very good idea: the more you indulge in them, the greater the thrill! Every good game should be easy to start and hard to master. Run through the tutorial and you'll see that in order to get to the higher levels, you will have to learn all the subtleties of the motorcycle controls. When your opponents hit the dirt, the crashes are quite entertaining. All in all, this is the best PS2 motorcycle game on the market

<www.thq.com/MX2002>

Batman: Vengeance: Holly Batfun!

Super hero fans are going to have a field day when they become the privileged drivers of the Batmobile. It is full of exciting gadgets! You can also enter fistfights. A convincing 3-D rendering enhances the animated cartoon look. There are mini-games, cinematics, and battles with archenemies like the Joker or Mr. Freeze. For the most part, it is a third person story. The camera follows the action smoothly but you can also control it when you want. This is a good, stylish follow-up for Ubi Soft's foray on the North-American market.

<www.UbiSoft.com/batmanvengeance>

Kinetica: fusing with the track!

When you become the speedscar, the expression "at full speed" really means something! This is the basic concept behind *Kinetica*. Holding one wheel in your hands and one wheel between your feet, you bomb down futuristic trails as fast as you can. Going from acrobatics to surprises, you are going to experience total happiness. Add to this a number of weapons, a super charger option where you literally hold onto the track and what you've got is

the most original racing game that has come out in a long while. There are plenty of shortcuts you will be forced to seek out, trying to escape your pitiless opponents. The learning curve is pretty steep but the more you play the more fun you'll get. One the charms of the game is the tempo: it is so incredibly fast! Kinetica is unique, so intense! The web site is very cool.

<www.scea.com/games/categories/racing/kinetica>

Nascar Thunder 2002 and F1 2001: Rev it up!

If you are attracted to more conventional races, the most recent products from EA will suit you. F1 and Nascar races are at opposite ends of the racing spectrum, but EA has successfully brought forward what makes them so fascinating.

In *Nascar Thunder 2002*, the innovative aspect is the career mode. You can choose your auto manufacturer: Pontiac, Ford, Chevrolet, or Dodge. And you can choose sponsors, who, of course, will want you to offer them as much visibility as possible. The way to keep them happy is to become a star driver. This game is almost like a sport RPG. With 43 cars on the track, accidents are unavoidable. The gashes and bashes to the car bodies are quite realistic. If you think oval tracks are OK, *Nascar Thunder 2002* for the PS2 is the best version you can get under the Nascar license.

In the world of American races, Nascar is number one and F1 is the eternal underdog. Just like football compared to soccer. Nevertheless, EA keeps working on its F1 race game. To make the title more popular, EA has changed from the simulation approach to the console style. The "normal" option, which makes driving easier, is a good example of the design decision. There are only three tracks available at the beginning of the game and the rest of the lot will unlock as you improve your ranking status. AI is more effective in this game than in any other race game: you never feel that the system is cheating on you in order to beat you. The environment reflects itself on the cars, which gives the atmosphere a plus. Definitely EA's best effort in the game genre.

<www.ea.com>

Spyhunter: drivers and spies wanted!

Midway's arcade classic is back on the PS2. Lots of action and a littler brush-up make it one of the best conversions on the market. You can drive up and down the environments at full speed, blasting opponents with Bond-like weapons. What else would you want? A transformer car? Ok, you got it!

Exerting your skills at driving the car as fast as you can is certainly the focus of the game, but remember you are a spy and you have missions to accomplish. The car's 3-D design is particularly well done. The sound track is based on a zillion versions of *Peter Gun*. *Spy Hunter* proves that when the job is well done, you can have plenty of fun for very little.

<www.spyhunter.midway.com>

ICO: unique and bizarre!

Sony's development team regularly comes up with titles that take specialists by surprise and that are beyond the usual game categories... more like interactive films. The effort is quite commendable! After *The Bouncer*, they are back with *ICO*, an exceptional adventure game. The experience is totally unique. The production is spotless. The visuals, the sound track, and the design of the riddles all collaborate in building an eerie, "otherworldly" atmosphere adding to the feeling of immersion. Camera angles are well chosen. The lighting is very effective. There are top-notch special effects and fantastic character animations. The game is a little short but it seems to be a new tendency. Most people don't have 30 to 50 hours to invest in a game. So beautiful, so agreeable, definitely in a class of its own!

<www.scea.com/games/categories/ actionadvent/ico>

NHL 2002: Magnificent!

Last year's version was acclaimed as the best hockey game of all times. *NHL 2002* is even better. Hold on to your skates, guys! The multi-user mode is the most exciting to date. Action is so instantaneous that you just sit and wonder how they did it! There is a career mode that spans over 10 seasons, so that you can build yourself a dream team. A card system has been added, just as was done in *Madden*. You can purchase cards from a 189-card bank if you have accomplished certain skating feats, like scoring three goals in the same match. The cards will help boost your player's abilities. At the end, you can run the EA Gamestory, a voice-over report about the highlights in the game. A brilliant idea! Frame rate problems, still present last year, have been eliminated. I could go on and on, praising the game till you get sick of it. Just go out and grab it!

<http://nhl2002.ea.com>

XG3 Extreme G Racing: If you long for Wipeout...

Forget about the first version. This year, the developers have discovered a way to express their vision really well. *XG3 Extreme G Racing* enjoys a well-deserved success. The speed element, which is crucial to this kind of game, is right there for you. Images are displayed at 60 frames per second. It reminds us fun we got from *Wipeout* back then! The design of the racetracks is done with great care. The *XG Mall* lets drivers buy weapons, gadgets and boosted engines. When your speedster takes you up to 750 mph and breaks the sound barrier, the combination of audio and visual effects will give you an extra kick! Quite something!

Tension will rise when you use your weapons and gadgets against your eleven opponents. But what will serve you best is your talent as a rider. *XG3* takes

advantage of the best aspects in *Wipeout*, but just with its controls and its special effects, the title holds his own. The environments, the motorcycles, and the weapons are top quality. You get a cool distortion effect when the heat from the exhaust pipes rises up in the air. The way the rain falls also adds to the feeling of immersion. The efforts they've placed on the special effects are admirable! As for the sound track, it is just as well polished. Try it out as soon as you can!

<www.extremeg3.com>

Armored Core 2: Another Age/Metal to metal!

Are you a forlorn mercenary with a major in robotics? If yes, you will have ample time to prove your skills during one of the 100 missions of *Armored Core 2*. The game's interface, ever since it came out on the PS1, has always been user-friendly. You can personalize your Mech to a great extent: there are over 100,000 possible combinations. You can even paste your own emblem over it! The graphics tools at your disposal have been tuned up.

This avatar offers better 3-D space rendition. Frame rate is solid at 60 fps. You can play using the cooperative mode, but the multi-player mode is definitely the best. You can import whatever you created under version 1. Quite cool! Have a look at the Flash application the developer included, it's cool too!

<www.fromsoftware.co.jp/top/special/web3d/ac2.htm>

Code Veronica X: goose bumps on the grill!

Capcom was blessed with a movie deal for the fifth anniversary of *Resident Evil*. In the latest game in the series, *Code Veronica X*, the cinematics have received great care and attention. The series has aged a bit, when compared to *Onimusha* or *Devil May Cry*. But it is still the best in the horror/action genre. The environments are more detailed than in the previous versions. The lighting is particularly well done. The levels have become even bigger than in the Dreamcast version. They will offer you a long, protracted descent in the abyss of horror! Watch out, riddles can be solved by certain characters only…

<www.capcom.com>

Madden NFL 2002: Touché!

In the *Madden* dynasty, *NFL 2002* is the best avatar so far. Every component is even better. I can't get over the quality of the graphics. They are just astounding. This is a true football simulator. Replay factor is almost unlimited. The franchise mode can extend over a period of 30 years. The card system is back. As a bonus, it has been extended to the cheerleaders! More

important: the passing system has been improved and so has the implementation of the defensive. Animations and textures are superior. This is really state of the art!

<www.ea.com>
<www.tiburon.com>

Theme Park: Roller Coaster/ An Interactive ride

For the first time, the *Theme Park* series gets an appropriate console treatment. It is even better than the PC version and this is probably due to the power inside the PS2. There is increased interactivity and a multitude of mini-games. What you have to do is to build and then maintain an attraction park. Think of it as simulating micro-management. Add a little more salt to the French fries and you'll see your clients ask for beverages. But don't overdo it, or else, they will get sick! Visitors always give you adequate feedback on your decisions: their facial expressions are quite meaningful. You can stroll inside your own park and even try out the roller coaster you have designed.

<http://playstation2.ea.com/gamepage_theme.html>

Sky Odyssey: Take off!

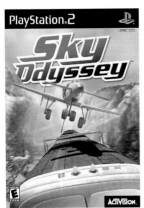

If you are ever so slightly interested in flying planes, you are going to fall in love with *Sky Odyssey*. Five modes are available and the adventure mode is the best. It is not really a flight simulator. The game is based on your ability to pilot different kinds of planes and in different kinds of climactic or geographic environments; most of them are under extreme conditions. For example you may have to jettison fuel so as to be able to go over a mountain pass during a heavy snowstorm; or you will have to refuel from a wild train gone loose. You must keep calm in the eye of the storm and execute stunts without a glitch. You will have the opportunity to fine tune or up-grade your plane, which will be necessary when you get to the acrobatics part under all kinds of weather. The graphics are good but what impressed me most is the variety and the magnitude of the environments. This is almost a Zen game for qualified pilots.

<www.activision.com/games/skyodyssey>

And they keep coming!

PS2 is coming to fruition. Titles are mushrooming. Developers are getting accustomed to the system's architecture. With over 20 million units sold, PS2 can look at Xbox and GameCube and wish them good luck!

Soul Reader 2

Vampire games have taken a bold jump over to the PS2. *Soul Reader 2* is a real epic. Raziel's adventures are all about power struggles among a dynasty of immortal creatures. The story line is full of fights and riddles. Expect about 20 hours of delightful mishaps! Just as in the first version, you have two parallel worlds to explore, but this time, you are given a map and a compass. Raziel is nimble as ever. The fighting system is a lot better. The cinematics, quite frankly, are a success. Really hot!

<www.eidos.com>

Smuggler's Run 2

Rockstar is still one of my favorite publishers. With the immoral *Grand Theft Auto 3* and now their riot simulator *State of Emergency* storming up the charts, they keep pushing the boundaries with amazing success. It all started with *Smuggler's Run*. All the winning elements from version 1 are there, but there are even better! Even if the levels are huge and the environments very detailed, the 60-fps frame rate is very steady. You now have access to a greater variety of vehicles and weapons. A number of modes are available, which gives the game some extra length. Very well built!

<www.rockstargames.com>

Half-Life

Half-Life has been shrouded with compliments even since it came out in 1998. It is a *chef-d'œuvre* and there's isn't much more I can say. This is the first console version.

<www.sierra.com/games/Half-Life>

Tony Hawk's Pro Skater 3: nothing like it!

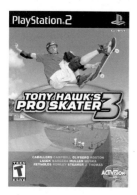

When several platforms appear in the same time, it is a bonanza for the developers who are quick enough to follow the pace and can produce the same title for all of them. This is what Activision did with *Tony Hawk*, last year's most popular license.

The game was already close to perfection. This year, it is even closer! There is a whole bunch of stunts, the levels are bigger, the gameplay has improved, and the look is better! The skateboarders' animations are more polished; the image speed is as steady as can be. There is a new screen interface for the 3-D store. You can change, personalize, or adapt your skateboard gear as you please. You can also create your own level.

The network mode offers an opportunity to challenge your pals on a LAN, or on the web if your console is Internet ready.

<www.activision o2.com/tony_hawk>

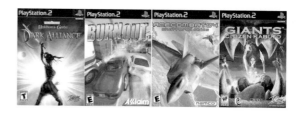

Baldur's Gate: Dark Alliance

Baldur's Gate was an extremely popular PC RPG title. On the PS2, the elements of success are the mythic battles between the Gods and the Demons from the Abyss.

<www.interplay.com/bgdarkalliance>

Burnout

Easy to learn, *Burnout* gives you lots of opportunities to literally blow yourself apart in very entertaining accidents! Whether you make right turns or left turns doesn't matter, it is just as much fun!

<www.acclaim.com/games/burnout>

Ace Combat 4: Shattered Skies

Ace Combat 4: Shattered Skies is the best console flight simulator. It is very agreeable to become a pilot in a universe usually reserved for Top Guns only.

<Ace Combat 4: Shattered Skies>
<www.namco.com/games/ace_combat_4.html>

Giants: Citizen Kabuto

The humor is fantastic and so are the level design and the gameplay. In *Giants: Citizen Kabuto*, you can play three races, with very different attributes. I love its diversity!

<www.interplay.com/giants/index.html>

Games to keep an eye on

Maximo: Ghosts to Glory
Virtua Fighter 4
Deus Ex
Drakan: The Ancients' Gates
Max Payne
Wipeout Fusion
The Getaway
Tekken 4
Black and White
Rubu
Giants
Stuntman

X-Box

The least we can say is that Microsoft did the research and development right. A vast round of industry consultations was organized before the Xbox was built. Developers expressed their techno desires and Bill Gates did his best to satisfy them. The end result is the most powerful console in history, and the easiest one to program. The company lavishly will spend more than half a billion dollars to promote its little marvel.

With the complete kit, you return home about 400 bucks poorer. But check the bundles and starter pack offered all over for interesting deals. Anyway, this is what the Nvidia graphics card inside it would cost you if you bought it for a PC. Add to this the $200 DVD, and you'll understand why Microsoft looses around $120 per console. Don't cry over Bill's fate. This is quite normal. He makes his money selling the games. The whole industry is based on the give the razor and sell the razor blade model...  Inspired by Nintendo's and Sony's business plans, Microsoft counts on its exclusive titles to attract customers. On November 15, the launch date in the America, 12 games ere available. But with up to 40 exclusive developers, the figure is now quickly growing. The launch in Japan takes place in February 2002 and for Europe, the set date is March 14.

The Xbox was the first console to come standard with modem and hard disk. The Internet connectivity may not be used much before mid 2002. In 2001, broadband access (high speed cable and DSL) was somewhere between 10 and 15%, with an installed base of around 5 million American homes.

This is going to revolutionize game distribution, allowing the purchase of games by installments, one episode at a time. The influence of the Xbox can already be felt on the industry. In a console market which had seen, only recently, the demise of Sega's

Dreamcast, Microsoft is like a young mustang kicking about wildly to make room for itself.

Halo:
best title on launch date

A number of voices cried murder when Bungie Inc. decided to stop the development of *Halo* on the PC and allocate all of its resources to the Xbox version. Microsoft had just bought Bungie and was looking for exclusive titles.

If you give *Halo* a real try, you will soon find out that the Xbox avatar announces a new generation of games. The background story is a classic: it is you against a bunch of extra-terrestrials. An old story, but a very urgent matter! You can play solo or in cooperative mode with a friend. Grab yourself a vehicle and you will change from a first to a third person perspective, which is one of the interesting aspects of the game.

There is nothing like the pleasure of roaming around in your jeep, with your friend taking care of the 360-degree piece of artillery, blasting the enemy lines! You have several other vehicles at your disposal, some of them coming from the enemy's side. The multiplayer mode allows you to hook up four Xboxes to four different screens and start a carnage session. If you get close enough to the enemy, you can bash him on the head with the butt of your rifle. Take this, you alien scum!

Character animation is excellent. Textures are superior. There are majestic sound effects. The graphics processor shows its muscle when it comes to display particle effects for convincing explosions. AI adapts to your playing style quite well. Real time physics, like your car handling, does a great job. Quite frankly, *Halo* is so pleasurable that any one who loves that game genre should try it. I tried it on a plasma screen in 16:9 anamorphic format, with Dolby 5.1 surround sound, and I was ecstatic!

<www.xbox.com>
<http://halo.bungie.org>

Other launch titles

Dead or Alive 3 is the title you'll hear fighting game amateurs talk about. Have a look at it and you'll understand why. In 3-D, *Munch's Oddysee* carries on with the glorious, fascinating tradition. *Project Gotham* is designed to fit virtual race top drivers.

Max Payne

Max Payne steals the show in the interactive version of the famous dark movie *The Matrix*. Works beautifully!

<http://maxpayne.godgames.com>

NHL 2002

One of the most exciting game on the market. Instantaneous action! Breathtaking!

<www.ea.com/easports/platforms/games/nhl2002/xbox.jsp>

Amped: Freestyle Snowboarding

Amped: Freestyle Snowboarding is a beauty! The Zen version of *SSX Tricky*. Relax off-trail and glide down in powder snow. I'm impressed!

<www.microsoft.com/games/amped>

Star Wars Starfighter: Special Edition

With its five different multi-player modes, *Star Wars Starfighter: Special Edition* is going to keep the Star Wars amateurs happy. It's got everything they want.

<www.lucasarts.com/products/starfighter>

Xbox games you want to keep an eye on

Jet Grind Radio Future
Medal of Honor: Allied Assault
Project-Ego
Soul Calibur 2
Brute
Unreal Championship
BC
Shenmue
Wreckless
Tony Hawk 3
Silent Hill 2

Gamecube

Is there a chance Nintendo can regain the market shares it lost to the PS1? Won't be easy! Sony has been making giant strides forward. The market has changed a lot over the past 10 years. The average gamer is now 28. So that, on paper, it looks like the pre-teen atmosphere of most of Nintendo's

products should not really meet the needs and expectations of that average consumer. Yet, at E3 2001, when the GameCube was launched, the cram packed room went quasi hysterical with excitement Nintendo may still surprises us all.

The GameBoy Advance GameCube: the dynamic duo

When you see the GameCube, the first thing you notice is how small it is! It looks like a toy. And obviously, this is what Nintendo wanted. Its philosophy hasn't changed over the years and it has met with unfathomable success. Competitors are not only trying to emulate the Pokemons' success story, but they are adopting the company's business plan. Quite understandably. Hasn't Nintendo sold over 1.4 billion games under its brand name?

Nintendo finally opted for the CD, but under a proprietary format. The Cube and controller have been developed under the auspices of Shigeru Miyamoto, the creator of the most beloved characters in the game universe. Shigeru has promised titles with Mario, Zelda, Donkey Kong, Star Fox, and has announced the return

of Metroïd. With a price tag of $200, the attack on the consumer carries a lot of clout. The GameCube came out of E3 2001 as the grand champion, despite the strength of its competitors. Nintendo has always downplayed the technical aspects, concentrating on the quality of the gameplay and the personal appeal of its amazing slew of character.

The domination of GameBoy over the portable market is a factor one shouldn't overlook. On launch day, the GameBoy Advance (GBA) sold more copies that the PS2 in a month. The competition cannot reproduce the synergy between the GameCube and the GBA. With the N64 and the GameBoy Color, Nintendo has already gained some expertise about how to combine the advantages of two concurring systems. It is certainly going to exploit this competitive advantage as much as it can. Game cartridge production and distribution used to be complex and costly: as much as hopeful publishers spent $30 per cartridge. With the cartridge system now out of the way, Nintendo holds excellent cards in its hands and is well positioned for the market wars ahead.

Star War: Rogue Leader: The force is with the Cube

I am old enough to remember the scene when Luke Skywalker exploded Darth Vader's hideout. Our collective imagination was going wild: we could picture ourselves flying a rebel ship, wiping out every soldier in the Empire forces. In fact, our passion for video games seems to have partly arisen from the urge to recreate that legendary scene! 20 years later Star Wars amateurs can pick up *Star War: Rogue Leader* and perform every action they ever dreamed of. And on top of that, the game is incredibly beautiful.

 You can recreate the attack on mighty Darkstar. In itself, this level is a wonderful gift for all the Star Wars License fans. In first or third person perspective, you can pilot a vast selection of rebel ships and get involved in ten heroic missions. Secret levels, extra ships and extra modes will come as a reward for your success. The quality of the visuals will drive you to the outer limit of your abilities: you are going to strive hard, just because you want to see what the developers have in store for you.

The controls react very quickly. The variety of weapons is of great tactical import. With the great number of characters involved, the pace picks up quickly; soon enough, it's a total rush. The battle of Hoth is very inspiring. This is superb title for the GameCube launch.

<www.lucasarts.com/products/rogueleader>

Super Monkey Ball: Sega's Monkey business!

 People can easily see the public fight between the 128-bit consoles. But it's easy to forget that another major war has started: freed from the drudgery of console production, Sega is now ready to compete with EA, the number one independent publisher. A new convert to agnosticism, Sega is going to publish its titles on all consoles… and beyond!

The GameCube battle starts with *Super Monkey Ball*. This is a sort of *Marble Madness 3-D*. What you control is not the monkey way up there in its bubble, but the floor as a whole. By moving it in the proper direction, you try to show your primate the right way to go. Several mini-games complete that slate.

Whether in solo mode or in multi-player mode, this is a game for the family. Easy to learn and hard to master, *Super Monkey Ball* can keep you busy for years! For its hundred levels and for its intuitive gameplay, this is a party game you must put on your list.

<www.sega.com>

Other launch titles

Super Smash Bros. is the upgrade from the best seller N64 version (five million copies). Hours of fun battles between Nintendo heroes! In *Luigi's Mansion*, Luigi is looking for Mario in a haunted manor that his brother thought he had won in a tournament…Irresistible!

Pickmin

Pikmin is the latest creation of Nintendo's genius, Shigeru Miyamoto. An original and captivating mix between strategy and adventure genres, with riddles galore.

<www.pikmin.com>

NHL Hitz 2000

Forget about rules... *NHL Hitz 2000* put the focus on swing shots and fist fights. The game is perfect in multi-player mode. Expect the public in the stands to shout out loud!

<www.nhlhitz.midway.com>

Batman

Designed and produced in Montreal, *Batman* offers lots of mini-games, great cinematics and spectacular fights. Great flair for the graphics! Good show!

<www.UbiSoft.com/batmanvengeance>

Extreme G3

Speed is quite palpable. Track design is very detailed and very well done. Environments, motorcycles and weapons are tops! Unrelenting and strenuous!

<www.extremeg3.com>

Games to keep an eye on

Star Fox Adventures: Dinosaur Planet
Metroid Prime
The Legend of Zelda
Eternal Darkness
Mario Sunshine
Resident Evil
Perfect Dark
Mario Kart
Soul Calibur

GameBoy Color and GameBoy Advance

In 2000, Nintendo celebrated sales results of 100 million units. In fact, 47% of all consoles sold in the industry are GameBoys. On the first day of sale, 650,000 units of the GameBoy Advance were available and they sold out. Because Pokemon is so popular, games for the portables rose from $216 millions in 1998 to  $619 in 1999, to $782 millions in 2000. From 1998 to 2001, the sale revenues for the GameBoy quadrupled, going from $300 million to 1.2 million.

Nintendo plans to sell 24 million units before March 2002. Add to these 78 million games and you can imagine the sort of resource planning it takes to get the distribution chain rolling. The marketing budget is $75 million! Nintendo represents 99% of the portable market. Within the first week after launch day, the GameBoy Advance in America sold 540,000 units, i.e. 76% of all console sales, with revenues of $45 million. This means over 50 GBAs sold per minute. In terms of game sales, Super Mario Advance was number 1, with revenues of $18,5 million.

The Game Boy Advance marches on

The same kind of sale craze has taken all over the world. The GameBoy, under its various avatars, is really the King!

The GameBoy Advance is not revolutionary. When your team enjoys a winning streak, you keep the same players and you do only minor adjustments! The screen, though bigger, is still reflective, using up its batteries in less than 15 hours. An active matrix screen (lit form within) would suck up even more energy, so it is still out for the moment. The processor is now a full 32-bit machine. Colors available climb from 56 to 511 simultaneous colors in character mode and 32,768 in bitmap mode. But beyond the technical specs, the truth of the matter is that you get the equivalent of a Super Nintendo, under a portable format. In the years to come, pushing this mini-bomb to the limit, developers are certainly going to surprise us for good!

On launch day, almost twenty titles were available. For Christmas 2001, the number had climbed to 60. The two added top buttons (left and right) extend the potential of the gameplay. There is a cord you can buy to use the GBA as a game pad for the GameCube or connect to another GBA and exchange data or use the four-player option. Look out for an osmosis and new game play possibilities between the Game Cube and the GBA with the same cable. The fact that the GBA is retro-compatible with the 450 GameBoy color games is worth notice. In my view, the only missing element is a cable to connect to a TV screen. But with such a setup, the GBA wouldn't be a portable any more!

Nintendo's competitors have now all been defeated, so I can't see what could stop the advance of the GameBoys!

<www.gameboyadvance.com>

Greatest hits in 2001 (GameBoy Color)

Pokemon Gold and *Pokemon Silver* have been bestsellers from the day the first came out. *Donkey Kong Country*, *Rugrats in Paris* and *The 102 Dalmatians* are in the top 10. And so is *Tony Hawk's Pro Skater*, the all category, all platform champion franchise. There are 400 titles available, from *Laura Croft* to *Rayman*, *NASCAR*, *M&M's*, *Lego* and *Spiderman* to *Frogger*; from *Chicken Run* and *Powerpuff Girls* to four versions de *Tetris*; all the sports you can think of, plus the *Looney Toons*. There is *Disney*, *Metal Gear Solid* and *Perfect Dark*. In 2000 alone, more than 180 titles were published. And the games keep coming…

Super Mario Advance

Nintendo offers two titles under that name. There is *Super Mario Advance*, a faithful conversion of *Super Mario Bros. 2*. And there is *Mario Bros.*, classic edition, in which the graphics have been rejuvenated some.

F-Zero: Maximum Velocity

This title was specially designed for the GBA. In this futuristic race game, the famous Mode-7, available on Super NES, is put to practice. Four players can play together with only one copy of the game, which is quite cool!

Tony Hawk's Pro Skater 2

Tony Hawk's Pro Skater 2 is a harbinger of what sort of graphics are coming on the GBA. The perspective is now isometric. The gameplay has been adapted to a portable configuration. There are some surprising sound effects. All in all, a complete success!

<www.activisiono2.com/tony_hawk/gba/>

Castlevania: Circle of the Moon

Castlevania has gone through several incarnations. The most accomplished was for the PS1. This is where the Advance version took its inspiration from. In this vampire story, you run, jump and glide and the heroes are whips, knifes and holy water! A proud heir to 1997 success *Symphony of the Night*, this is one of the best titles from the launch day list.

<www.konami.com/main/ctlvania>

Rayman Advance

Rayman started its career as a glorious 32-bit side-scroller on the PC. For the launch of the GBA, Ubi Soft has seized the opportunity to optimize it for the conversion. The magic is intact! Ubi Soft is setting a good example with its choice of five different languages. One day, all games will follow that model.

<www.UbiSoft.com/games/gameinfo.php?id=104>

Championship Racing

Championship Racing is a mini version of *Gran Turismo*. There are thirty- two race tracks, forty-five models and seven auto manufacturers, many of them unknown on the North-American continent. This is the first race game for the Advance, and its multi-player mode certainly adds to its assets. Don't miss it!

<www.thq.com/gt_advance>

Other titles to give a try

All platforms considered, *Advanced War* is one of the best strategy games. *Golden Sun* is an RPG with impressive graphics. *Mario Kart Super Circuit* is a new, slightly modified version of the Super NES classic. Finally, I can't resist recommending *Doom*, the game which started the revolution on the PC. With the GBA version, think about the 245 levels you are holding in the palm of your hand. Incredible!

The five best game consoles and 20 best games

The question everyone is asking is "What new console should I buy?" Unfortunately, it's like asking "What should I eat today?" It all depends on your tastes, needs, and budget. Sega's Dreamcast, for example, is the best dollar value, but no longer appeals to anyone.

There are so many games on the market that identifying the best 20 titles is nearly impossible. You can't please everybody. I'll just suggest the titles I personally find superior on all levels: quality and degree of immersion, length, game play, graphics. Note: the prices listed below are the manufacturer's suggested retail prices. You'll have to compare retail prices in your area.

The new PS1 model

Price: $99.00
LCD Screen: $129.00
Games available:
   more than 1100
Game prices:
   from $19.99 to $39.99

The elegant PS1 with its portable LCD screen lets you play CD-ROM games in the car for the first time by plugging into the cigarette lighter. The integrated mini speakers work wonderfully well and the headset output makes parents happy. Ideal for kids' bedrooms. The list of excellent games for the 80 million PS1s on the market is impressive. *Tekken 3* is still considered THE classic combat game. The three Oddworld titles are superb, original and intelligent. A rarity! *CTR* is a version of Kart games from the excellent *Crash Bandicoot* series for the whole family, and hilarious to boot. *Spiderman* is the best title featuring a superhero. Way cool!

The mature Playstation 2

Suggested price: $299.00
Games available: 300
Game prices: $49.99

With 25 million units sold, the PS2 is by far the most mature new generation platform. Excellent titles are now regularly published. For all those aspiring to it, PS2 is definitely the machine to beat. *Gran Turismo* revolutionized the very concept of race games. Absolutely stunning! *Metal Gear Solid* is the most sophisticated and technically accomplished best-seller around. *Devil May Cry* has made more than one player fall over backward, and *Tony Hawk 3* is considered by everyone to be the best sports game in history. All masterpieces!

The Xbox is a must

Suggested price: $299.99
Games available: 19-30
Game price: $49.99

This Microsoft machine is simply the most powerful console on the market. Xbox is the first console to come as a package with a modem and hard drive that

will revolutionize the way game are delivered in the medium or long term. *Halo* redefines the shooter genre on a console. Intense! *DOA3* is the game most talked about recently by combat game lovers. *Munch's Oddysee* continues the tradition of its three extraordinary preceding titles in 3-D. Unique and fascinating. *Project Gotham* is custom made for virtual racing aces.

The surprising GameCube

Suggested price: $199.99
Games available: 22
Game prices: from $49.99

You should have seen the enthusiastic and nearly hysterical reaction of the adult-packed room when the GameCube was introduced at E3 2001. Nintendo might surprise more than a few of you. The ways in which interaction might be possible between the GameCube and GameBoy Advance have already been explored between N64 and GameBoy Color. Rest assured this was only the beginning. Nintendo will make good use of this unique advantage. *Rogue Leader* was the must-have at the GameCube launch, *Super Smash Bros.* is the sequel on steroids of the irresistible N64 version (5 million copies sold). Hours of joyful combat in sight between Nintendo heroes. Sega starts off on the right foot with *Super Monkey Ball*. Brilliant! Luigi looks for Mario in a haunted house he thinks he's won in a contest, and the fun begins!

GameBoy Advance rules

Suggested price: $69.99.
Games available: 60
Game prices: from $39.93

GameBoy Advance lets you play games of a quality equivalent to Super Nintendo titles on a portable console. A cable (sold separately) lets you exchange data between GBAs and also offers an up to 4 player multi-player option. The fact that it's retro-compatible and makes the nearly 500 GameBoy Color games

compatible with it is not to be ignored. *Advanced War* is one of the best strategy games on all the consoles combined. *Golden Sun* is a completely convincing role playing game with impressive graphics. *Mario Kart Super Circuit* is simply the classic Super NES reworked to suit. I can't resist recommending the game that started a PC revolution: 245 levels of *Doom* in the palm of your hand. Incredible!

The Dream Lives On ...

12.

Computer Games

E veryone seems to want to be involved in interactive games these days. And this despite the
lukewarm results of the last few years' efforts by
American hardware inventors.

The great egalitarian dream of Open Source and
the Indrema console, based on the Linux programming language, bit the dust on April 6, 2001. The company never managed to raise the funds required to
launch the endeavor. The plan was to offer developers
a new kind of relationship. A free development kit
would have been made available to individuals and
companies alike. The hope was that an open development platform, supported by Linux fans, would
spread among the game developer community. It was
all for naught.

<www.indrema.com>

For the time
being Nokia (well
known for its cel-
lular phones) is
picking up where
Open Source left
off with its Media
Terminal. Same Linux, same philosophy, except this
time the company has resources, experience and a
proven marketing record. The approach, however, is
different. The Media Terminal is actually an interactive
TV terminal in disguise, with a strong game and digital
entertainment option. A hard disk allows users to
record TV programs, music, photos and personal
videos. A modem provides access to the Internet and
content deliverable by high-speed cable. Peripherals
like cameras and printers are also compatible.
Surprisingly enough, it is the only black box that's Flash
compatible (the animation standard from
Macromedia that's used for games). It's the best proof-

of-concept offered today. What the general public thinks of it, however, remains to be seen.

<www.nokia.com/multimedia/
mediaterminal.html>

Aside from Japan where telephone games are a real phenomenon, standard WAP (Wireless Application Protocol) is simply not taking off. Cellular phone owners don't actually mind having a game or two to occupy their down time, but they aren't ready to pay for the service. Let's just say the economic model leaves a lot to be desired.

The same seems to apply to portable PCs and all hand-held gadgets of the Palm Pilot variety. One day there will be a sort of Game Boy/telephone/organizer with Internet access and all the trimmings. In the meantime, everyone is busy preventing this dream from becoming a reality: If it's on the Web, it's for free.

The PC

A short history

The illustrious ancestor of interactive games, the PC is still the R&D platform of choice. The PC also has the unique advantage (with the exception of Dreamcast and Xbox) of being connected to the prime mover of innovation itself, the Internet.

Creativity unleashed
on the perpetually evolving platform

It all started with text games, which were actually just extensions of board games like *Dungeons and Dragons*. One example, *Zork*, swept away more than one geek on Apple IIe. A new world of possibilities opened up, and from that point on designers went all out. A number of MUD (Multi User Dungeons) appeared, *Dragon Realms* being one of the most popular.

Electronic Arts wasn't the powerful multinational company it is today, but even from the very beginning it was synonymous with hip and cool. *Archon, Archon II, M.U.L.E., Racing Destruction Set, Seven Cities of Gold, Adventure Construction Set, Lords of Conquest* and *Robot Rascals* are all titles that marked this first era of PC games.

Things evolved more quickly after the arrival of Commodore 64, which, after all, offered color graphics and sound. Role games, for example, could use the computer to manage the wide range of data inherent to the genre and, a short time later, even the smallest regions of these universes could be illustrated in a basic way. Characters and their traits could be defined in tens of pixels. It was Lord British (Richard Garriot) who created the first truly efficient RPGs with the Ultima series. Hundreds of games came out on C64, *Pirates* and *Wasteland* among the best remembered.

A new generation of companies then took over: Bullfrog, Westwood, and id Software all had a common, radically different approach to programming, graphics, and marketing. The revolution was about to begin.

A few months before id Software's *Wolfenstein 3-D* came out, Origin published *Ultima Underworld: The Stygian Abyss*. This event launched the second phase/era of PC games. A real, though somewhat primitive world of 3-D immersion was offered to the public for the first time. Bullfrog, for its part, released *Populous* and *Syndicate*. These games brought us a new vision of the future, both in terms of presentation and through their themes and options.

But it was with *Doom* (*Wolfenstein 3-D* refined and on steroids) that a larger and more varied audience could finally be reached. *Doom* was an irresistible shooter, although it didn't become the game of the century. It had style, attitude and, above all, was easy to play.

But the innovations didn't end there. The next offering was a multi-player death match where users could transform certain aspects of the game to their liking. Moreover, a revolutionary marketing strategy crowned the achievment. The developer/distributor, id Software, allowed you to download one level for free, and once you were hooked, made you pay for subsequent downloads.

The *Doom* phenomenon is still cited today as the innovation that brought about a cyber culture which, even though underground, inspired a number of entrepreneurs to expand to the Internet, fuelled by dreams of riches and fame. Admittedly, this worked for a while.

The modern day alchimist: John Carmack

John Carmack, with the help of his team, was creating games that he wanted to play. This attitude gave us the most sophisticated 3-D engines in the industry, and games the public could identify with. Grateful gamers deluged Carmack with money.

<www.idsoftware.com/corporate/index.html>

Another game that, in many respects, was the opposite of *Doom* was rising to similar heights in 1993-94. *Myst* is to this day the most highly sold PC game in history. This adventure game with 3-D graphics the likes of which the public had never seen was purchased by anyone wanting to test the power of their new computer. The fantastic success of these two titles, and the economic consequences of their success, inspired a slew of young entrepreneurs to set up dozens of gaming companies.

Doom, Quake, Heretic, Half-Life, F.A.K.K.2 and American McGee's *Alice* are all designed along the same lines and known as action games and FPS's (First Person Shooter). These games mostly test out gamers' reflexes in real-time. A few puzzles are included to let you catch your breath. These games, however, are essentially based on frenetic action and the impending thrill of being confronted by your friends in duels to the death. Soon, however, RPG and strategy games would make their appearance and speak to a whole other section of gamers' brains.

But first a word on the *Wing Commander* series, which created a sensation in its time because of the high quality of its cut scenes. The interactive portion of the game consisted of spaceship battles that had to be won in order to gain access to the next filmed scene. This type of soap opera for sci-fi fans passed for the next phase of evolution in the art of interactivity. Today it looks more like a pterodactyl. Its mediocre cinematic adaptation probably killed the series off forever.

All the while Lucas Arts was putting out one classic after another, my favorites being *Day of The Tentacle*, *Sam & Max Hit the Road*, *Full Throttle* and obviously the *Monkey Island* series. If you've never played any of these titles, take the plunge. They're intelligent, funny, and an absolute must-see. One of my favorite titles of all times is the most recent *Grim Fandango*.

<www.lucasarts.com/products/grim/>

Blizzard and Westwood took advantage of a lull in the wonderful world of carnage games to introduce strategic real-time games with *Warcraft* and *Dune*. *Starcraft Command & Conquer* followed, and the community was injected with new energy, which hasn't let up yet. *Diablo 1 and 2* adapted the isometric view of these two games and created an original and finely executed version of the carnage game, which was phenomenally successful. A multi-player Internet dimension added to the glory of this now legendary title.

Unreal introduced a new game engine to the industry, giving even id Software cause for concern. *Unreal Tournament* offered an extravagant number of options, special effects, weapons, multi-user gaming styles and level design, as original as they were impeccably produced.

Excellent simulation games like *Civilization* and *The Sims* also saw the light of day during this short but intense period of PC game evolution. Today's trend is to mix genres like *Sacrifice*, a group tactical game, or *Tribes2*, with Internet-only games à la *Everquest*. New ideas will continue to emerge, and the last 25 years of interactive game history will eventually be seen only as a launching pad towards the mythical Star Trek holodeck.

Windows and its must-haves

Microsoft has been offering solutions designed for the specific needs of PC game developers since Win95 and Direct X, finally introducing its own console, which is both ironic and understandable. The range of different PC configurations cost developers a fortune, and it's often a futile enterprise since, one way or another, a bug will sneak in and the game will crash. PCs are, nevertheless, the industry R&D platform of choice. The PC's constant evolution is responsible for the fact that the most beautiful and original games can be found on this platform.

The great success
of 2001
PC's great successes

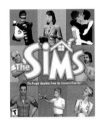

Diablo II, *Age of Empire* and *The Sims* are the reigning trio of the year, while critically acclaimed games like *Homeworld* and *Deus Ex* have not really found an audience save for die-hards. Is home piracy accountable for this? It's certainly not quality that's lacking. *Quake III: Arena*, *Half-Life: Counter-Strike*, *FAKK 2* and *No One Lives Forever* are exceptional shooters. *Giants: Citizen Kabuto*, *Alice*, *Crimson Skies* and *Sacrifice* are veritable gems. *Everquest: The Scars of Velious* and *Ruins of Kunark* still have an audience of 400,000, of which anywhere from 50,000 to 150,000 are simultaneously playing online 24 hours a day. *Baldur's Gate II*, *Icewind Dale* and *Shogun: Total War* are also superb. The adventure game is still alive and kicking with *The Longest Journey* and *Escape from Monkey Island*, and casual gamers made *Who Wants to Be A Millionaire*, *Barbie* and *Roller Coaster Tycoon* runaway hits.

The PC games
I particularly enjoyed

Good and Evil confront each other

A friend cried during a demonstration of this game at GDC (Game Developer Conference). Well, I didn't actually see it, but I believe him. A real gamer always imagines what would be a perfect game for him (or her). Lionhead studio actually permitted itself this luxury. The Englishman Peter Molyneux invented the "God Game" genre and when, after five years of work, one of Molyneux's "visions" appears on the market, one can't help but stand up and take notice. *Black & White* pushes the concept of being a god to the max, and offers a unique experience to those willing to invest the time. You are responsible for your creatures and, like a parent, witness your offspring act and react according to the upbringing you've given them. You can tickle them, stroke them, or punish them with a good slap of the hand. Your creature is endowed with the most highly developed artificial intelligence algorithms ever put in a game, and it will behave completely independently, surprising you at every turn. It can therefore spread joy and happiness (white) or become a blood-thirsty monster (black). The game is far from philosophical. The final goal is to convince the entire population that yours is the only and real god they should adore, and any and all means are appropriate to achieve this. You can also take your creature online to play group games or to measure it against the rest of the B&W ecology. Stories of emerging autonomous behavior have started to appear on the Web, and some of them will soon be part of urban legend. If the history of video games or the advances made in this form of techno-art interest you in the least, you owe it to yourself to spend time with this truly unique and extraordinary title.

<www.bwgame.com>
<www.black.ea.com>
<www.white.ea.com>
<www.lionhead.com>

It's Hell!

Sales of *Diablo II* reached their peak last year. The latest offering, *Lord of Destruction*, gives the developer, Blizzard, an opportunity to improve this now classic title with the introduction of new elements. The enhancements mostly concern the gameplay aspect, and the results are very convincing.

The most astonishing transformation is that you can now accumulate twice the amount of possessions. Gone are the days when you had to let go of perfectly valuable items because of limited storage space. An option that allows you to quickly transfer from one weapon to another is also welcome as it allows even more intense immersion in the game. There are also new elements such as weapons, shields and, of course, intriguing spells.

Lord of Destruction also introduces two new types of characters, the Assassin and the Druid. The first is a barbarian, a martial arts specialist who uses magic to inflict the greatest possible damage when he attacks. The Druid seems to be a combination of the Necromancer and the Barbarian; his powers, which include mutation, are varied and extremely interesting. Each has 30 unique talents and spells. The new monsters are cool. The environments are fairly destructible, adding an increased level of interactivity. The screen can now be increased to a resolution of 800 x 600 which should make players feel less restricted..

Diablo II fans have a lot to be excited about. To non-fans who consider the series only a string of mindless clicks, watch out! *Diablo* is back, and stronger than ever.

<www.blizzard.fr/diablo2exp>

Max Payne
tears down the house

The film noir genre now has a video game counterpart. *Max Payne* manages to provide us with a skilful mix of the best of John Woo movies. The game has been in development since 1996, enabling designers to see the emergence of the script concept. Popularized by *Half-Life*, scripts are real-time events triggered by players scattered through the game and who provide an extra level of player immersion. *Max Payne* extends the concept and uses it to push the story forward. The scripts are wonderfully integrated into the game.

It's dark, but beautiful. The textures, environments, soundtrack and actors' performances all contribute to a shadowy atmosphere that really works. The graphics and special effects are surprisingly realistic. The environment's degree of interactivity is developed to a level rarely seen to date. Toilets flush, beer flows, windows explode into shards of glass, and when your victims are brought down they knock into surrounding objects with impressive precision. You'll encounter questionable characters – braggarts, contract killers, mafia dons, junkies and prostitutes – every step of the way. Thank goodness you're armed to the teeth!

To be successful a game must have a Unique Selling Point (USP). Max Payne has a killer USP. The use of third-person perspective allows players to slow down the action and avoid bullets à la Matrix. It works like a dream! Add the ability to perform acrobatics, and the result is extraordinary! A real interactive action film (and the reverse will soon be true – *Max Payne* is about to be immortalized on celluloid by Hollywood).

Max Payne is the best PC action game of the year, and will be available cross-platform. Players will also be able to create their own PC levels thanks to the MaxED tool.

Textures are available at:
<www.3drealms.com/index.shtml>
The first patch is downloadable
on the developer's Web site:
<www.remedy.fi>
The official Web site:
http://maxpayne.godgames.com

500,000 years of history to rewrite

A Vivendi executive once confided that *Empire Earth* cost the company a small fortune. May his consolation come from the certitude that the money went to the right place. Without redefining the genre, *Empire Earth* is a truly unique endeavour. Ambitious? Absolutely! After all, it deals with the entire history of humanity. From pre-history to a Terminator-type future, you can let yourself go and redefine history as your talents allow. If you're a fan of *Age of Empire*, you owe it to yourself to try this title by the same designer.

<http://empireearth.sierra.com>

A jewel of the genre

When the small Canadian company Bioware launched the original *Baldur's Gate* the RPG style was considered dead or dying. These developers did not rest on the laurels of their brilliant success – 2 years later they delivered an absolutely stupendous product. The tiniest details have been lovingly reworked. If you like quests, there are more here than you will ever be able to find. You can personalize the interface as well as the levels of difficulty. The game is a culmination of the best of the *Dungeons and*

Dragons universe, with its mythical battles between the sons of the gods and the demons of the abyss. If you didn't try the original, it's high time you discovered the best of the genre, long under-appreciated. Absolutely extraordinary!
<www.bioware.com>
<www.interplay.com/bgate2/index.html>

Beware! Mystic Nazis...

This happened to me when *Quake III* came out too. I'm the idiot who forgets to fight because I'm too busy admiring the game textures. Brilliant... *Castle Wolfenstein* is so beautiful that it's easy to want to stay and be a tourist. The ambience, however, is not so healthy. Himmler and his occult-obsessed Nazis are ready for anything. It's obviously up to you to foil their diabolic plans. Wait till you see the flame thrower who helps you along the way. A multi-player mode based on team work is what's at the heart of the game. Try the demo and see for yourself!

<www.activision.com/games/wolfenstein>
<www.planetwolfenstein.com>

A PC giant

The graphics, humor, gameplay and level design are fantastic. The real time lightning is also something to behold. The game engine can illustrate gigantic environments, and in no time flat throw you into a relentless race. *Giants: Citizen Kabuto* is ambitious and different. Three years of arduous work were required to create this little masterpiece. Variety is the star feature, since you can choose any of 3 entirely different and interesting races. You'll always be busy with one task or another, but never in a repetitive way. It must be said that to appreciate this game in all its aspects you'll need a high-end PC and 3-D card. The release of the PC game trilogy composed of *Alice, Sacrifice* and now *Giants,* is certainly the best possible excuse to upgrade your system. One of this year's best and most innovative PC games.

<www.interplay.com/giants/index.html>

Dashing through the skies

Crimson Skies is a brilliant action game that allows players to truly feel like aviation aces of old during all 24 mission options. Forget about any connection to flight simulators that force you to watch the oil pressure gauge or make complicated landings. Even though Microsoft's new Sidewinder Force Feedback Pro is the joystick of choice, controls are simple, and the emphasis is placed on the pleasure of flying in an action-filled sky. The game's atmosphere is also very engaging. You travel in a world based on the 1930's, populated with gentlemen pirates, film stars, heroes and moustachioed villains. *Crimson Skies* holds your attention with outstanding scenery, well-spoken dialogue and a well-gauged difficulty curve. Players have access to more and more levels as they progress. Eleven incredible modes are available. Each scenario with all its principal elements (goals, number of enemies, wingers, etc.) is presented in comic strip style. Up to eight players can shoot at each other in the network or online version. An exceptional title!

<www.microsoft.com/games/crimsonskies/>

Adrenalin rush

Install *Undying,* turn off the lights, turn the sound up and I guarantee an adrenalin rush as powerful as any film of this type can provide. *Unreal*'s updated engine gives us interior and exterior environments where superb textures are skilfully used. The music and special effects are exemplary, and add a great deal to the dark and haunted atmosphere. The enemies and other characters encountered are highly believable and drag you from one horrific situation to another. Knowledge in the use of conventional weapons and magical spells will help you handle the monsters and ghosts that rise up along your path. You'll often hear your enemies before they jump out at you, which also adds to the suspense. The action takes place mostly in and around a haunted mansion, but the principals often meet their demise in a worrisome parallel world. *Unreal* is proof that the horror/survival genre works best in first person mode. Careful — adrenalin can be addictive!

<http://undying.ea.com/>

Space Caretaker

Startopia is a simulator with a special twist. You're in charge of a space station and the crowd of extra-terrestrials and tourists who stop to visit. You'll have to do everything in your power to create and maintain what will become the most popular area in the space station. The cartoon-style 3-D animation is superb. The entire production, in fact, is of extremely high quality.

The tutorial is a must, and fun too. You'll learn how to master technology like the biodeck, and how to create androids. You also hire employees and track the colony's progress. Nine distinct races live side by side aboard the station, and physical and cultural differences quickly become the source of problems. You'll have to doctor up a hundred or so of these creatures during your first mission.

To keep everyone happy, you'll have to build dance clubs, bars, music workshops and small atriums to remind them of their mother planet. An economic simulation is at the heart of all of these operations. You'll have to go through Arona, a character you'll grow to simultaneously love and hate. The influence of the recently deceased Douglas Adams, who gave us the *Hitchhiker's Guide to the Galaxy* series, is felt here. Twisted humor abounds.

A number of interfaces, which you will have to master, give you quick access to the various modules. The camera, with its extreme zoom-in and zoom-out, is really effective. The game has two modes, 10 pre-designated missions, and a sandbox (a workshop which allows you to play freely.) You can also play online and on a LAN TCP/IP. Fans of this genre absolutely have to try *Startopia*.

Download the demo at:

<www.muckyfoot.com/startopia/demo.html>
And visit the official site at:

<www.startopiagame.com>

Truth is... elusive!

Game design is the creative nerve of the industry. It is, however, becoming more and more difficult to invent or even renew the different types of games. EA's last baby, *Majestic*, is extremely innovative. This game is played strictly online. Based on an X-Files-type theme (but without ETs), conspiracy is everywhere and seems to infiltrate governments at the same rate paranoia takes over our mind. Majestic's gameplay breaks the confines of the PC – once you've signed on, expect to receive phone calls, faxes and emails which help the story move forward. You'll have to visit Web sites and view videos that the game will scatter along your path. If game progress as an interactive art form interests you, you owe it to yourself to try *Majestic*. It's so revolutionary that the developer's offices were the target of arson, and it seems the designer died in the blaze.

<www.majesticthegame.com>

Update: The game was put on hold after the September 11 event, to be permanently shelved after a last attempt to market it in an old box. At best, game designers will scavenge ideas from this highly original concept that didn't find its public.

Of war and games

Since September 11, companies are walking on eggshells with regard to marketing war games. Yes, the military uses strategic games to test out battle theories. Yes, PC flight simulators are sophisticated enough to serve as training tools. Video games do their best to raise the level of simulation and immersion to emulate reality. This is what applied science is all about.

It had to come to this one-day or another. War games are starting to appear again. Democracy and a free market go hand in hand. If these games don't correspond to the public's taste, they'll stop being produced, that's all! In the meantime, *Commandos 2: Men of Courage* and *Command & Conquer: Yuri's Revenge* are now available. Good timing – both games are excellent.

Men of Courage places us at the moment in history where the rise the 3rd Reich seems inevitable. The commandos' mission is to destabilize Hitler's armies as best they can. Careful, you'll have to pay attention and think hard on the road to victory. The terrain to negotiate is well-defined and your units can elect to work with specialized characters like Natacha the seductress and Whiskey the dog. You can control several game windows simultaneously. The multi-player mode allows you to work online with friends to accomplish your goals. The 360-degree environment is completely accessible, and the level of interactivity impressive. An extremely solid but demanding title!

<www.eidos-france.fr/games/embed.html?gmid=78>

Westwood developers offer us the game's biggest expansion yet. Yuri, an expert in psychic weapons, has decided to take matters into his own hands and avenge himself on the Soviets as well as the allies. You board a time-travel machine and there you are, halting the enemy's progress. You have now signed on for about 20 hours of intensive game play. *Yuri* can also be played in multi-player mode. If you're a fan of the series, it's a sure bet.

<www.ea.com/worlds/eaworlds.jsp>

It's Hell, but give us more!

The level of realism found in Rainbow 6-type tactical games just moved up another notch with the arrival of *Ghost Recon*. The 15 missions in solo mode are as diverse as the atmosphere is intense. Sound effects guarantee constant immersion. Artificial intelligence will give you as much trouble as any self-respecting enemy. What's more, the multi-player mode allows you to move in groups on missions where cooperation between members of your unit is essential for success – seize this opportunity to visit the new Ubi Soft server made available to gamers. The other modes are just as solid. Treat yourself, you disillusioned mercenaries!

<www.ubi.com>
<www.ghostrecon.com>

The art of combat

If you missed the release of *Shogun, Total War* a little over a year ago, it's high time you brought yourself up to date. This tactical game, with thousands of simultaneous fighters, turned many heads in its time. The expanded version entitled *Mongolian Invasion* is now available along with the original title under the name *Warlord Edition*.

This type of product allows the original to be improved with the addition of all kinds of new possibilities for devoted fans. Launch your hordes of Mongolians, Samurais and Ninjas in enormous battles where your tactical talents will be put to the test. Artificial intelligence has been refined to guarantee a balance between opponents. Three other campaigns, a multi-player mode for six opponents, and a wildly effective soundtrack complete the offering. The added script and battlefield editor makes this a purchase that will keep the Shogun sleeping inside you busy for a long while.

<www.totalwar.com>

Not for the faint-hearted!

This title is for hardcore gamers who have already invested a great deal of time and money in their obsession. When the original version of *Tribes* came out, news of a team online carnage game spread like a virus. Finally, the spirit of fraternity in war films, where a well-defined combat unit can defeat opponents in greater numbers, had become a reality. *Tribes 2* offers new vehicles, tons of weapons, more game modes and a battle field and campaign editor that will make all virtual generals drool. The training level is a must for novices because the action is merciless. *Tribes 2* is a complex game, and the ability to fly with the use of a the jet pack only increases the odds. Veterans will immediately feel at ease, and the way communities can be created has never been as

intuitive or efficient. More than 300 servers are already available throughout the world, and many have up to 40 fighters simultaneously engaged in killing each other. Battalion... charge!

<www.sierrastudios.com/games/tribes2>

Pleasant fallout

Fallout Tactics: Brotherhood of Steel demands an uncommon degree of immersion. This game's storyline lies somewhere between *Fallout 1 & 2* which plunged us into a dark, post-nuclear world where the forces of a market in the process of breaking down confronted each other. This new variation benefits from near-perfect production. Level design, cinematics, sound effects and characters succeed in creating a universe even more convincing then the original titles. Whether you are busy leading your squad or working with the RPG elements, you'll have your hands full. This game is intense even at its easiest level. Most of the missions lead you towards multiple endings dictated by your actions. Here's a game that's not afraid to advertise that it is designed only for the most sophisticated players. It also happens to fulfill its mission admirably. Seriously good!

<www.interplay.com/falloutbos/index.html>

Even better carnage

The craze continues for what was originally only a demo of the *Serious Engine* game engine. Nothing revolutionary, just tons of monsters to kill off in a *Doom*-inspired atmosphere with a humoristic twist á la Duke Nukem. An on-screen counter makes it possible to identify up to 200 simultaneous assailants. Even though this game is half the price of the others, I can guarantee you will feel sated when you've gone through all 14 levels. No mercy!

<http://serioussam.godgames.com/>

The return of the prodigal son

Myst has always divided PC game aficionados into two camps. On one side are the millions who consider the title the apex of interactive games, with all the graphic splendor of its strange universe and well thought-out puzzles. The other side just doesn't understand the attraction of exploring a universe they consider lifeless and endowed with a low level of interactivity. Cynics would add that at the time the game came out, you absolutely had to be a puzzle lover to figure out how to play it on Win95.

On the other hand, the series' incredible success can't be denied. With more than 10 million copies sold over the last seven years, *Myst* is the most popular PC title in history. Something to note: half its fans are female. Novels based on the *Myst* universe have been published, and dozens of sites are still active, sustaining the interest of fans for the D'ni civilization, which is at the heart of the saga. The sequel, *Riven*, took four years to develop, and *Myst III* another four. Hey, if it ain't broke, don't fix it! These two titles are still top sellers. The original designers, Rand and Robyn Miller, are not involved in this version, but the new producers took great care to capture the same atmosphere while applying the latest graphic innovations.

The new game engine just about abandons the slide-type view to adopt a 360 camera angle that allows for more in-depth exploration of the universe in sumptuous 32-bit and up to 1600X1200 resolution. The lighting effects are superb and level of detail surprising. The story takes place 10 years after the events of *Riven*. Atrus and Catherine are back, and you must help them defend themselves against a certain Saavedro, who wants to avenge the disappearance of his civilization. The overall effect is one of immersion in a strange world where puzzle-solving is well integrated into the story's progress. *Myst* remains the absolute best non-violent series around. Fans should rush out and get it.

Virtual drivers wanted

Skill and strategy are featured in *NASCAR Racing 4*. This title is truly for automobile race freaks. Each and every part of your race car can be adapted to your specifications, whether you understand what the effect of the modifications will be or not. We are, in fact, a long ways from the *Ridge Racers* and *Daytona's* of this world. Consider yourself warned! We are in the presence of a true simulation and, as we have seen recently, the least error can have dramatic repercussions. An entire season can be brought to an abrupt end two laps from the finish line. Sierra has fortunately included a very exhaustive user's guide that will help steer novice mechanics. You'll have access to 21 race tracks, lead up to the Winston Cup 2000. The sensation of speed is very well rendered and the accidents are completely convincing. Invest in a force-feedback steering wheel to experience this game in all its interactive splendor.

<www.papy.com>

The most long-awaited sequel

History has spoken – *Half-Life* is the most popular FPS (First Person Shooter) of all times. I usually use the expression carnage game for this genre, but in the case of *Half-Life*, we had to use more than just our reptilian brain to get through it. The enemies' formidable artificial intelligence, coupled with event scripts, has revolutionized the genre and created an instant classic. *Blue Shift* is the second official expansion and you won't feel left out in the cold. This time, you play a security guard caught between a rock and a hard place. You'll cross the former title's main characters such as Gordon Freeman (the non-intentional cause of the inter-dimensional gap), the man with the suitcase, and the soldiers whose goal remains the same – clean up the mess. The hideous Xen monsters are obviously still around. Gearbox's developers (responsible for the mega success *Opposing Force*) adapted the original recipe with flair. Even though shorter than the original, the CD contains an HDP (High Definition Pack) providing players with a higher quality graphics version of *Half-Life* and *Opposing Force*, which remain the most widely played multi-player games on the Internet. Finally, a purchase offer too hard to resist.

<www.sierrastudios.com/games/hl-blueshift>

3-D spice

Brought to the screen by David Lynch, *Dune* is, along with *Star Wars*, the most popular science-fiction saga. *Emperor: Battle for Dune* is the sequel to the 2-D strategic game *Dune II*. This time it is entirely produced in 3-D. The joy of seeing the house of Atreides, Fremen and Sadaukars once again is increased by outrageous videos featuring actors, taking us back to the era of *Wing Commander III*. The game takes place in a universe that respects Frank Herbert's books in every possible way. Adversaries are well balanced, each house possessing its particularities and strategic advantages. The automation of resource management is a welcome addition and allows us to devote ourselves to the central issue of the war. The addition of a map gives us a big-picture view. The environments are as impressive as the explosions and other special effects. Westwood's first foray into 3-D is a huge success.

<http://westwood.ea.com/games/emperor/index.html>

Choo choo train!

In the good old days kids who got trains for Christmas were ecstatic. Entire universes were created in living rooms and bedrooms by those lucky few. You can now plunge back into that atmosphere with *MS Train Simulator*. The interface is simple and works well. You can choose from three types of trains (two steam engines, three diesel engines, and three electric trains). Controls are similar except for the steam engine, which is more complex and requires the addition of water and coal – a real challenge. Six itineraries are offered, including the famous Orient Express through Europe. The graphics and sound effects are completely convincing.

This game is not for fans of relentless action. But if you are a train freak, don't hesitate to climb aboard!

<www.microsoft.com/games/trainsim/>

Strange and inviting

In the early 80s the *Dungeons and Dragons* phenomenon was somewhat comparable to today's Goths: a faction of young people, more or less misunderstood, who thrived on being different and took great joy in participating in a culture adults could not understand. *Icewind Dale* takes you back to this universe where you must identify the evil that is gnawing at the kingdom. To accomplish this you'll have to clean out crypts filled with the living dead, explore the ruins of Elven, make friends with giant ice kings and obliterate a great number of Drows. All in the midst of the choice RPG element: your character's development. You explore enormous dungeons, defeat immeasurable adversaries and eliminate hordes of monsters, only to notice that this is only a fraction of what the game offers in terms of adventure. In the meantime, you become increasingly powerful, and the magic you collect will help you face more and more demanding challenges. Your character's development curve is perfectly proportioned. The *Bioware/Black Isle* crew really invested a lot in this title. The battles, resources management, strategy and timing are all well balanced to offer superior entertainment.

<www.interplay.com/icewind/index.html>

With it's own story, attention given to the minutest details, and greater artificial intelligence than the first title, the enhancements made to this game are so positive that veterans will want to experience the entire adventure again from the beginning. Players who master this genre will quickly move to the new *Heart of Fury* mode which makes enemies more violent and resilient, and gives greater experience points. Like *Baldur's Gate II*, the containers for potions, papyrus and crystals become accessible throughout *Icewind Dale* once the expansion is installed. New spells are also available, and like all the other enhancements are of undeniable quality. An exemplary sequel to the saga created around Bioware's *Infinity Engine*.

<www.interplay.com/icewind/>
<www.bioware.com>

An RPG innovator

I admit I have a weakness for the *Fallout* series, which many consider the best and most original Role Playing Game (RPG) around. *Arcanum* is the result of three years of work by the same developers, regrouped under the name Troika Games. The literary sub-genre of cyberpunk gave rise to a Victorian version of itself, called Steampunk. *Arcanum* makes unique use this futuristic past. The confrontation of magic and technology are at the heart of the title. The level of personalization is breathtaking. You can change your characters as freely as your heart desires. The class system imposed by most RPGs is ignored here. You can choose whatever talents and weapons you want.

The story angle is wide, and the world in which the game takes place immense. The sense of freedom is real, and sub-quests abound. The combat system is based on the Diablo school of thought. You can alternate between real time and turn based mode at any time. The story editor means you can add to the 30 to 100 hours of game play offered by *Arcanum*. Don't forget to install the patch.

<www.sierrastudios.com/games/arcanum>
<www.troikagames.com>

Become a god!

Pharaoh was good, but *Zeus* is excellent. The first thing one notices is the simplicity of the interface. This new ease of play is constant throughout the game. With shorter missions, you can invest anywhere from 30 minutes to 10 hours playing, depending on your schedule. The new modes give users the option of creating cities simply for the pleasure of observing them and watching their evolution. The open mode is particularly fascinating because it offers access to all the resources, and gives you the freedom to do what you like with them. Building a city is now easier, but creating the perfect megapolis is still a challenge. If controlling the progress of a civilization interests you, this is the game to try. If you're already a fan of the genre, don't miss *Zeus*. The *Poseidon* extension is a complete success and extends the pleasure.

<http://zeus.impressionsgames.com/>

Golf for all seasons!

The *Links* series is the best known golf simulator. Microsoft surpasses it with this new version. *Links 2001* is powered by a new 3-D graphics engine and it's a gem. The physics applied to the ball are impressive. Six courses, 16 types of players, and the fact that up to 63 networked computers can play, tops it all off. The *VGA Tour* makes it possible to play online for $100,000. But the birdie here is the inclusion of the Arnold Palmer course editor. The same one the creators of the game used. The engine gives players absolute control over what they've created. A decent hole will probably take you a week to build, but you'll be able to invite your friends over to play in your own private golf course. The course editor alone is worth the price. No golf fan should miss this.

<www.microsoft.com/games/links2001>

All about monkey business...

The release of *Escape from Monkey Island* gives me an opportunity to promote this type of game generally, and as produced by Lucas Arts in particular. These adventure games are the best and funniest in history. For years Lucas Arts has been offering us one little masterpiece after another. *Grim Fandango* is a thriller that takes place in the Mexican underworld. It's brilliant and beautifully crafted. Become the leader of a (non-criminal) motorcycle gang in *Full Throttle*, and what can I say about the insane *Sam & Max* and wild *Day of the Tentacle*. All excellent titles you can now acquire for peanuts. The actors' performances, deliriously funny dialogue, impeccable style and wild stories make these the games the most widely praised by game developers themselves.

<www.lucasarts.com/products/monkey4>

Give up on the ordinary!

Since the easy-going *Earthworm Jim*, the developer (Shiny) has been offering us bizarre jewels like *MDK* and *Messiah* without quite ever living up to its initial success. It certainly isn't due to a lack of originality or ambition. This company thrives on innovation. The undeniable quality of the 3-D engine and interface sets up the strange atmosphere of *Sacrifice* right from the start. Unlike conventional real-time strategic games, the action takes place in the 3rd person, propelling you into the heart of the fray. *Sacrifice* is frenetic, pagan inspired and visceral. You'll have to collect souls for five gods on ten different levels, discovering new spells and units that come with the different combinations. A game editor lets you create your own solo or multi-player levels. Magnificent!

Way cool baby!

The years PC surprise comes at the last minute and leaves everyone amazed with its charming heroine, action to spare and a real sense of humor (rare, in games.) Most surprising is that it's a shooter... wow! Reminiscent of 60's spy films, spirited Cate Archer must save humanity from a Machiavellian plot that turns organic beings (like humans) into living bombs. Ridiculous and hilarious! Exemplary game play and artificial intelligence that really works, coupled with particularly well-made character animation means you will enjoy every level, each filled with wonderful ideas. The admirably well acted dialogue and the period soundtrack perfectly complete the atmosphere. A happy mix of *Thief, Half-Life* and *No One Lives Forever* is intelligent, funny and entirely brilliant.

<www.noonelivesforever.com>

Alice... a wonder!

Just like *Alice*, your curiosity will be rewarded as this title is filled to capacity with unique finds. The level design breaks all bounds. The architecture, fantastic characters and textures are wonderful. You'll go from surprise to amazement,

just like in the original story. But this time it is tinged with Goth-inspired atmosphere, and our little friend is locked up in an insane asylum. Charming! A Hollywood film is already in the making. The artistic direction is impeccable and will keep you glued to your screen. Your desire to explore will become insatiable as you experience one novelty after another going from level to level. The game designers throw surprises at you, and play with your perceptions by keeping you constantly on your toes. The actors' performances are as top level as the soundtrack. A wonderful addition to the PC year.

<www.alice.ea.com>

Complex but fascinating

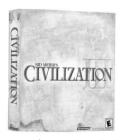

Fans of more cerebral entertainment also have something to celebrate. *Civilization* is considered to be the best strategic game of all times. Its creator, Sid Meier, shows that you can take a theme as great and as complex as the whole of human history and make it fun and accessible. Today his name is a guarantee of success where gameplay is calculated in terms of months.

Civilization III keeps the tradition going beautifully. Managing a civilization is no small thing. Starting with a simple tribe in 4000 B.C., you have to conquer the world and build an empire despite the adversity that won't take long to appear on the scene. Meier puts the experience gained while producing his other games to good use. The concept of sphere of influence (introduced in *Alpha Centauri*) means that your efforts in the cultural world will cause not only your sphere of influence but also your borders to expand. It's a vital and brilliant concept.

The interface has been improved and the options of commercial transactions and diplomacy completely reworked. The Civilopedia, which is the game database, has also been reworked with positive results. The developers, Firaxis, did not think it a good idea to add a multi-player option, but the story editor is back. This kind of game is mainly for devotees of the genre. They'll be thrilled.

<www.civ3.com>

An intergalactic breath of fresh air

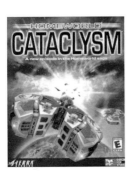

The original *Homeworld* was one of the best games of 1999, allowing the developer, Vancouver Relic, to successfully enter the marketplace. This real-time strategy game was, in fact, revolutionary for its use of 3-D space, which made real, epic-like battles possible. Its camera system, music, atmosphere and style made it a unique and beautiful space-opera. *Homeworld: Cataclysm* continues in the same vein, and even succeeds in offering a few enhancements. The option that enables players to compress time to a factor of 8 is a find that makes collecting material less taxing. The interactive user guide is wonderful and will

quickly put you at ease. The five levels of difficulty get you gently immersed in the game.

<www.sierrastudios.com/games/homeworld/cataclysm>

The Red Menace

The U.S. is invaded by the Soviet empire armed with psychic weapons. Since Rambo is busy trying to make a new career for himself, the responsibility of saving America falls on your shoulders. The developers, Westwood, haven't reinvented the real-time strategy game, but they've brought back the most successful aspects of their first two productions. *Command & Conquer: Red Alert 2*, is a brilliant balance of tactical intelligence, with a very interesting arsenal and use of technology like Russian Tesla and Yankee Prism. Obviously, the solo missions are only training sessions for D day, where you test yourself against opponents online. The formula works wonderfully well. New additions to the online version add to the fun, and its extra-solid production make this title a sure bet for fans.

<http://eagames.ea.com/#>

The School of Capitalism

When it bought Hasbro, Infogames took over several traditional game franchises like Scrabble and Monopoly. *Monopoly Tycoon* easily borrows *Roller Coaster Tycoon's* recipe for success and accomplishes the feat of modernizing this classic. The dice are gone, but the entrepreneurial spirit lying dormant inside you will no doubt be teased awake. The 3-D's retro look is a perfect complement to the game's atmosphere. And the city built according to your economic scheming is oh so elegant.

Since there can be anywhere up to five players working hard to be more successful than you, expect strong competition. The tutorial is excellent, and the Sandbox mode allows you to amuse yourself trying out the different game possibilities without any pressure. The race to City Hall is really interesting. I can easily imagine the boring television debates of our electoral campaigns replaced with a game of online *Monopoly* with real candidates. It would be very easy to see who really has leadership and administrative talent.

<www.monopolytycoon.com>

Tons of fun!

For all the fans of the genre *Mechwarrior 4: Vengeance* is a must-have. The series is a true dynasty, and the gaming gods have blessed this new version. The creators of *BattleTech* (FASA) are in fact responsible. They listened to their fans and incorporated their suggestions. The result is based on a story of betrayal and steel giants that flay out at each other all the way to the scrap yard. The most obvious enhancement is the speed of the mechs themselves. The days of slow motion mastodons are over. *Mechwarrior 4* moves along at great speed, and this change of pace is welcome. Sidewinder owners have an advantage over traditional keyboard and mouse players. The rotation of the mechs' torsos is more natural with a joystick and will help you survive the frenetic battles awaiting you.

<www.microsoft.com/games/mechwarrior4>

The fine line between dream and reality

The adventure game refuses to die. The last embodiment of the genre, *The Longest Journey*, is an homage to the very best of this style. The Scandinavian developers, Funcom, created a product that is in no way inferior to those created by masters of the genre, Lucas Arts and Sierra. Rather than the spirit of childish fun experienced in those company's titles, the themes addressed here are more mature. The heroine of the adventure lives in an environment constructed of impressive 3-D renderings. In her 23rd century, somewhat "steampunk" world (a mix of Victorian architecture, Art Nouveau, and science-fiction) our heroine sees the line between reality and her imagination become more and more blurred. The story alone is worthy of your attention. The design matches the gameplay in quality. With more than 40 hours of playing time, *The Longest Journey* is twice as long as the average game in this genre. For fans, it's a definite must-have. Positively yummy.

<www.longestjourney.com>

Tacticians attack!

The official release of the latest addition to *Ground Control: Dark Conspiracy* gives me the opportunity to draw your attention to this real-time 3-D strategy game. You successively become the chief tactician of two military factions. Choose between 12 types of units you'll deploy during your 15 missions, where battles take precedence over resource management. Camera control is beautifully accomplished, allowing the genre to evolve into a 3-D environment, a great improvement over the previous 2-D limitations of *Starcraft* and *Age of Empires*. The attention to detail is impressive – the camera zoom-in and zoom-out feature will enable you to verify this. *Dark Conspiracy* offers 15 new missions, new battlefields on three different planets, and new units. Can be networked or played online.

<www.sierrastudios.com/games/groundcontrol>

A good sense of tumor!

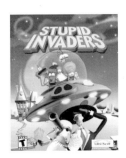

Scatological humor is certainly easy, but I'm not the type to turn my back on enjoyment. I burst out laughing more than once playing *Stupid Invaders*. The 2-D series transposed into 3-D is just beautiful. The cut scenes alone are worth the price. This adventure game consists of puzzles you have to solve using objects you find in the 500 backgrounds on your path. The solutions are usually pretty easy. The dialogue is by a writer of *Ren & Stimpy* fame, a guarantee of stupidity and cringing humor. Save often, as many of your actions will lead to cartoon-type endings where everything explodes, unless it's an anvil that drops from the sky... It's usually hilarious. Sorry, but I grew up on Bugs Bunny cartoons and they've marked me for life.

<www.UbiSoft.com/usa/games/stupidinvaders>

Tempered steel

Military simulation games are few and far between. They're a huge and difficult task. *Steel Beasts* was initially a postgraduate university project to create a terrain rendering engine in 1996. The direction changed when the two most sophisticated tanks of the American and German armies were added to the environment. The battlefields of Europe, Asia, and the Middle East are offered as playing fields for the M1A1 and Leopard 2A4. Montreal's Strategy First continue to unearth the best strategy games on the planet, and *Steel Beasts* is no exception. The developers concentrated mainly on gameplay. Played in a 1st person perspective, player immersion in the subtleties of tactics takes precedence over knowing what each button and lever in the tanks do. Most time is spent negotiating the terrain, deploying your units and blasting enemy tanks. But careful, the artificial intelligence is formidable and a single well-placed shot is enough to get yourself eliminated. More than 40 missions range from tank-to-tank duels to large scale battles. More than 20 tutorials help you master the learning curve. Initially only available online and praised by the critics, the boxed version is now available on store shelves. The community of online multi-players generated by this game is extremely active.

<www.strategyfirst.com/steel/steel-eng.htm>,
<www.esimgames.com/steelBeasts.htm>
<www.steelbeasts.com>

Viva Santa Banana!

Imagine an electoral campaign where our leaders would play a game of *Sim City* on live television as an aptitude test. My impression is that we'd see their real talent as administrators. *Tropico* goes beyond that. It's a political simulator where you have to fight and finesse to become El Presidente of a banana republic in the 50's. The goal is simply to gain power through every possible means available to you. If only martial law could be declared and elections fixed... but that's not the case. You have to learn to negotiate with different factions. The ever-present law of the jungle brings you back to earth in no time flat. One game mode provides specific goals to attain, while the other gives you ample latitude (size of the island, population, resources and goals) while letting you know about the trouble you're about to get into even before it rears it's ugly head. All you have to do is choose the profile of the dictator you want to become and off you go. All your public needs is your vision and political flair. But be careful! The more you give, the more they want... and you can't please everybody and his uncle. You'll realize fairly quickly that the key is to keep your coffers filled. This exercise might even give you a glimmer of respect for our poor politicians, who more often than not find themselves in no-win situations.

<http://tropico.godgames.com>
<www.poptop.com/Tropico.htm>

Edutainment

When I received a game with the mention Ages: 9 to 24 months, I was surprised and amused. I nonetheless tested it out and have to admit that the adventure of learning can, in fact, begin at this young age. Parents will truly enjoy witnessing their child's interactive/computer awakening.

Lucas Learning

Well-known for the phenomenal success of *Star Wars*, George Lucas has accomplished exceptional work in his "edutainment" division, Lucas Learning. Here is a series of games parents and children can discover together. Irresistibly drawn in by the Star Wars theme, children will learn universal concepts in a non-violent atmosphere. Among my favorites is *Pit Droids*. What at first seems like a simple exercise in directing traffic of nice but stupid droids quickly becomes a puzzle of exponential complexity, demanding all your skills in logic and deduction. The possibility of creating your own puzzles and exchanging them online also makes the game attractive.

<www.lucaslearning.com>

Lego

Lego is one of the most well known brands in the world. Adapting it to video games, though inevitable, was no easy task. The lego *Chess* game is brilliant, while *Stunt Rally, Crator* and *Lego Island* allow kids to build all kinds of virtual environments and venture into them. *Alpha Team* is an adventure game where kids have to prevent the evil Ogel from using his mind control tools to conquer the world. A true action game! You are the leader of a team of spies/commandos adept in gadgets who must accomplish more than 40 missions, each more distracting than the other. The game's production is excellent. Children will learn the basics of logic and deduction... but don't tell them that! Lego was also first to put out a Harry Potter related game.

<www.lego.com/software>

The Disney avalanche

Disney cartoons get the game, soundtrack and pajama treatment. Let your kids choose between *Tarzan, Toy Story, Atlantis*, etc. All these titles pretty much follow the same formula, and each is as entertaining as the last. There is even a section with access to the Internet. Parental supervision is, however, suggested for this portion of the game. It's an interesting way to introduce the Web to children. The platform games are entirely respectable and are published for PC, PSI and Dreamcast. The number of titles this entertainment multinational puts on the market is impressive. The company's talent for innovation is also evident with *Phonics Quest*. This game uses voice recognition (microphone included) to initiate kids 5 to 8 to the subtleties of the English language. An excellent initiative. *Music Mix Studio* even uses the microphone to let young DJs, musicians and soon-to-be producers create their own songs and music videos. Very hot indeed!

<www.disneyinteractive.com>

The case of Apple

At the beginning of the Mac story, Steve Jobs turned up his nose at games because he thought he could sell Macs to businessmen and didn't want to stigmatize his buyers with the specter of adolescent and not entirely serious machines like the Commodore. We now know what history dictated... the Mac has been reduced to the realm of publication graphics and high scale music software (Pro-Tools). Jobs' lack of intuition is inexcusable, and Mac game fans are still paying for his error. Thank goodness he's put himself back on track with his acquisition of Pixar, proving that he at least believes in a form of 3-D art. Poor Mac gamers wait an eternity for versions of the most popular games, if they arrive at all... and even with the support of John Carmack of id Software, it would be surprising if this changed.

Already released

Baldur's Gate: Tales of the Sword Coast (GraphSim)
Centipede (MacSoft)
Diablo II: Lord of Destruction Expansion Set (Blizzard; hybrid PC/Mac release)
Escape from Monkey Island (Aspyr)
Monopoly Casino (MacSoft)
Myst III: Exile (Ubi Soft)
Pong: The Next Level (MacSoft)
Tomb Raider Chronicles (Aspyr)
Tony Hawk's Pro Skater II (Aspyr)
Unreal Tournament: Game of the Year Edition (MacSoft)

Soon to be released

American McGee's Alice (Aspyr)
Baldur's Gate II: Shadow of Amn (MacPlay)
Breakout (MacSoft)
Clive Barker's Undying (Aspyr)
Deer Hunter 5: Tracking Trophies (MacSoft)
Fighter Squadron: The Screamin' Demons Over Europe (MacPlay)
Fly! II (MacSoft)
Giants: Citizen Kabuto (MacPlay)
Icewind Dale (MacPlay)
Jeopardy! Second Edition (MacSoft)
Master of Orion (MacSoft)
Myth III (MacSoft)
QBert (MacSoft)
Red Faction (GraphSim)
Sacrifice (MacPlay)

Starfleet CommandVolume II: Empires at War
   (MacPlay)
Summoner (GraphSim)
The Sims House Party Expansion Pack (Aspyr)
Tropico (MacSoft)
Vampire: The Masquerade—Redemption
   (MacSoft)
Wheel of Fortune Second Edition (MacSoft)
World War II Online (Strategy First)

I hate to bring it late like this, but you're right, I can seem to be over enthusiastic about video games. It is an editorial stance of some sort. There are too many great games published to waste time, space, and energy on ripping a game apart. Journalists use the fact that they love sarcastic prose as an excuse. And maybe they should: because of the price they are getting paid for their work, sarcasm has always been one of the pleasures of their trade.

The Web is central to the evolution of gaming

13.

Games and the internet

n the mid 1990s, game companies thought the end-all answer to their Internet strategy was to offer titles like Quake to hardcore players who would pay to play online. A dozen game sites adopted this model and ended up closing up shop. Then came a slew of sites aimed at occasional players with free, simple games. This trend is also starting to hit the skids. Industry consolidation has already begun.

Recent History

In a few months time, Electronic Arts bought Pogo.com (which was no. 2 in terms of traffic for online games) for $50 million and integrated it into its empire. With the exclusivity agreement signed with AOL, EA's investment in its online division comes to $150 million.

Vivendi's subsidiary, Flipside (no. 1 in traffic) acquired Uproar (no. 3 in traffic), which had previously merged with Iwin.com (once a top 10 site), for $140 million. Vivendi predicts that its merged occasional game operation will produce $70 million in revenue in 2001.

Infogrames, for its part, bought Hasbro Interactive and at the same time got Atari and the Games.com site for around $100 million worth of shares and cash.

Wouldn't you know it, these sites are now getting a second chance by offering à la carte pay-to-play games aimed at occasional as well as sophisticated gamers. This time, they're counting on well-established brands. Big investments are in the works. Borrowing from the cable model, EA has started to offer, for $5 a month, subscriptions to packages of online games consisting of one prestigious title bundled with other more ordinary ones. The titles include *Motor City Online* and online versions of *Lord of the Rings, Harry Potter,* and *The Sims.* Sony continues to work on *Star Wars Galaxies* with George Lucas, and Activision is busy creating *Star Trek Online.*

THQ, which seems not to be able to make any mistakes these days, has decided to adopt a more modest approach. It has joined up with its long-time partner, the World Wrestling Federation (WWF) to offer *With Authority!,* the equivalent of a card exchange game. THQ provides players with a (basic) card collection and then charges $6 for each additional pack. These cards show their favorite wrestlers, each in their own unique pose. THQ shares the revenues with WWF, but avoids the costly marketing and online costs of a Web site dedicated to adventure.

Verant Interactive, Sony's interactive subsidiary, has created *Everquest,* the most popular online game with around 375,000 users paying $9.89 a month to play. As of today it's the model to follow, as Sony pockets twice as much money as it spends maintaining its MMOG (Massive Multiplayer Online Game).

That's all the rest of the pack needed to hear, and recently, more than twenty new MMOGs were announced.

RealNetworks comes into play

In an effort to consolidate its market share, well established in the realm of video and music down-loading, RealNetworks will apply its expertise to online games by offering a technology that allows developers to sell and quickly download their games to consumers online. It is expected that online games will see their number of players increase from 39 million in 2000 to 74.7 million in 2004.

RealArcade's principal asset is making game developers' lives easier by making products directly accessible to their clients. The old model of the all-powerful publisher who has control over everything will be put to the test.

Developers will also be able to circumvent retailers by downloading their games on the RealArcade site. RealNetwork's technology compresses the games so they can be downloaded more easily by consumers who can play free demos or pay for the whole game. RealNetworks obviously keeps a percentage of the transaction fee (a business plan model that will be tried by a lot of companies in coming years). The technology makes downloading simple by allowing consumers to stop the process mid-stream and resume it at their convenience.

For hardcore players, RealNetworks will offer a networked matching service by joining up with GameSpy. The company will also provide chat services and a games column. Finally, a game engine (designed to help developers by being easily downloadable) will be offered for free.

RealNetworks' compression technology can considerably reduce the size of large files. For example, a 350MB game can be reduced by 30% to 80% for downloadable files. An average MP3 file is anywhere between 3MB and 6MB. But for the time being the company will be unable to post games available only on standard CD-ROMs because they require around 650MB. The time to download them is too long compared to music files.

To date many publishers including Havas Interactive, Sierra On-Line, Activision, not to mention dozens of game developers like Valve, have announced they will publish games through RealNetworks. Intel has also stated it will sponsor a few games that will show off the power of its microprocessors on the Real.com site.

During the site's trial period, consumers downloaded some 5 million game demos, 3% of them paying for the entire game.

A WildTangent game: Betty Bad

Since its release, Real Arcade has distributed 15 million games. By opening up a new game publishing market for small developers, RealNetworks faces competition. Wild Tangent is another company that has been offering a similar service for over a year. Its game and compression engine was developed by the same people who put Direct X on the market, and the results are already more than interesting.

<www.wildtangent.com>

This year the company also pulled off a coup by hiring Paul Steed, one of id's most reputed artists. A more artistic and hardcore gaming trend has already started to emerge at Wild Tangent. The company's core effort is geared towards delivering 3-D games online, and the first demos are promising.

Macromedia owns 2 technologies used to develop small games for occasional players: Shockwave and Flash. They're free, inventive, and wildly popular.

Try out all the new ideas at

<www.shockwave.com>
<www.flasharcade.com>
<www.flashgamer.com>

Online Games

Imagine a business plan predicting your product will initially sell for $70, where new owners will have to pay $10 a month if they want to continue playing. We're talking 150,000 users, which means approximately $30 million of revenue per year. Not bad for a niche product. These games are called MMOGs (Massive Multi-player Online Games).

Online games based on persistent worlds (the story goes on and evolves whether you're there or not) are now made up of three convincing concepts. EA's *Ultima Online*, Sony's *EverQuest*, and Microsoft's *Asheron's Call* all make good use of these games' intrinsic appeal.

<www.uo.com>
<www.station.sony. com/everquest>

At the moment this market doesn't seem to be slowing down since numerous sites are always being added to the list, the most important being Strategy First's *World War II*, Funcom's *Anarchy Online*, and EA's *Motor City Online*. South Korea is also a hot spot for this genre.

<http://216.74.158.92/>
<www.motorcityonline.com>

To get an idea of the spirit of these types of games, visit <www.stratics.com>.

The first 3 MMOG'S started a revolution

For developers these games are technically demanding and costly to maintain (the biggest part of the work actually begins on launch day). Curiously, they seem to create communities that are much more faithful than any other type of Web following. During peak times, more than 100,000 players from all over the world simultaneously link up to live *Dungeons and Dragons*-type adventures that used to be reserved for nerds.

As a matter of fact, launches of the latest two (*WWII* and *Anarchy Online*) were conducted in the midst of confusion typical for this type of product. Companies become victims of their success. When 50,000 people simultaneously try to log on to share a 3-D real-time universe, the least you can say is that there's going to be a bit of pushing and shoving to get in. But with the spectacular success of *EverQuest*, everyone is getting into the race.

Everquest ingnited the market

EverQuest was launched March 16, 1999, and 10,000 people signed on the first day to instantly make it the number one online game. In only 6 months 225,000 copies had been sold, and 150,000 subscribers were investing more and more time in this virtual universe. Today, *EverQuest* and its official expansions (*Ruins of Kurnark* and *Scars of Velious*) have sold more than 700,000 copies. The 300,000 subscriber mark was reached near the end of 2000. *EverQuest* now has a following of 450, 000 active players. This is unheard of!

Urban legends or the new economy?

Nicknamed *Evercrack* by fans and critics because of the severe addiction it creates, the game is already responsible for several sociological aberrations. For example, items and characters won in the game can be found on online auction sites (E-bay) and bought by gamers who freely spend real cash to increase their arsenals or raise their social status within the game. Some gamers quit their real jobs because they can earn more money looting *EverQuest*'s resources and selling them to newcomers ready to pay the price. A good player can earn up to $2,000 per week in trade. Fascinating! And people wonder why they watch less television! Two support sites exist for partners who feel neglected because of the game.

<www.egroups.com/group/EverQuest-Widows>
<http://clubs.yahoo.com/clubs/
spousesagainsteverquest>

Players seem to endow their characters (avatars) with increasing importance. Fans are even creating guilds on their own Web sites. Gatherings and conventions of subscribers who meet while playing are becoming more and more common.

Go MMOG youg one !

If this interests you, explore *Norrath*. You'll need a few days to visit the 13 cities and races that inhabit the first four continents. The original title is delivered with the expansion *Ruins of Kumark*. Creating your character is an extremely intuitive process. Choose from among 12 races and professions including bard, druid, magician, warrior, sorcerer, shaman, etc. You'll then be given ability points you'll have to distribute among seven attributes (strength, endurance, agility, dexterity, wisdom, intelligence and charisma). Christen yourself, choose your gender and your god, and you're ready to join in the fun!

<www.station.sony.com/everquest>

Conclusion:
Trends

What about the French connection?

The French video game industry bought nearly 35% of the American industry, thanks to a series of spectacular acquisitions. Nevertheless, the French still seem incapable of producing a homegrown hit on the American market, based on its own intellectual property. France produces a meager 1 % of all games sold around the world. To make matters worse, the 2001 report from ECCSELL (European Consoles and Computer Software Edutainment and Leisure Leaders) shocked the French game community.

<www.sell.fr/eccsell/fr_2001.html>

Among the 30 best sellers, not one French publisher was to be found. A similar situation arose when Sony bought Columbia Pictures a while back.

Vivendi/Universal, Infogrames and Ubi Soft are all in acquisition mode. Havas' coup when it took over Sierra and the crown jewel developers Blizzard and Valve, responsible for *Diablo* and *Half-Life* respectively, shocked the American industry. The British who, it must be said, produce some of the most original and best games in the world (11 % of PS2 and PC games), are also getting swallowed up by big French publishers. Infogrames had already rung some alarm bells in Britain when it took over Ocean, Gremlin and Accolade. There was a real sense of panic when it was leaked that one of the last independent Brits, Eidos might also be swallowed. Ubi Soft joined the fray by successively taking over Sinister Games, Grolier Interactive U.K., Red Storm and Blue Byte, and then casting covetous glances at Activision. Even tiny Titus purchased a part of Interplay and took control of Virgin Interactive.

All this must be put into perspective. In 2000, total sales of Infogrammes, Ubi Soft, Cryo and Titus combined did not even equal half those of Electronic Arts. What's more, Infogrammes and Titus lost money in 2000, which might not bode well for their performance on the stock market, still traumatized as it is by the dot-com crash. In fact, contrary to the American trend where EA shares increased by 50% on the NASDAQ, the price of French publishers' shares plummeted. A dangerous turn of events because this is precisely where these companies financed their acquisitions.

Following on the heels of traditional media, the interactive entertainment industry is currently in full consolidation mode. But while executives play the speculation game, even venerable *Business Week* magazine has deemed the century to come as the century of creativity. Sooner or later all 21st century corporations will have to produce original content.

Obviously they all are already doing this. But in the video game sector we have to concentrate on the creation of intellectual property specific to games (*Pokemon, Tomb Raider, Metal Gear Solid, Everquest* or *Final Fantasy*). It seems French companies have not yet assimilated the cultural differences inherent to their new global market.

Ok, it makes economic sense to start by acquiring established licenses. This is the path Ubi Soft chose by linking up with Disney, Batman, Jacques Villeneuve, Pamela Anderson and even Hooters. However, their first forays onto American soil with *Rayman* and *Speed Devil (Buster)*, did not quite achieve the goals set for

them, despite the fact that they were favorably received by the critics.

As far as Havas is concerned, the situation is a bit different. It remains to be seen whether their amazing edutainment success, *Adibou, Adi* and *Adibou'chou* will be attractive to Americans. Competition is fierce in and American children certainly don't have the same cultural background as the creators of these enormously successful titles. What's more, the latest offerings in this market were produced for consoles (mainly PS1), a sector in which Havas has not yet established a presence, but will have to if it wants to become a real player.

Infogrames has already made a few unsuccessful tries. *Outcast* was a monumental flop even by admission of their president, Bruno Bonnel, with whom I discussed the matter at Milia 2000. Their flagship *Alone in the Dark* didn't fare much better. With Gameloft and Game Citizen, established with great pomp in Canada only to have jobs slashed and be repositioned more modestly, it seems the French have a lot to learn about North American gaming culture.

Even in Europe, 40% of games are produced in England, 38.8 % in America, 20.2 % in Japan and only 0.5% in France! What's going on?

After the fall of dot.coms...

One thing is certain; the collapse of dot.coms set off alarm bells in the so-called new economy. Fiber optic networks will not be installed at the expected rate. Large-scale delivery of digital content will not become a reality for another 10 years or so. In fact, no one is even sure any longer that this is what the public wants. With Microsoft and Sony building their campaign based on the assumption that broadband is the way to go, the road to profit could be bumpy.

Gamers, on the other hand, want and will continue to demand a fail-safe connection to the Internet. What's more, consoles will reach the PC players enamored by MMOGs, which are very demanding with their thousands of players in 3D worlds. Real time voice exchange is also on the rise. Non-stop real-time remains a necessity to achieve the level of immersion gamers expect. And that's not all...

... what does the future hold for us?

The road toward the Star Trek holodeck will no doubt be a long one, but already R&D departments of several high tech companies are making headway. The American army can already print images directly onto the retina thanks to a specially designed laser apparatus. Imagine the level of resolution! Video games have also been the source of inspiration for some science-fiction authors. To get an idea of what the video game culture might look like in future, you owe it to yourself to read *Snow Crash*, by Neil Stephenson.

A Cyberpunk classic not to be missed to get a feel of where this culture is heading

The number of players continues to increase because preceding generations are still playing. People are also starting to play at a younger age, and casual players constitute a bigger and bigger piece of the pie. You'll also have to start getting used to the humiliation of getting your ass kicked by the cyber-grrrls of the world. Women actually make up one-half of casual online players.

2000 was a transition year, where game companies focused on controlling expenses and reorganizing internally to deal with the irreversible market consolidation. Relationships between the different parties solidified to match the trend towards globalization. 2001 was a rerun, but expectations were higher. Everyone was counting on the exceptional launch of three new consoles (GBA, Xbox, GameCube) to breathe new life into the industry. Tons of money were spent to promote these new platforms, including $500 million by Microsoft, which will boost the popularity of the industry as a whole.

Cell phones, personal palm devices and the increased connection between all these gadgets also offer new possibilities for gamers on the run. The addition of a hard drive to consoles, and the arrival of high bandwidth, are the basic elements of another revolution that will allow new game concepts to emerge.

The way players interact with games will also evolve. Voice recognition technologies are quickly developing, but it's the use of a camera capable of transmitting a player's movements to his character that could drive users wild.

For its part, Sony unveiled the Gscube (PS3?) based on no less than 16 PS2 with two Gbytes of direct Rambus DRAM. The graphic synthesizer contains 32MB of memory compared to PS 2's 4MB. A monster capable of displaying the likes of Monster Inc. and Final Fantasy in real time.

The new generation of consoles are already so powerful that slightly modified versions connected to a network of satellites could be used to disseminate basic knowledge like AIDS information to developing countries. The World Economic Forum (WEF) would like to use such new innovations to bridge the technological gap between nations. It seems a modified PS2 is more stable and easier to use than a PC, and can be introduced anywhere there's a television set. The DVD player and hard drive could also be used in education.

The arcade market is in free fall, save for Asia, which is still the place of choice for fans of tournaments and LAN parties. Clubs are being formed and challenges issued. One can easily imagine international tournaments played from arcades scattered throughout the world.

In the meantime, it's clear that Moore's sacrosanct law stipulating that the number of transistors in circuits doubles every 18 to 24 months, is about to hit a wall. The microchip engraving technology in use today will come up against a diffraction phenomenon and researchers are already looking toward nanotechnology, quantum physics and photon optical processors for solutions. But let's get back to Earth, where the next version of the Internet is being discussed.

We're talking about a transfer speed of 40GB making it 300 times faster, plus fiber optic connections and new routers capable of managing billions of bytes per second. With nearly 500 million users worldwide, and all the hand-held devices and telephones getting Web access, a new protocol will be needed to increase the number of addresses. Christened IPv6, this new standard will allow 6000 billion addresses to be created. People will be able to play anytime and anywhere!

Too close for cultural comfort

On a lighter note, game designers are always looking for ways to expand the envelope. This can sometimes produce perplexing results.

Japanese arcade games are known to be weird by American standards, but they can occasionally launch a craze that finds cultural resonance. It happened with Pokemon musical games, for example, where you can dance or play an instrument.

Lately things have gone a little over the top. Would you dare be seen in public playing the new butt-poking arcade game *Boong-Ga Boong-Ga* that is sweeping Japan? Known in English as "Spank'em!" the game leaves little to the imagination. Players can choose between eight targets, including "ex-girlfriend", "ex-boyfriend", "gold digger", and "prostitute". Other characters include "mother-in-law", "child molester" and "con man".

> "This is a fun game of spanking the people who make your life miserable. When you spank the character that you choose to punish, the facial expression of the character will change as they scream and twitch in pain. The funny face expressions will make people laugh and relieve stress."

The player is not expected to spank the protruding bottom, but to poke it enthusiastically with the attached plastic finger. On screen the character's face grimaces and screams while you're busy poking. The harder you poke, the higher you score. At the end of the game, the machine prints out a card explaining the player's "sexual behavior". Ouch!

Violence

The stigma of violence will continue to haunt the industry since it's highly likely American politicians needing attention will continue to pound on the message. Self-regulation is the only viable avenue — recalling games like Shakespeare's *Hamlet* and Homer's *Odyssey*, both of which are incredibly violent, won't work. And then there's professional wrestling... need I say more? We all agree that children should be protected from violent and sexual content, but we must also admit that the television environment is much more permissive and accessible. ESBR ratings are printed on game boxes, but it's up to parents to manage their children's upbringing.

Game violence: 2 different standards?

My position on the subject of violence in video games is the same now as when the controversy began. I'm not "in favor" of violence in video games, but I'm absolutely "for" freedom of expression!

Still, I would like to remind readers that 80% of games on the market are not violent, and that recourse to extreme violence is generally indicative of designers being short on ideas. These games are usually monumental flops anyway, and disappear without a trace a soon as the publicity machine accompanying their release stops. The case of *Kingpin* is a prime example.

The antidote to the violence virus is, in my opinion, education rather than repression. I can't imagine wrestling being outlawed, or boys stopped from playing cowboys or with swords. While the tendency to pound the message in seems to be growing, it might be more appropriate to take a step back and expand the debate. A media literacy course designed to increase understanding of the workings of the media in our society, taught to adolescents, could yield surprising results. Take a look at:

<www.pbs.org/wgbh/frontline/shows/cool/>

A T-shirt seen in the hallways of E3 illustrates that video game violence is polarizing our society more and more. A young programmer was proudly wearing the shirt which read "Video games don't kill people...I do!"

Over the last few years computer games have been singled out time and again as incentives to violence. The parents of three Paducah, Kentucky teenagers killed December 1, 1997, are suing Web sites, several game companies and the distributors of the film The Basketball Diaries released in 1995, for $130 million. One of the attorneys in the case, Jack

Thompson, has laid out his plan of action. "We intend to hurt Hollywood. We intend to hurt the video game industry. We intend to hurt sex porn sites." The case alleges Michael Carneal, who was 14 at the time of the shooting, was influenced by, among other things, violent computer games he'd played. Games like *Doom*, *Quake* and *Mortal Combat* are being singled out and Sony, Sega and Nintendo also stand accused. The lawsuit was dismissed last April. A federal judge ruled that video games are not subject to product liability laws.

But to no avail. Families of the 13 killed at Columbine High School filed a lawsuit against video game companies and sex-oriented web sites. The suit seeks $5 billion in punitive damages from 25 entertainment companies. Named in the lawsuit are:

Nintendo of America, Sega of America, Sony Computer Entertainment, AOL Time Warner, ID Software Inc. and GT Interactive Software Corp, creators and publishers of the game *Doom*.

"Absent the combination of extremely violent video games and these boys' incredibly deep involvement, use of and addiction to these games and the boys' basic personalities, these murders and this massacre would not have occurred," says the lawsuit. This case was also dismissed.

Let's also regulate wrestling and newscasts

Lt. Col. David Grossman (retired from the U.S. Army) whose expertise in the area of human aggression and violence includes service as a West Point psychology professor, a professor of military science, the author of a Pulitzer nominated book and numerous peer reviewed encyclopedia entries on this topic, brought forth the following theory in his statement before the New York State Legislature:

"The violent video games teach criminal behavior: i.e., shooting human beings, to include motor skills, aiming skills, target selection, and trigger control. The video games and their advertisements exhort the reader to engage in criminal behavior while teaching blatant disregard for human life: being rewarded for harming and killing humans, and: "Kill your friends... More fun than shoot-

ing your neighbor's cat... Destroying your enemies is not enough ... you must devour their souls."

It's true that the U.S. army does in some cases resort to FPS (first-person-shooter) computer game adaptations as tactic simulators to train troops. Adapting games aimed at the general public seemed a good economic alternative to developing a combat simulator. Simulation is the key word here, and yes, they are getting more and more realistic. This is, after all, applied science and as we know we can't stop the wheel of progress. Mr. Grossman is calling for coercive laws destined to help parents keep video games far from their children.

Controversy continued to surround the tragic Littleton events. *Time Magazine* headlined violence and the PC culture. In an act of derision, the video game columnist Jessica Mulligan decided to sue God for bad use of free choice in the creation process! For opponents of regulation, this debate probes deeply into freedom of expression and individual responsibility. It's easy to see that both sides are firmly entrenched. But are computer games really synonymous with violence?

According to Dr. Henry Jenkins of the MIT Media Lab, approximately 80% of young American boys play video games. According to recent estimations, 15 to 20 million people play network games. This last category, which is experiencing exponential growth, largely consists of non-violent games such as parlor or strategy games.

To be precise, 20% of console games have violent overtones and 9% of games feature firearms. On the PC platform, approximately 15% of games have violent overtones. Therefore, the great majority of games do not resort to violence. On the other hand, the success of this industry is based on games with violent overtones and a great number of technological advances can be attributed to them. The first real-time LAN network and Internet games were combat games (*Doom, Quake*).

The controversy surrounding the Littleton tragedy has caused the industry to rally around IDSA, one of the principal professional organizations in this sector. IDSA members account for 85% of the $6.35 billion in computer and video game software sold in the US in 2001.

Habits of young consumers under high surveillance

Their main arguments are based on self-regulation and purchaser responsibility. According to Doug Lowenstein, President of IDSA, a recent poll showed that 46% of gamers are less than 18 years of age, while 25% are over 36 years old. Moreover, more than 90% of video game purchasers are adults. Most games are not dangerous for the majority of people. They can even have a positive, cathartic effect.

At the same time, according to a poll by CNN/USA Today/Gallup, 58 % of adult American citizens are in favor of government regulation of video games.

Senator McCain opened the Senate Commerce Hearing on Marketing Violence Toward Children by pointing out the nation's responsibility with these words: "As a country, we are not parenting our children. We are not involved in our children's lives. We are not putting them first. In the absence of parental guidance a rising culture of violence is engulfing our children. This is an extraordinarily complex problem, with many contributing factors. It is not simply video games, music, movies or access to guns. Instead, it is all of these factors plus many others which combine to create a deadly mixture which feeds a culture of violence."

One of the difficulties developers have always faced is showing victory over adversity in a visual way. Be it Mario who stomps on a mushroom, or a mercenary who has eliminated an alien...an action must take place to neutralize the danger so the game can move forward. From *Miss PacMan* to *Quake Arena*, developers have all come up with their own solutions to this problem, more or less tastefully and/or successfully.

Are we shooting the messenger? In the second half of the 20th century, North-American culture has had a tendency to point an accusing finger at many forms of entertainment as being the cause of our society's ills. In the 1950s, comic strips like *Tales from the Crypt* were criticized for their images and stories of horror. Many types of music – rock 'n' roll, heavy metal, rap and now Goth rock — are often accused of tearing at the seams of our social fabric.

Now it's the turn of video games to take the blame. Nevertheless, millions of people play these games every day without becoming deranged serial killers. 99.9% of these enthusiastic players see games, films, and television for what they are: forms of entertainment that appeal to their imagination and temporarily draw them into a fantasy world. The staunchest critics are often those who have never tried out this type of activity. They certainly can't understand the enjoyment and strong emotions the average player finds in them.

Until now, no real proof has been offered that video games contribute to the rate of violence among young people. During the last five years, young people's passion for video games has become a cultural phenomenon. During the same period, the teenage homicide rate has declined.

There are no statistics to support the assumption that violent video games can harm well-balanced teenagers. For a disturbed child who confuses dream with reality, it's possible that video game immersion could have a negative effect. It would however be deplorable to develop public policy to deny access to popular content based on the psychological deductions of a handful of individuals. The use of content in bad faith is a price we have to pay if we want to live in a free society.

At the same time, designers shouldn't limit themselves to using the ever-growing power of technology only to create realistic violence. The public's concern about violence and the power of the market

Parent's choices are clear: repression, education or free for all

will lead the industry in other directions. A new generation of games integrating education and entertainment will emerge from this controversy. We will get interactive film and television content that will allow people to communicate through new means. This entertainment will appeal to all demographic groups, including women.

Whatever happens, let's hope the general public remains logical and makes enlightened decisions based on facts and not on rhetoric.

Can video games be good for children?

A study of the British Government's Economic and Social Research Council (ESRC) states that the level of coordination and concentration of video game players can be compared to those of high-level athletes. Young people who play regularly but not obsessively (18 hours a week) are purported to have more friends and be better adapted than those who enjoy more traditional forms of entertainment like television or reading. In fact, in a series of questionnaires and psychological tests, gamers did better than sports enthusiasts and other designated groups. They had, among other things, a higher chance of finishing high school. They will end up with more highly paid jobs, and are more intelligent than average. And remember, I'm not the one saying this...

<www.esrc.ac.uk>

Young gamers number 80 million and make up America's No. 1 demographic group. The youngest are still in diapers and the oldest just turned 20. Last year, America's teens spent $100 billion and influenced their parents' spending to the tune of another $50 billion. While baby boomers are still struggling with Windows 98 and Office, their children, born with a game pad in hand, learn how to keyboard before they learn to read. Video games become their common denominator. What's more, the Internet lets them discover new trends on their own, as soon as they emerge. For the first time in history, children are more knowledgeable, more informed, and more comfortable than their elders with the innovation that is at the center of our society's evolution. Children are teaching their parents. Now that's a real revolution!

attracting both the elusive casual gamer and women, thanks to the game's intrinsic social component of communication between individuals. The danger lurking in these new tools is that some people will have more interesting lives online than in real life. That's what happens when you explore virgin territory... you never know how the natives will react. See you next year!

Au revoir!

Back to where we never left!

Here we are. The year ends on a wonderful note for all gamers who have never before had such a multitude of choices. It's been a record year in sales, and the most incredible part is that this year Sony and Microsoft will offer their versions of online games from a console. *The Sims* online should be a hit and finally succeed in

Mediagraphy

The history of the gaming industry has already been the subject of many books and websites. Here are the main ones…

History of video games

The Ultimate History of Video Game

From Pong to Pokemon. The Story Behind the Craze That Touched Our Lives and Changed the World, Steve L. Kent, Prima Publishing, 2001, ISBN: 0761536434, 624 pages.

Phœnix

The Fall & Rise of Videogames, Leonard Herman, Rolenta Press, ISBN: 0964384825.

Electronic Plastic

Electronic Plastic, Jaro Gielens (Editor), Buro Destruct (Editor), Lopetz, Büro Destruct, Robert Klanten, Die Gestalten Verlag, 2001, ISBN: 3931126447, 176 pages.

The First Quarter

A 25-year History of Video Games, Steven L. Kent, BWD Press, 2000, ISBN: 0970475500, 466 pages.

Websites

<www.videogames.com/features/universal/hov>
<www.videotopia.com>
<www.emuunlim.com/doteaters/index.htm>
<www.ammi.org/exhibitions/cs98/index.html>
<www.klov.com>
<www.dadgum.com/giantlist/list.html>

The history of Nintendo

Game Over

Press Start To Continue, David Sheff and Andy Eddy, GamePress, 1999, ISBN: 0966961706.

The history of the PlayStation

Revolutionaries at Sony: The Making of the Sony PlayStation and The Visionaries Who Conquered The World of Video Games, Reiji Asakura, 241 pages, McGraw-Hill Professional Publishing, 2000, ISBN: 0071355871, 494 pages.

The history of Atari and Pong

ZAP!
The Rise and Fall of Atari, Scott Cohen, 1984, ISBN: 0738868833, 139 pages.

Websites
<www.atari-history.com/mainmenu.html>
<www.pong-story.com>

The history of arcade Games

Supercade, Van Burnham and Ralph Baer, MIT Press, 2001, ISBN: 0262024926, 448 pages.

Arcade Fever, The Fan's Guide to The Golden Age of Video Games, John Sellers, Running Press, 2001, ISBN: 0762409371, 160 pages.

Sociological and economic analysis

From Barbie to Mortal Kombat
From Barbie to Mortal Kombat, Justine Cassell (Editor), Henry Jenkins (Editor), MIT Press, 2000, ISBN: 0262531682, 380 pages.

Playing for Profit
How Digital Entertainment Is Making Big Business Out of Child's Play, Alice Laplante, Rich Seidner (Contributor), éditeur, 1999, ISBN: 0471296147, 287 pages.

Trigger Happy
Videogames and the Entertainment Revolution, Steven Poole, Arcade Publishing, 2000, ISBN: 1559705396, 256 pages.

Credits

We would like to thank Acclaim, Activision, AIAS, Bioware, Blizzard, Capcom, Compaq, Croteam, DMA Design, Dreamworks Interactive, ECTS, Eidos, Electronic Arts, Ensemble Studios, ESBR, Factor 5, Firaxis Games, Fox Interactive, Game Commander, Gathering of Developers, GDCA2M, Gearbox Software, Gray Matter Studios, Guillemot, Havok, Id Software, IDGA, IDSA, Ion Storm, Infogrames, Interplay, Konami, Lionhead Studios, Lucasarts, Microsoft, Midway, Monolith, Namco, Naughty Dog, Neversoft, NIME, Nintendo, NovaLogic, Nvidia, Oddworld Inhabitants, Origin, Polyphony Digital, Presto Studios, Pyro Studios, Rainbow Studios, Rare, Raven Software, Red Storm, Relic, Remedy, Ritual, Rockstar Games, Sega, Shiny, Sierra Online, Silicon Knights, Sony, Squaresoft, Strategy First, Take-Two, Tecmo, THQ, Trio-Tech, Ubi Soft, UWink Inc, Valve Software, Verant Interactive, Virgin, Vivendi Universal, Westwood, 3D Realms, 3DO, 3Q, for allowing us to reference their intellectual property.

Atari®, Pong®, Lynx™ logos and images courtesy of Infogrames Interactive, Inc., © 2002 Infogrames Interactive, Inc. All rights reserved. Used with permission.

We would also like to thank Stuart Harrisson (pages 32, 33, 51, 58, 127, 128, 134, 135, 139, 140, 144, 145, 149, 154, 155, 163, 164, 165, 171, 173, 176, 177, 259, 269, 270, 272 and 274) and Mike Krahulik (pages 113 and 235) for their illustrations.

Index People

Index Console Games

Mega Man Series: 186
MLB 2002: 185
Oddworld: 187
Spiderman: 187
Tekken 3: 187

Sega's Dreamcast

2001 HITS: 192
Alien Front Online: 195
Bass Fishing 2: 196
Crazy Taxi 2: 199
Daytona USA: 199
Grandia II: 195
House of the Dead 2: 200
Jet Grind Radio: 193
Metropolis Street Racer: 197
Ooga Booga: 195
Outtrigger: 198
Phantasy Star Online: 193
Project Justice: 198
Ready Rumble 2: 200
Resident Evil: Code Veronica: 197
Shenmue: 197
Skies of Arcadia: 194
Sonic Adventure 2: 194
Soul Calibur: 200
Spider-Man: 198
Virtual On: 200
WSK2K2: 195
Worms Armageddon: 200
Worms World Party: 196

Sony's PS2

2001 BIGGEST HITS: 201
Ace Combat 4: Shattered Skies: 220
Armored Core 2: Another Age: 217
ATV Offroad Fury: 208
Baldur's Gate: 220
Batman: Vengeance: 215
Burnout: 220
Dark Cloud: 209
Dead or Alive 2: 211
Devil May Cry: 205
F1 2001: 215
Final Fantasy: 203
Gauntlet: Dark Legacy: 212
Giants: Citizen Kabuto: 221
Gran Turismo 2: 201
Grand Theft Auto III: 203
Half-Life: 220
ICO: 216
Jak and Dexter: 204
Kinetica: 215
Klonoa 2: 212
Madden NFL 2002: 218
Metal Gear Solid 2: 202
MDK2 Armageddon: 210
Music Generator 2: 213
MX 2002: 214
Nascar Heat 2002: 214
Nascar Thunder 2002: 215
NBA Street: 204
NHL 2002: 216
Onimusha: Warlords: 206
Rayman 2: 207
Red Faction: 213

Index Computer Games

Apple